Daily Guideposts, 1990

GUIDEPOSTS®
Carmel, New York 10512

ACKNOWLEDGMENTS

All Scripture quotations, unless otherwise noted, are from The King James Version of the Bible.

Scripture quotations marked (GNB) are from The Good News Bible, The Bible in Today's English Version. Copyright © American Bible Society, 1966, 1971, 1976.

Scripture quotations marked (MLB) are from The Modern Language Bible: The Berkeley Version in Modern English. Copyright © 1945, 1959, 1969 by Zondervan Publishing House. Used by permission.

Scripture quotations marked (TLB) are from The Living Bible, © 1971 owned by assignment by Illinois Regional Bank, N.A. (as trustee). Used by permission of Tyndale House Publishers, Inc., Wheaton, IL 60189. All rights reserved.

Scripture quotations marked (NAS) are taken from The New American Standard Bible, © The Lockman Foundation 1960, 1962, 1963, 1968, 1971, 1972, 1973, 1975, 1977.

Scripture quotations marked (NIV) are from The Holy Bible, New International Version. Copyright © 1973, 1978, 1984 International Bible Society. Used by permission of Zondervan Bible Publishers.

Scripture quotations marked (NKJV) are from The New King James Version of the Bible. Copyright © 1979, 1980, 1982 by Thomas Nelson Inc., Publishers.

Scripture quotations marked (RSV) are from The Revised Standard Version of the Bible. Copyright © 1946, 1952, 1971 by the Division of Christian Education of the National Council of Churches of Christ in the U.S.A., and are used by permission.

Verse on page 167 is from "Upon That Whitsun Morning" ("A Mighty Sound from Heaven") by G. B. Timms (1910-) (v.1). Copyright © 1975 from *English Praise;* reprinted by permission of Oxford University Press.

Spiritual Treasure series which appears on the calendar page of each month were written by Sue Monk Kidd.

Family Prayers which appears on the calendar page of each month were written by Robin White-Goode.

The "Day Brightener" by Phyllis Michael on page 343 is copyright © 1989 by Phyllis Michael and is used by permission.

Designed by Holly Johnson
Artwork by LMD Service for Publishers
Indexed by Mary F. Tomaselli

Printed in the United States of America

TABLE OF CONTENTS

INTRODUCTION

And they that be wise shall shine as the brightness of the firmament....
—Daniel 12:3

Just as every schoolchild knows that the sun is always shining somewhere, so every Christian knows that God's radiance is always flooding the universe with love and power. This light falls upon all of us equally, and each of us has the opportunity—even the duty—to reflect it as best we can. Not only back to God, but to one another.

In our daily lives, light often reaches us through windows. And so you will find that symbol of light streaming through open windows many times in the pages that follow.

The first window of light is on the monthly calendar page. There you'll find *Spiritual Treasure,* taken from Matthew 6:20 where Jesus urges us to store up treasure in Heaven. Through the words of the Sermon on the Mount you will be helped to reflect His goodness all through the year.

Then on the first of each month, in *Through an Open Window,* Eleanor Sass describes the insights that have come to her through the windows of her New York apartment. Every midmonth, in *Windows Into Wonder,* Marilyn Morgan Helleberg helps us discover the mysterious dreams, visions and miracles of the Bible and their message for us today.

During Holy Week, in *His Final Gestures,* Carol Kuykendall focuses on the last words and actions of Jesus and shows us how they can help us live *purposefully* each day. Writer Elizabeth Sherrill illumines for us the season of Pentecost in *The Coming of the Spirit.* In a three-day summer series, Eric Fellman takes us on *A Family Adventure* into the great outdoors. In the fall, Ruth Stafford Peale brings us warm insights from the light of *Our Travels Together,* with husband Norman Vincent Peale. When Advent comes, Terry Helwig lights the candles of Christmas in a *Journey to Inner Bethlehem,* where we discover our hidden potential waiting to be born.

Many other favorite authors will be opening windows of spiritual growth for you during the year: Sue Monk Kidd, Marjorie Holmes, Arthur Gordon, Marion Bond West, Van Varner, among them. Old and new Fireside Friends will make occasional house visits with you. And *Day Brighteners,* little upbeat thoughts and verses, will appear from time to time as bonuses to your day's reading.

A new feature this year, *My Monthly Prayer List,* is on the calendar opening page. Here in a boxed space you can briefly record monthly prayer needs and concerns for yourself and others. Also in the same box, a *Family Prayer* is given so that readers of *Daily Guideposts* can say one united prayer each month, for the homeless, for our national leaders, for educators and schoolchildren, and many more. Every midmonth a reminder will invite you to review your prayer-box requests. In addition, at the end of each month are *Thank-You Notes to God,* a place to record a brief thought, feeling or prayer at the end of each daily reading.

This year, our authors *and* their families are waiting to meet you in the biography section, *A Family Affair.* And once again to provide that extra help in devotional reading, turn to our comprehensive three-part index *The Reader's Guide* to locate that special devotional.

We who have worked together to prepare this volume hope that every single page will help you blow away the dust of daily living from your own windows, let His Glory shine through that you might reflect it back to others.

May each day of this Year of our Lord Nineteen Hundred Ninety bring you every happiness—and steadily closer to God.

—The Editors

JANUARY

S	M	T	W	T	F	S
	1	2	3	4	5	6
7	8	9	10	11	12	13
14	15	16	17	18	19	20
21	22	23	24	25	26	27
28	29	30	31			

SPIRITUAL TREASURE

Seek God First

But seek ye first the kingdom of God, and his righteousness....

—Matthew 6:33

January is the doorway to a brand-new year. In fact, the word *January* comes from the Roman mythological figure *Janus,* who was the guardian of portals. This month as you step across the threshold into 1990, leave the old year behind and take with you a fresh resolve to seek God first. Each day apply this question to whatever situation arises, "How can I place God's way first?"

This simple question will turn your heart into a portal, one that is open wide for God to fill with spiritual treasure the whole year long.

My Monthly Prayer List

Family Prayer for January

Lord, a new year has begun. Help me to face each new challenge with Your strength and confidence. Let's begin!

THROUGH AN OPEN WINDOW
Seeking God's Plan

For I know the plans I have for you, says the Lord, plans for welfare and not for evil, to give you a future and a hope. —Jeremiah 29:11 (RSV)

In New York City where I live, I consider myself one of the fortunate ones because I have a room with a view. From my seventh-floor apartment, I can look over the neighboring rooftops for several city blocks. Above these rooftops there's an enormous expanse of sky. The sky is what I see upon awakening each morning, sometimes cloudy, sometimes bright. It reminds me of the words of the Psalmist, "The heavens declare his righteousness, and all the people see his glory" (Psalm 97:6). It's a good beginning for my morning quiet time, and unless the weather is really blustery, I open my window wide, breathe in deeply and quietly ask, "Lord, what is Your plan for me today?"

Sometimes an answer comes immediately—a simple suggestion to call a certain friend for lunch, or the hint of a solution to some problem that's bothering me. Other times God just seems to say, "Be still." So by sitting down quietly with my Bible and notebook, I try to relax and empty my mind as completely as possible and wait for Him to speak to me.

God does have a plan for each of us: "I will instruct thee and teach thee in the way which thou shalt go: I will guide thee with mine eye" (Psalm 32:8). We have to wait, listen, be patient, be receptive. At the beginning of each month, therefore, in this brand-new year of 1990, I'd like to share with you some of the thoughts and insights that have come to me through my "open window."

Now and in the months that follow, won't you join me? Whatever view lies outside of your window, you can still open the window of your soul. Every day ask God expectantly to show you His plan for your life. I promise you, He will.

Dear Father, every day this year I want to seek Your plan. Help me to find it. —Eleanor Sass

Tuesday

2

Lift up thine eyes westward, and northward, and southward, and eastward.... —Deuteronomy 3:27

During my one and only cruise, I saw a "Peanuts" cartoon posted on the ship bulletin board. It pictured Charlie Brown and Lucy on a cruise ship. As they stand on deck, Lucy says, "Life is like this cruise ship, Charlie Brown. Some people take their deck chairs to the front of the ship so they can see where they are going. Other people take their deck chairs to the back of the ship so they can see where they've been. Which kind of person are you, Charlie Brown?" He answers, "I'm the kind of person who can't get my deck chair open."

I smiled. For it seemed to me Lucy was right. Some folks are future-oriented, focusing on the possibilities of tomorrow. Others are past-oriented, focusing on the experiences of yesterday. (And some, like Charlie Brown, never seem to look in either direction.)

What kind of person am I? I wondered. I recalled that the first day on board I'd sat in a deck chair at the back of the ship. The next day, I'd sat in one at the front. And actually neither much suited me. One view without the other offered a limited perspective. The third day, though, I'd discovered a small deck at the top of the ship which offered a vision of the entire horizon. I could see where I'd been *and* where I was going. It was the best view of all.

On this second day of the new year, why not take your chair to the top of the ship for a glimpse of the whole horizon? Remember where you've been, learn from it and give thanks. Then reach for where you want to go, challenge yourself and take hope.

Lord, at the launch of this new year help me achieve a wider perspective by looking both at the waters I have traveled and the waters I have yet to cross. —Sue Monk Kidd

Wednesday

3

I, even I, am he that blotteth out thy transgressions for mine own sake, and will not remember thy sins.
—Isaiah 43:25

I was doing a little digging in Bible lore when I happened across a listing called "Famous Bibles." Here was a rundown of memorable editions of Scripture through the centuries, everything from the first complete Bible published by Wycliffe in 1384 to the King James Bible of 1611 right on up to the many versions published in our lifetime.

Some Bibles, I discovered to my surprise, are known today for their inadvertent printer's errors, mistakes that even serious-minded Bible scholars have found amusing. "The Affinity Bible," for instance, is so called because it contains a table of affinity that says: "A man may not marry his grandmother's wife."

There was one scriptural mistake, however, that I found more thought-provoking than amusing. It appeared in what is now referred to as the "Forgotten Sins Bible" of 1638. Luke 7:47 reads: "Her sins which are many, are *forgotten*." The printer should have used the word *forgiven*, and yet, I thought when reading that, what a better mistake it would have been if the passage had read, "Her sins which are many, are forgiven" and the printer had then added two words of his own: "and forgotten."

To forgive and then to forget—what powerful healing there is in that!

Help me to correct my own mistakes, Father, and then get on with the business of living. —Van Varner

Thursday

4

In my Father's house are many mansions....
—John 14:2

Some years ago a famous industrialist asked me to come and see him. His wife had died, leaving him with a terrible sense of grief and loss. He wanted assurance that he would be reunited with her someday.

"Do you truly believe," he asked me, "that after we die another life is waiting for us?"

I told him that I was absolutely convinced. I said we had the promises of the Bible, the Resurrection of Jesus Christ, the deepest instincts of countless people throughout history. I said I had no doubts about it whatsoever.

"But what about scientific proof?" he wanted to know. I said, "Let me tell you something about the greatest scientist our nation ever produced: Thomas A. Edison. I knew his widow, and one day when I was in her home I said to her, 'Tell me about your husband. What sort of mind did he really have?'

"She said, 'Exactitude was the mark of my husband's mind. He was not sentimental. He had to know something for sure before he would say it or record it. It had to be proven.' Then she told me that when her husband was dying, he could barely speak. His doctor, who was also a family friend, noticed that the great inventor was trying to say something. He leaned close and heard Edison whisper, 'It's very beautiful over there.' Those were his last words."

I said to the industrialist, "Edison would not lie. He would not fabricate anything. He would report only what he saw. Is that scientific proof enough for you?"

"Yes," he said. "I think he glimpsed the land where my wife is waiting for me."

I think so, too.

Dear Jesus, thank You for Your promise that someday we will be with You in "the Land that is fairer than day."

—Norman Vincent Peale

Friday

5

And he is not served by human hands, as if he needed anything.... —Acts 17:25 (NIV)

Esau came into our lives at just the right time...for him. Arriving a few weeks before the death of our old Labrador retriever Rocky, this bubbly Lab puppy helped fill our void. He lavished attention on my wife Sally, wedding his shadow to hers. My attempt to hone him into a fine retriever was rewarded by tail wagging and slurping as he bounced around me. But he saw no sense in bringing back something I had just thrown away.

Until after dinner he pays little attention to me. Then he arrives for his evening petting. I have no choice. His head leans against my leg, then flops on my lap, or bores into my ribs until I stroke it. My attitude has always been, "Since you never pay attention to me any other time, why now?"

The other day I was just too tired. I resisted until he finally gave up. As he walked away he stopped and looked back. Those sad brown eyes seemed to say, "I don't understand why you are passing up this chance. It's not for me that we do this, it's to give you something at the end of your day."

Now I know we always think it's the dog that needs the petting. Maybe so... but just maybe we need to do it even more. To share that love, to give that touch of caring, to sense the bond that is there.

Sometimes I seem to feel that I'm doing God a favor by taking time to be with Him. Now at twilight I'm going to put my head in His lap and allow Him to stroke away the rough edges of my day. Because I need it.

Lord, let Your touch strengthen the bond between us.

—Scott Harrison

Saturday

6

The sun has one kind of glory while the moon and stars have another kind. And the stars differ from each other in their beauty and brightness.

—I Corinthians 15:41 (TLB)

A star, though it seems magical at times, is nothing more than a self-luminous, self-contained, relatively stationary mass of gas, visible at night from Earth. And yet, if we look closely, we can always find a star twinkling a little faster and shining a little brighter that can light our way, as the star of Bethlehem did for the wise men almost two thousand years ago.

This coming year I'm going to try harder to appreciate the real "stars" in my life:

My son, when he offers to teach his little brother a new skill.

My daughter, when she cleans up the kitchen without being asked.

My neighbor, who offers to drive my children somewhere.

My friend, who listens to my heart and asks nothing in return.

My father, who builds yet another beautiful object for my home.

My coworker, who takes the time to explain something with infinite patience.

This week, as we celebrate the Epiphany, why don't we make up a list of the stars in our lives, send them a star-shaped thank-you note and let them know how much we appreciate the way they light up our lives.

Lord, help me not only appreciate the stars in my life, but to be a star myself to all those around me. —Patricia Lorenz

Sunday

7

We always thank God for you and pray for you constantly. —I Thessalonians 1:2 (TLB)

Every town takes pride in its sons and daughters who grow up to distinguish themselves, especially very small towns. I make note of this fact because I recently visited the village of Benton, Pennsylvania, which a native quickly informed me was the birthplace of Frank Laubach. If you don't recognize his name, perhaps you are familiar with his world-famous work with the illiterate. "Each one teach one" is the motto of the movement he started that continues to this day. All told, he helped create reading primers for adults in 165 languages.

Frank Laubach (1884–1970) also wrote a Christian classic entitled *Prayer: The Mightiest Force in the World*. It shows another side of the man who was a missionary and preacher before he gained renown as an educator. Memorable is a section on prayer experiments. In it he suggests silently "shooting" prayers all day long at everyone we meet, including strangers on the street, asking God to be near them, to help them with their problems, to lift their spirits. Not only will your prayers be a positive force for the recipient, Laubach wrote, but the endeavor "is for me the finest tonic I know. When you are utterly tired from work or study, flash prayers at people. Your nerves will tingle with the inflow from heaven...."

If you want to know more about Frank Laubach, visit Benton, Pennsylvania. If you want to know more about his deep faith, read his book. If you want to know more about intercessory prayer, find some target people today and shoot prayers in their direction. According to Laubach you don't have to know them or their needs. Just supply loving concern; the Holy Spirit will do the rest.

Help me, Lord, to never ration
Your gifts of love and compassion.

—Fred Bauer

Monday

8

And let us not be weary in well doing: for in due season we shall reap, if we faint not. —Galatians 6:9

Last January, I planted two seeds. The first was a tomato seed, and within a week a small plant appeared and began its phenomenal growth. All summer long and into the fall, I gathered delicious, vine-ripened tomatoes. What a lavish return from one tiny seed! *How I wish that every seed of kindness I plant would produce a return like that!* I thought.

The second seed was from an apple that was particularly crisp and delicious. I thought to myself, *I wonder if this seed will produce apples as good as this one?* So I planted it and soon got a little sprout. But I haven't gotten any return yet. I'm learning that the apple tree will take some time, and waiting takes patience and faith. Two seeds, but each requiring a different effort.

Some seeds of kindness do not produce fruit in a short time, but I'm willing to wait for their long-term investments: in my family, in my friends and even in my relationship with God. These will bear fruit, not for a brief season, but for years to come. Even now, time spent with my children years ago is still bearing glorious fruit! God has His law of harvest. So don't give up; plant your seeds of kindness. They won't disappoint you.

Dear Lord, give me the faith, not only to plant, but to wait for the harvest. Amen.

—Lee Webber

Tuesday

9

Looking to Jesus the pioneer and perfecter of our faith....
—Hebrews 12:2 (RSV)

Alaska is often referred to as "The Last Frontier." When I hear this, I am reminded of pioneers erecting simple cabins from materials at hand and foraging for food among a plentiful plant and wildlife supply. Well, we've got the wilderness—365 million acres of it—populated by only half a million hearty souls. As for living off the land, I have an Alaskan cookbook brimming with unusual recipes: kelp mint marmalade, jellied moose nose, spaghetti and sea lion meatballs, fillet of whale with mushrooms, braised bear chops and seagull egg pie.

The fact is, though, most Alaskans lead typically modern lifestyles. There are still a few true pioneers among us, but the rest of us just "play" at it. For example, when a friend gave us caribou meat, we *conveniently* had the butcher cut and wrap it rather than attempting it ourselves. Another friend who owns a remote cabin reaches it *quickly* by plane instead of trekking across rugged terrain. Our wood heat comes from trees felled *easily* with a gas-powered chain saw, replacing hours of backbreaking labor with an axe.

Conveniently, quickly, easily... words that pioneering stock never heard. Yet I live with these terms every day and still find myself stewing over delays, disruptions and anything that impedes my progress. I've begun to expect my life, my relationships and even my faith to come prepackaged special delivery.

Maybe a "frontier attitude" is exactly what I need to restore to my own rusty vocabulary, words such as *patience, courage, effort, determination, dependability.* There just might be hope for the likes of me, after all, here on the Last Frontier!

Jesus, Pioneer of our faith, work side by side with me as I tackle my personal frontier.
—Carol Knapp

Wednesday

10

Cast thy burden upon the Lord, and he shall sustain thee....
—Psalm 55:22

A few years ago, Christopher de Vinck wrote an essay called "Power of the Powerless: A Brother's Lesson," which appeared in *The Wall Street Journal*. De Vinck wrote about growing up in a house where his brother Oliver lay on his back in bed for thirty-two years. Oliver was blind and mute. He was spoon-fed every morsel of food, and didn't have the strength to lift his head or the intelligence to learn anything.

But the family's love and devotion never wavered. De Vinck said being brought up in a house "where a tragedy was turned into a joy" made a deep impression on him. He remembers his mom saying, "When you go to heaven, Oliver will run to you, embrace you, and the first thing he will say is 'Thank you.'"

But de Vinck believes his parents were the real heroes. How did they manage to change Oliver's diapers for thirty-two years? How did they cope with spoon-feeding him three times a day every day of his life? De Vinck asked his father this very question. His father said he did not feed Oliver for thirty-two years, but just asked himself, "Can I feed Oliver *today*?" The answer always was, "Yes, I can."

De Vinck's words have taught me not to look so far into the future. The next time I encounter difficulty, I'm going to ask myself, "Can I manage this for just today?" I have a feeling my answer will also be, "Yes, I can."

Lord, please help me not to fret about the future, but to remember that You have given me the necessary strength to live out today.
—Terry Helwig

Thursday

11

I keep working toward that day when I will finally be all that Christ saved me for and wants me to be.
—Philippians 3:12 (TLB)

In late December I decided not to make any New Year's resolutions because I *always* broke at least one before January 2—usually the one that said, "I will not eat junk food."

Then I read these resolutions written in the 1700s by the Puritan preacher Jonathan Edwards:

I am resolved...

To live with all my might while I do live;

Never to lose one moment of time, but improve it in the most profitable way I possibly can;

Never to do anything that I should despise or think meanly of in another;

Never to do anything out of revenge;

Never to do anything which I should be afraid to do if it were the last hour of my life.

I prayed about them and adopted them as mine. I know I can't follow them perfectly, but they are worthy goals, and I can try to make them part of my daily life.

Perhaps you'd like to adopt these resolutions as your goals, too. Like me, you may not keep each one perfectly, but we can keep trying. Isn't that what following Christ is all about?

Lord, thank You for wisdom from the past to guide our futures.

—Penney Schwab

Friday

12

Fireside Friend 

Give ear to my words, O Lord.... —Psalm 5:1

When I was unemployed, I thought that if only I had a job, I would be happy. It seemed obvious that a paycheck and a workplace were just what I needed to improve my life dramatically. So I prayed, "Dear God, just let me get a job and I will never complain about anything again." Needless to say, only weeks after getting a job, I was unhappy with some of my coworkers, swamped by my workload and even annoyed that my chair wasn't comfortable enough!

When I was single, at times I thought, *Dear God, if only I had a husband, then my life would be so much better.* In reality, only a few months after Paul and I were married, an argument about the right way to slice carrots for salad had me wondering if *this* was the happily-ever-after I'd prayed for.

Who knows what I might have wished for next as the "answer" to all my problems if a well-meaning friend hadn't given me a needlepoint pillow that read, "Happiness is not getting what you want—it is wanting what you get."

Surprisingly, that simple message even enabled me to give up my recurrent "If-I-lost-ten-pounds, my-life-would-be-perfect" fantasy. It also caused me to stop making my prayers into a "gimme" list for God, and instead to be appreciative for the many good things already in my life—including my cozy apartment (small enough to not require too much work to keep clean), my good health (including a zest for food) and a caring husband (despite the fact that he cuts carrots wrong!).

God, help me to remember to thank You for what I do have rather than remind You of what I don't have. —Linda Neukrug

Saturday

13

And on mine arm shall they trust. —Isaiah 51:5

Fear was creeping up on me as I sat in my living room. I needed to confront a neighbor who I felt had slighted me, and as I tried to pray about it, confusion mounted and my prayer felt empty. Suddenly, our new stray cat Minnie jumped on my lap. It took me a moment to realize that she was fearful. She stood almost paralyzed, staring at something with her ears flattened and her eyes widened.

Finally, I located the source of her fear. Minnie had seen my china cat sitting under a table. The statue looked quite lifelike. I picked it up to let my cat see that it wasn't real. She immediately buried her head under my arm and refused to look. I stroked her and talked to her and gradually she lifted her head, still clinging to my arm. Ever so slowly Minnie sniffed the large china cat. Then she cautiously placed one of her paws on the statue's pink nose. She looked at me in astonishment and then with pleasure. She began to purr. I put the china cat back under the table, and Minnie hopped down and sauntered over to sniff it once more... maybe even to become friends.

Watching her walk confidently around the statue I thought,

Father, I do believe You can teach me about fear and trust, even from a cat!

I went to the door. I would call on my neighbor and reach out past my fear. And with His help, maybe even find the way to restored friendship.

Dear Lord, when I'm paralyzed with fear, let me remember the lesson of the china cat, trust You and take a risk....

—Marion Bond West

Sunday

14

I do set my bow in the cloud.... —Genesis 9:13

Some of us were reminiscing about childhood episodes that we remembered because of their religious content or significance. I recalled the Sunday evenings in our cottage at the beach where we all sang hymns in a lively and good-humored way, each of us choosing his favorite.

One friend said, "I remember one rainy Sunday evening on the farm where I grew up. We were sitting on the porch when a magnificent double rainbow appeared in the eastern sky. It blazed so brilliantly that Dad went and got his Bible and read aloud the passage where God says that the rainbow shall be a token of a covenant between Him and the earth. Then Dad quoted from memory a passage from the Apocrypha that I've remembered ever since:

> *Look upon the rainbow and praise him who made it;*
> *very beautiful it is in the brightness thereof. It*
> *compasseth the heaven about with a glorious circle,*
> *and the hand of the Most High hath bended it.*
>
> (Ecclesiasticus 43:11-12)

My friend added thoughtfully, "I love that phrase: 'The hand of the Most High hath bended it.' I believe that same hand can bend my life and my personality in the same way, if I'll just let it."

Finally, he said, "I think about that every time I see a rainbow."

From now on, so will I.

Thank You, Heavenly Father, for shaping us closer to the image of Yourself. —Arthur Gordon

Monday
15

WINDOWS INTO WONDER
Miracles, Common and Uncommon

Your old men shall dream dreams, your young men shall see visions. —Joel 2:28

I've always been both intrigued and mystified by the dreams and visions in the Bible. Wrestling angels, burning bushes, chariots of fire, a blinding light on the road to Damascus. Those mysterious events excited me. Yet they also seemed a bit too otherworldly for my computerized, mass-produced, nail-it-down world. They seemed to happen only to specially chosen great people, far removed from me in time and space. But as I started rereading the many dreams and visions in the Bible, I discovered a wonderful thing: *You and I are included in that chosenness!* Those great, awe-filled events are for us, too. Each of them can be a window through which we may glimpse the miraculous in the thousand unnamed miracles of our everyday, bread-and-butter existence!

As I immersed myself in Bible dreams and visions, I began to see that, in every case, God gave the person something specific and tangible to take back into ordinary life. A guiding torch, a new name, a fresh start, a safe place...no wonder our spiritual ancestors knew such a close companionship with their Creator! I saw that it could happen to me, too. I went searching for miracles amid the shimmer of the spectacular... and found the same radiance shining through the grace-touched moments of my least significant days.

Will you go searching in the miraculous with me? Each mid-month, we'll let a Bible dream or vision become a *window into wonder*, through which to catch a fresh new glimpse of God's nearness. Then we'll bring something back from each encounter, something that connects with our everyday experiences to remind us of the closeness of our ever-present God.

Lord, may seeking You in the extraordinary help me to find You in the commonplace. —Marilyn Morgan Helleberg

January Prayer List Reminder

Return to your Monthly Prayer List on the calendar opening page and review your requests. Give thanks for prayers answered, renew old prayers and add new concerns today. Then pray once again our *Family Prayer for January.*

Tuesday

16

Therefore I write these things being absent....

—II Corinthians 13:10

Nobody writes letters anymore. Sure, it's nice to get a phone call, but it's not the same. Five minutes after you hang up, it's gone and forgotten. You can't reread a phone call to be sure you didn't miss something written between the lines or to relish the turn of a phrase. There's no commitment in a phone call, either—Americans call perfect strangers every day, but they write only to people they really care for. At least they used to.

People are afraid to write. Their spelling's not good, their handwriting's a scrawl. Yet all over America, other people are riffling through the day's mail, hoping for just one letter amid the junk and bills, one sign that another human is willing to invest a half hour in them, even if there is no news to tell. A world without letters is a shallow, uncaring, lonely world.

Aunt Jessie doesn't care about my spelling. She cares very much about me. My father-in-law hates to read, unless it's about his grandchildren. We're all willing to invest in one another, to proudly sign our names right under the word *love*. If you're willing to do that, believe me, no one will ever notice or care about your spelling!

Father, help me find time today to write to one person I care about.

—Toni Sortor

Day Brightener

Better keep yourself clean and bright; you are the window through which you must see the world.

—George Bernard Shaw

Wednesday

17

If thou canst believe, all things are possible....
—Mark 9:23

As I tucked my seven-year-old daughter in bed, I noticed a sad tilt to her mouth. That afternoon she'd had trouble learning the steps in ballet class and was pulled aside for special help. She was still smarting. "I'm no good, Mama," she said. "I don't think I want to go back."

I patted her hand and opened the book of fairy tales we'd been reading, hoping it would take her mind off the matter.

We read the story of Rapunzel, a beautiful princess who was imprisoned in a tower by a wicked witch. Every day the witch told Rapunzel that she was ugly. Convinced of her ugliness, Rapunzel lost her spirit and gave up hope of leaving the tower. Then one day a prince climbed the tower. Rapunzel saw her image mirrored in his eyes and discovered that she was beautiful. From that moment she was free.

As I closed the book, I thought how easy it was for people to become convinced of their "ugliness," imprisoning themselves in negative thoughts. Maybe they simply needed someone to mirror to them the beauty in their lives.

I looked down at my daughter. "Even the best dancers sometimes take a long time to learn new steps," I said. "You are a beautiful dancer."

"Really?" she asked.

"Really," I said.

Ever so slightly the curve in her mouth lifted. "Maybe I'll go back next week," she said.

Lord, help me to affirm the gift and possibility I glimpse in the lives around me. —Sue Monk Kidd

Thursday

18

Now you are my friends.... —John 15:15 (TLB)

I work for a large radio-TV station that employs more than three hundred people. Every day I see the same faces in the halls, yet I know less than half of them by name.

At a Christmas party a few years ago, I got to know one of the reporters. I learned that he and his wife were expecting their first child. We talked about our jobs; Ron learned a little about writing radio commercials and I learned a little more about the newsroom. Now, whenever we see each other in the hall, we may stop and chat or give a friendly wave.

Every week of this new year, I've decided to learn the name of one person I work with. Then when I see them in the halls, I can address them by name with a comment like, "You sounded great on the air this morning." Or, "I heard TV sales are up. Congratulations!" Or, "What's new in the newsroom?" A new friend every week. Doesn't that sound like a marvelous way to spend a new year?

Why don't you give it a try? Think how full your life will be at the end of the year with fifty-two new friends!

Lord, give me the courage to meet new people...and then to treasure and nurture our friendship each day. —Patricia Lorenz

Friday

19

Let your light so shine before men, that they may see your good works, and glorify your Father which is in heaven. —Matthew 5:16

One of the finest museums in New York is the Cloisters, a collection of medieval sculpture, art and stained glass housed in authentic remnants of various medieval cloisters. Perched above the Hudson River, it's a peaceful haven in this crowded, noisy city. Taking guided tours through the gardens and rooms, I enjoy discovering the symbols in the art that say so much about my faith.

A feathery pelican crowns one capital, tearing her breast with her beak to feed her young—a reminder of Christ's sacrifice for His children. Joseph the carpenter works in his shop with a mousetrap at the window—a symbol of the trap that Jesus made for the devil, or so the guide tells us. The disciples and evangelists are carved on the base of a stone sarcophagus with the image of a recumbent knight on top, because the dead rest on the body of the Church...literally.

But what particularly delights me is the guide's explanation for why stained glass was so popular in church architecture. "It's the only artistic medium," she explains, "that doesn't reflect light. Instead what we see is the light shining *through* the glass illuminating the figures." I see the light shining *through* John the Baptist, Mary Magdalene, the apostles Peter and Paul, and making them glow—like the true light of the Son in all His followers. I like that image. When we serve Him, we shine to the extent that He is working *through* us.

Lord, let me shine in Your service. —Rick Hamlin

Saturday 20

Fireside Friend

Freely you have received, freely give.
—Matthew 10:8 (NIV)

I once heard a folktale about two brothers, one single and the other married with a large family. The single brother, upon looking at his crops, thought, *Why, it's not fair for me to keep this abundance to myself. My brother has so many mouths to feed.* So, in the middle of the night, he crept to his brother's barn, filling it from his abundance. The married brother, in turn, looking upon his crops, thought, *Why, it's not fair for me to keep such abundance to myself. I have many children who will care for me in later years. My brother has none.* So, in the middle of the night, he crept to his brother's barn and filled it. Each brother was amazed in the morning to find his own barn as full as it had been the day before. This went on night after night, until the hour the brothers met each other, arms full of grain, and realized the real abundance they shared.

All my life I, too, have had wonderful, caring people who "filled my barn" with their abundant kindnesses, without counting the costs for themselves. People like my teacher Mrs. Olson, who, when she separated my best friend and me from a childhood spat, told us she hated to see us fighting and that she loved us. Her words stuck in my mind—to think a teacher loved me! Then there was Mary Jane Whiting, the family friend I called "Grandma." Knowing I was scared to go away to college, she made sure I had a letter in my mailbox the very first day I was there. And of course, there was my own mom, who in her foster care work always showed me there was room for one more at our table—and that age, race or disability didn't make any difference.

Now that I'm grown up, I try to give back what I've been given: by saying "I love you" when it counts; by trying to show love in my actions; and by trying to make sure there is always room for one more in my heart. Because I've learned that in families, like the two brothers in the folktale, whatever you give comes back to you. And from all those who've helped me over the years, I've learned that families can be built not just of flesh and blood, but of great armfuls of abundance given without counting the cost.

Lord, let me remember to give as the brothers gave—expecting nothing in return. Because all of Your children are my family.

—Tammy Rider

Sunday

21

He that had gathered much had nothing over....

—II Corinthians 8:15

My wife Sharon showed me our savings balance and I got a queasy feeling in my stomach. My mind began to spin. *What will we do in our old age? Will we have all the material comforts we need? Will we have enough to pay our bills and still enjoy life?*

Sometimes I feel guilty because I don't have every day of my life "covered" in advance as some of my friends do. They have elaborate insurance and savings programs. One of them even has his tombstone engraved and sitting on a prepaid lot!

"The Bible doesn't promise God's blessings in advance," Sharon reminds me, and I know she is right. If God guaranteed our security, why would we have to trust Him?

"Let's increase our savings," Sharon says, "a little bit at a time."

"And to that, add an increase in our trust, too," I say sheepishly.

Dear Lord, I would like to know in advance how everything is going to work out, but then I wouldn't need to trust You. Help me to be wise in my planning, but never to hoard things—except my trust in You!

—Daniel Schantz

Monday

22

Make a joyful noise unto the Lord, all ye lands.
—Psalm 100:1

"Asthma is a fact you'll have to live with," my doctor told me. "Listen to your body. Think happy thoughts. Prevent an attack before it comes." I thought she was crazy. How could asthma be prevented by "listening to my body" when all I heard was a wheeze?

Three weeks later, I caught a cold—a bad sign for any asthmatic. This time, I did as my doctor ordered. I listened for changes in breathing, and when I began to wheeze, I emptied my head of frightening thoughts and substituted pleasant images. But my mind kept returning to how miserable I felt.

Sensing my panic, my husband took me downstairs to his special chair and put on his favorite record. I tried again. This time, I concentrated on the soothing sounds from the stereo. At that moment, the melody soared, and I was reminded of glorious words that seemed to go perfectly with the music—David's song of praise in Psalm 100. I repeated the psalm over and over as the joyful music played. Almost without my noticing it, my breathing eased.

I haven't eliminated asthma from my life, but I have made adjustments. I rest more. I exercise. And I walk more closely with God. Praising God, I've discovered, is potent medicine.

You, too, can head off stress-related ailments with a healthy dose of "Prayer's Potent Medicine." Do the following:

1. Cut down on fatiguing activities.
2. Relax. Turn on soothing music.
3. Pray often to banish fear, especially those psalms of praise you know by heart.

God of joy and glory, melt the clouds of sickness and sadness, drive the dark of doubt away. —Linda Ching Sledge

Tuesday

23

Fireside Friend 

You younger men, follow the leadership of those who are older. —I Peter 5:5 (TLB)

I am an American Indian, a member of the Coastal Band of the Chumash Nation. Recently when some land along the California coast was given back to us, a ceremony was held. My father, who was ninety years old at the time, was not well enough to attend. As a respected Chumash elder, he is often called upon to lead the people in prayer. Many are Christians, who also have strong ties to their cultural heritage. On the day of the ceremony, Dad sent his walking stick with us to represent him. Dad had made the walking stick himself, with a hand-carved dolphin for the handle and a rainbow band of rope around the staff.

When our family arrived at the gathering, we found that the other ninety-year-old elder was also ill and had sent his eagle walking stick to represent him. The walking sticks were placed in the ancient ground overlooking the Pacific Ocean. In a very beautiful way they told us that the blessings of the grandfathers were with us on that day—and that they would always be with us.

I am very grateful today for the elders in my life: for their wisdom, their life experience, their example. They have given me so much. Today I will make time to call or visit at least one elderly person in my life—just to say how grateful I am.

Perhaps you might want to do the same. Or perhaps you might pull out the family album and reminisce and remember some wonderful ancestral influences in your life. Or you may be the elder who would like to share some gratitude with a younger person today. Thank God now for each and every one....

Father, I pray especially for the elderly in my life today. Bless them with good health, comfort them in their afflictions and give them peace in their old age. —Georgiana Sanchez

Wednesday

24

And which of you by being anxious can add one cubit to his span of life? —Matthew 6:27 (RSV)

Not long ago our family watched the movie *The Wizard of Oz* on video cassette. Dorothy and her two companions, the Scarecrow and the Tin Man, were following the yellow brick road when they came to a dark forest. They began to see something terrible behind every tree. Clinging to one another, they sang, "Lions and tigers and bears, oh my! Lions and tigers and bears, oh my!" But it turned out there were no tigers and bears. And the lion that turned up was nothing more than a big pussy cat. We all laughed at how much effort they wasted being fearful of nothing.

The next morning at breakfast I started worrying aloud about a talk I was to give at a luncheon that day, creating in vivid detail all the things that could go wrong. The audience wouldn't like me, I'd forget what I wanted to say, etc. Suddenly three voices around the table began to sing, "Lions and tigers and bears, oh my!"

Whenever anyone in my family starts imagining the worst possible scenario, seeing something terrible behind every tree, they generally get serenaded with that little jingle. What better way to remind one another that most of our fears are unfounded, that most of our lions turn out to be pussy cats in the end.

Father, do not let me be swept away by fear, but grounded in faith.

—Sue Monk Kidd

Thursday

25

Cast thy bread upon the waters.... —Ecclesiastes 11:1

I have a good friend, Art Fettig. Early every morning, weather permitting, Art walks along a river in our city park to a point where the river becomes a waterfall. One morning recently he tossed a pebble into the stream and watched ripple rings spread farther and farther apart. Finally one ripple reached the crest of the waterfall and over it went.

Later, Art told me, "At that point I made a wish that I might do something that day to cause an action like that pebble in the river. I wanted to make waves in the world that would spread out and touch a million lives for the better."

"Wow!" I said. "A *million* lives? That's a mighty ambitious wish!" But the longer I thought about it the more plausible it seemed. Every day each of us, consciously or unconsciously, tosses "pebbles" into other peoples' lives by our words, our actions, our attitudes.

Art's words tossed a pebble into my life, making me eager to spread ripples of love and encouragement, touching others' lives for the better. And, because of Art, I'm tossing a pebble into *your* life. Can we, together, keep those ripples spreading? Then Art will have his wish, many times over.

Dear Father, keep us ever aware that our influence for good—or for evil—goes farther than we know. May all our actions honor You.

—Aletha Jane Lindstrom

Friday

26

For all have sinned, and come short of the glory of God. —Romans 3:23

After spending four days in bed with a viral infection, twelve-year-old Kendall got up, asked for some macaroni and cheese for lunch and climbed into a chair to focus our powerful telescope on the school playground where her friends were at recess.

"Golly, Mom! I can see them playing Four Square, and it looks like Karen and Susan are arguing about who is in which square," she reported enthusiastically.

Later, as I tucked her back in bed, she seemed less enthusiastic. "It feels kinda funny thinking you could watch me at recess when I don't know you're looking," she said.

"I could!" I teased her, pulling the covers up under her chin. "But probably I won't." As I rinsed macaroni off the lunch dishes, I thought about the uncomfortable prospect of having someone focus a telescope on me at my most unsuspecting moments. The truth is Someone does. It is God! He catches me arguing about the rules or reaching for the piece of pizza with the most pepperoni or rushing all the way through the grocery store without smiling at a single person.

"Character is what you are when you think nobody is looking," I recently read. God watches and knows my character. He knows I'm wired to fall short of His mark, yet He accepts me just the way He sees me. With a giant thankful sigh, I closed the dishwasher.

Lord, I am humbled when I realize that You focus Your telescope on all of us. You see everything and You still love us.

—Carol Kuykendall

Saturday

27

Praise the Lord from the earth…fire and hail, snow and frost…. —Psalm 148:7–8 (RSV)

As I stepped outside the house to get the cows up to the barn for milking, the ground was just turning white from the first snow of the year. I pulled my collar up around my neck and buried my hands in my pockets. There is something mystical and peaceful about the first snow of the year. It's almost as if God is tucking the earth into bed after a long summer season.

The cows were lying in what not so long ago was their summer pasture and source of nourishment. Now they, as well as the pasture, were covered with snow. As the cows started to the barn, their breath steaming in front of them, I felt a peace come over me as pure as the blanket of white covering the earth. Farming isn't easy, and at times the stress seems overwhelming. But for me, in this one brief moment, standing in a winter wonderland, I felt a tender closeness to God, a feeling of being purged of all duress. I breathed deeply, filling my lungs with cold, fresh air. It felt good to be alive.

I walked into the barn and turned the radio on. The evening news was just starting its broadcast and I was back to reality. But for a few brief moments I had been alone with God. What a cleansing feeling it had been. Right now, why don't you close your eyes, cover your ears and for a few brief moments imagine yourself with no cares and God with His arms around you.

Dear God, as I go through my busy day, help me to remember Your arms are around me every step of the way. —John Coen

Sunday

28

Whoever humbles himself like this child, he is the greatest in the kingdom of heaven.

—Matthew 18:4 (RSV)

After six years, open house at the grade school no longer held the fascination it once did. By the time my wife Joy and I had scrambled to the third classroom and squeezed into the pint-sized chairs, I was not anxious for another review of a fourth-grader's schedule and goals for the coming year.

But Nathan's teacher had a surprise. "I promised your children you'd all help write the class poem," she said. Ignoring the chorus of parental groans, she said the poem was free verse and we must all contribute by finishing a sentence that began *"I wish...."*

The list from the parents was self-centered:

"I wish I could be happy and problem-free."

"I wish I had had the chance to be a national-class competitor when I was young."

"I wish I had a home of my own."

After collecting and reading our selections, the teacher quietly opened her folder and read what our children had written:

"I wish my grandma didn't die."

"I wish my daddy didn't drink so much."

"I wish my mom and dad would just love each other like before."

None self-centered. The silence that followed was deafening and the sparkle of more than a few tears lit our faces.

I know it is a cliché to say, "Out of the mouths of babes," but maybe clichés persist because they contain truth. If you don't agree, I dare you to try an experiment. Ask a group of children to complete the "I wish" sentence. The list you get will surpass any sermon on faith, hope and love.

Let me approach the world like a child today and leave it a better place for having seen through their eyes again. —Eric Fellman

His hands shall also finish it.... —Zechariah 4:9

Halfway through college, at a time when I was very discouraged, I heard a lecture by Pearl S. Buck. "It's fun to start a book," she said, "and fun to finish it, but oh the middle! Never give up halfway," she warned. "The only way to accomplish anything is to finish what you start."

She told us there were times when writing *The Good Earth* she was tempted to throw it out the window. "I had all kinds of excuses for quitting. It was dated. Editors said nobody wanted to read about China anymore. I wasn't sure it was really any good. But I stuck it out. Whether it was ever published or not, I had to finish that book!"

That was the novel that won the Nobel Prize.

Haunted by her words, I lay awake half the night, wrestling with my own excuses. I had made up my mind to quit college. I was poor and lonely and homesick; the transfer to this bigger college, which should have been so thrilling, was a disillusioning shock. It was hard to break in, nobody knew I existed and the courses were harder. Besides, the Depression was getting worse; Dad had lost his job, Mother wrote. And though it would be the last thing she wanted, I told myself I was needed at home.

It seemed the perfect excuse—to be noble and flee this pain! But though I tried not to listen, I kept hearing those words: "Finish what you start."

Words that kept me from making a mistake I'd have regretted. Words that have been invaluable all my life—as a wife, a mother and a writer. It's romantic to start a marriage, but not so romantic as years go on, with its problems and disappointments. It's thrilling to have a baby—babies are adorable. But babies grow into children who must be disciplined, who can cause you pain and trouble. It's dramatic to start a career. But it takes time and hard work to succeed, and personal sacrifice. There will be times when you think, "It's not worth it."

Everything has its price. Sometimes the price is too high—this may be something God doesn't even want you to do anymore. And if you've really learned something in the process, quitting isn't total failure.

But don't be too quick to use that as an excuse. If you're having trouble finishing something you really believe in, ask God to help you. Then go back to your desk or your home with renewed dedication, determined to see it through, knowing the true rewards can come only if you finish what you start.

Dear Lord, thank You for this reassurance. When I get discouraged, remind me of my goals. Help me to finish what I start.

—Marjorie Holmes

Tuesday

30

The power which the Lord hath given me to edification, and not to destruction. —II Corinthians 13:10

Years ago, I gained enough job seniority as a skilled machine operator to leave the evening shift and work days. I felt I should give something back to the community for watching over my family while I was absent nights, so I volunteered at the local community center. The director assigned me to the young teen club of twenty boys and girls. I was a bit dismayed, having hoped for something less challenging. But together, we hiked, picnicked, played baseball, presented a career night and initiated something new: preparing a dinner for the parents. It was a success!

Then, two years later, work orders slackened and I had to stop my community work and get back on the night shift...this time as a floor sweeper! Hurt and resentful, I wondered about my future, and the young teens. *What kind of example would I be to them now? A man pushing a broom?*

I didn't get the answer right away. But after many long nights of broom pushing, it came. Sure, floor-sweeping wasn't my idea of the most prestigious job, but it was a job worth doing—especially if I gave my best. That was the example I needed to set: a man doing a menial job with pride and dignity. I did my best to set it.

Have you lost something you were comfortable with...a good job position, a house you liked or even a friend? Maybe that loss is God's way of setting you on your way toward greater gain.

Lord, You taught me by taking away. Thank You for showing me a new pathway. —Oscar Greene

Wednesday

31

The foolish ones said to the wise..."Our lamps are going out." —Matthew 25:8 (NIV)

"Hand me the lamp, young'un," Grandma said, reaching for the kerosene jug on the floor of the pantry.

I lifted the old lamp from its place on the shelf. Carefully Grandma removed the glass globe, trimmed the wick and began pouring kerosene into the base. "Got to keep her filled—just in case this newfangled stuff gives out," she'd say, waving at the light bulb overhead.

Often that "new stuff" did give out—when autumn storms shook the trees, when spring winds swept over our farm in wild fury. That's when Grandma would set that kerosene lamp in the center of the kitchen table, where its rays helped push back the darkness. And her satisfied smile was visible even in the dim light.

Sometimes I feel like I'm running out of "oil": I volunteer for one too many committees; I try to get by on a few hours of sleep; I forget to take my vitamins; I neglect reading my Bible; I convince myself that hot dogs really are nutritious. But soon I find I'm irritable and tired and discouraged. I snap at the kids, grumble when my husband Gary's late for dinner. I am less creative and more sarcastic. That's when I seem to hear Grandma saying, "Got to keep her filled." So I take time for a long walk in the woods or a leisurely bubble bath. I thumb through a magazine, treat myself to Mexican food, play checkers with my son Brett. I read the Gospels, pausing to hear the roar of the Sea of Galilee and the murmurs of surprise when Jesus heals the blind man. I turn my prayers into praises. And, like Grandma's kerosene lamp, I soon find I'm "filled up" and ready to shine!

Cure me, Father, of the emptiness caused by hurry and stress. Today I will stand still—and be filled. —Mary Lou Carney

Thank-You Notes to God

1 ________________________________

2 ________________________________

3 ________________________________

4 ________________________________

5 ________________________________

6 ________________________________

7 ________________________________

8 ________________________________

9 ________________________________

10 ________________________________

11 ________________________________

12 ________________________________

13 ________________________________

14 ________________________________

15 ________________________________

16

17

18

19

20

21

22

23

24

25

26

27

28

29

30

31

FEBRUARY

S	*M*	*T*	*W*	*T*	*F*	*S*
				1	2	3
4	5	6	7	8	9	10
11	12	13	14	15	16	17
18	19	20	21	22	23	24
25	26	27	28			

SPIRITUAL TREASURE

Be Reconciled

First be reconciled to thy brother.... —Matthew 5:24

As lacy valentines turn up in stores, thoughts turn to those you love. But what about those folks who are difficult to love, the ones on the outskirts of your life? Think of the person with whom you've exchanged harsh words, someone who rubs you the wrong way, the one you've shunned because of past hurts. This month work at reconciling the distance between you. Build a bridge with a friendly note, a warm smile or the words, "Let's start over."

Building a bridge from your heart to another makes a way for love to flow, not just out, but back in.

My Monthly Prayer List

Family Prayer for February

Jesus, help me to love the poor, the homeless, the needy. Show me how I can make a difference this month.

Thursday

1

THROUGH AN OPEN WINDOW
Believe Him

Faith is the substance of things hoped for, the evidence of things not seen. —Hebrews 11:1

As I opened my window this morning, I noticed the little pamphlet on my bedside table, "God's Promises." I'd read it before going to sleep last night. It reminded me that there was a time when, even though I was a churchgoer, I doubted some of the puzzling sayings of Jesus Christ. "He couldn't possibly have meant what He said about faith moving mountains into the sea," I insisted to my friend Diane.

Then, a few weeks later, Diane admired the lace handkerchief I'd tucked into the breast pocket of my blue linen dress. "All the women in Paris are wearing fancy handkerchiefs in their suit or dress pockets," I volunteered.

"Have you just returned from Paris?" she asked.

"No."

"Then how do you know this?"

"A coworker who was there last month told me."

"You don't doubt your coworker's words?"

"No, my friend wouldn't lie," I answered.

Diane took out a pad and pencil, wrote something and handed me a piece of paper that read, "John 20:29." "Look it up when you get home," was all she would say.

That evening I looked it up and read, "Because thou hast seen me, thou hast believed: blessed are they that have not seen, and yet have believed." I knew what Diane was saying: I had put unquestioning faith in my friend's words about a frivolous fashion fad, so why was it hard to believe in the words of my greatest Friend, Jesus?

This month, as a little spiritual exercise, I'm going to search the Scriptures for His promises. As I study His words, I am going to bring to it an unquestioning faith. And when I feel that faith waver, I'll pray, "Lord, I believe; help thou my unbelief" (Mark 9:24).

Just for a start I've listed a few here:

I am with you alway, even unto the end of the world (Matthew 28:20).
I go to prepare a place for you (John 14:2).
I will not leave you comfortless (John 14:18).

The promises of Christ. What better guidelines can we have for His plan for our lives? Do you have a small faith today about something that looms large in concern? Then pray with me:

Lord, I believe in *You. Help me to* believe *You.* —Eleanor Sass

Friday

2

Fear not; I will help thee. —Isaiah 41:13

Sunlight glistens on his whiskers as Mr. Groundhog cautiously pokes his head above his earthy burrow. He eases to his haunches, twitches his fuzzy ears and listens for signs of danger. Then... horrors! He sees this big, black, spooky thing looming in front of him. *Whoosh!* He's gone. His shadow has sent him fleeing back to the safety of his den. This means, according to legend from Great Britain and Germany, that winter will last another six weeks.

I, for one, like a sunny day—especially in February. How silly to let a shadow spoil it. *But,* I wonder, *how many times have I retreated from opportunity because I was frightened by a shadow called "uncertainty" or "inadequacy"?* Perhaps my fear is as unfounded as the groundhog's.

I have an idea! This Groundhog Day, despite the scary shadows in front of me, I'm going to take one small step toward something I want to accomplish. I'm going to accept that invitation to speak, even though I'm nervous. How about you? Are you thinking about accepting a new job, going back to school or trying to break an old habit? Then why don't you make that phone call or write the letter that could change your life. After all, even the timid groundhog eventually raises his head, takes a whiff of clover and scurries from his hole.

Dear Lord, this Groundhog Day, give me the courage to confront my shadows. —Terry Helwig

Saturday

3

Let the wicked forsake his way...and let him return unto the Lord.... —Isaiah 55:7

The last time I saw my old friend he was back in the Southern city of his youth, back as well to the church where he'd been baptized.

"Are you hungry?" he asked me as we sat in his small, one-room apartment. I said I wasn't, but he got up and fixed me a tuna salad sandwich anyway. Then we sat and talked while I ate. We recalled how we'd met over thirty years before, after he'd written for the magazine I worked for about his own personal account of having been a professional pickpocket. We talked about his three hard terms in prison, and how eventually the insistent prayers of a good woman had found their mark. "Prayed me right out of business," he said with a glint.

Whenever we met and talked, there was never any doubt in my mind that his criminal past was behind him. "Amazing how the Lord can change a man," he'd say to me often. Sometimes we'd talk about his days as a pickpocket, but even when I'd ask, he wouldn't say anything about the techniques of picking pockets, only that no pocket or handbag was safe from the hands of a truly artful thief.

One time he did tell me something that I've thought a lot about since. It was about eyes. He was telling me that if he was in a crowd and there were "fuzz" (police) around, he had to be careful not to look straight at them. "The eyes are incorruptible," he said. "They talk truth."

Now my friend was deep into his eighties. The good woman with the insistent prayers was dead and he missed her, but I was glad this gentle man with the courtly manners had come back to the place that once he had been too ashamed even to visit.

"Amazing how the Lord can change a man," he said, leaning across the table. And his eyes, looking straight into mine, talked truth.

Father, may my eyes clearly reveal the truth that is You.

—Van Varner

Sunday

4

They that worship him must worship him in spirit and in truth.
—John 4:24

Sunday morning was more hectic than usual. It seemed to be a fitting end to a chaotic week. Too much surgery, too many patients and too many committee meetings. I slid into the seat my wife Sally had saved for me as the minister finished his announcements.

"Let us now turn our hearts to God," I heard him say as I carefully placed my feet to keep from stepping on Dino's tail. Dino, a greying golden retriever, is a seeing-eye dog who leads our friend Lisa into church each Sunday. He lay quietly at her feet beside me. "All stand to sing hymn number two seven eight," the minister continued. I fumbled with my book, nearly dropping it, as I searched for the page. The congregation was on the second line by the time I found my place.

I'm just not with it! I thought as I tried to join in. But then the beat of the singing seemed to take on a physical presence. It wasn't a miracle—it was Dino's tail wagging against my leg. It stayed with the tempo of the hymn only long enough to get me going. Then it speeded up even faster. I looked down to see Dino's brown eyes shining with devotion as he looked up at his master. Although Lisa couldn't see that devotion, she could feel the warmth and joy of Dino's presence close to her.

Could my Master feel my joy at being near Him? Did a sense of warmth radiate from me to Him?

I closed my eyes and looked upward.

Lord, may I worship You with a simple adoration and love.
—Scott Harrison

Monday

5

But by the grace of God I am what I am....
—I Corinthians 15:10

When I was a child, the comic character Popeye was one of my favorites. I especially loved when he sang, "I y'am what I y'am...I'm

Popeye the sailor man." I thought it was marvelous that this zany character knew exactly who he was and never tried to be anyone else. He even liked himself.

Unlike Popeye, I wasn't certain who I was or what I was supposed to do in life. Even as a teenager and young adult, I wasn't certain about my identity or what was expected of me. I often observed others who seemed to know who they were, and I tried to be like them. All to no avail.

For several years in high school, I hated my size 8½ feet and wanted feet like my cousin, who wore a cute 5½. Once at a dance, I felt rejected and hid for a while in a tiny bathroom so no one would know I wasn't having fun. After I married and had children, I became convinced that I was a total failure as a mother because I screamed some days and dreaded other days (especially rainy ones) with a houseful of bored children. Some days I just didn't like anything about myself.

It didn't come easily for me, but after years of reading God's Word, and finally believing it, I know now that I am *chosen* (Ephesians 1:4), *beloved* (Romans 1:7), *forgiven* (Ephesians 1:7, 4:32), *blessed* (Ephesians 1:3), *accepted* (Ephesians 1:6), *redeemed* (Ephesians 1:7), *a joint heir* with Christ (Romans 8:17), *justified* (Romans 8:30). The list goes on, and all through the Bible we're told exactly who we are! Some days I don't *feel* like it, but I choose to believe, even sing loudly like Popeye, *"I am who I am... I'm Marion, a child of the King!"*

If you're having trouble with who you are today or just experiencing one of those "down days," pray with me:

My Father, the great I Am, thank You for my identity in Christ Jesus. Amen.

—Marion Bond West

Tuesday

6

These things have I spoken unto you, that my joy might remain in you, and that your joy might be full.

—John 15:11

"Bust the blahs out of your life by practicing more joyful facial expressions!" the professor encouraged the people attending his workshop on the importance of humor in our lives. "Our faces communicate more messages than our words, but starting about age five, we get self-conscious about using facial expressions, and our facial muscles start to atrophy. Loosen them up! Use them to express yourself. Open your eyes wider. Lift those eyebrows. Show some enthusiasm. Etch in a few laugh lines!" The man sounded a bit more like a barker at a carnival than a university professor, but he got me to thinking.

Driving home, I began to wonder what my face reflects and glanced up to catch a glimpse of myself in the rearview mirror. Looks kind of sullen and anxious, I decided as I pulled up to a red light. Is that what the person in the next car sees? How about the cashier in the checkout lane, or the gas station attendant? Do they know I have the Holy Spirit within me? Does my face reflect His joy? I couldn't shake the questions from my mind and I have to admit, since that day, I've been lots more conscious of my facial messages.

How about you?

Lord, I promise to smile more often today, reflecting Your Love. And who knows? My facial messages might be contagious.

—Carol Kuykendall

Wednesday

7

He who has begun a good work in you will complete it.... —Philippians 1:6 (NKJV)

A few months ago I was watching a TV show about how movies are made. I laughed when the actors had to "take" and "retake" scenes until they got them right, but I could tell it wasn't funny to them. It was frustrating and embarrassing. "Let's do it again," the director would yell, "till we get it right." He was patient, but he kept after the actors to do their best.

Then one night I saw the finished movie. I was amazed at how smooth and natural the finished film seemed to be. No one would ever have guessed how much trouble went into producing it.

Now, when I get frustrated with my own failure, I think of that movie. I remind myself that my life is still in the production stage and that I'm going to make many mistakes.

"Let's do it again," God whispers, "till we get it right."

When my life is over, I'm hoping that God will edit out my goofs, and the finished product will seem natural and beautiful. The pain and frustration will disappear, leaving only the scriptwriter's story.

Are you punishing yourself for yesterday's flubs? If so, you are wasting energy that could be better used to replay the scene. Check the script of God's Word. Ask the Director for guidance, and begin again.

Lord, You know how hard I try, but I keep making mistakes. Don't let me give up until I am all You had in mind when You made me.

—Daniel Schantz

Thursday

8

I can do all things through Christ which strengtheneth me. —Philippians 4:13

Selling a house is a big undertaking. The trim needs painting, windows must be washed, tile fixed, carpets shampooed, trees clipped... and the list goes on. We can't afford to hire it out, so guess who has to do all the work? It's a real predicament. This month, I'm going to pray about it in a notebook by using a four-step problem-solving method I call *C.O.P.E.* Here's how it works:

Connect with God in your own way. Write a prayer or your thoughts in a notebook, bringing to God your concern.

Observe the scene and the people involved in your problem (including yourself) as if you were watching a play. Then write a description of the situation.

Partition. Break your problem into bite-sized pieces. Ask yourself: What is urgent? What can wait? What one part (however small) can I solve this month? This week? Today? Resolve to take that action.

Expect a good outcome. Write the Psalmist's words, "The Lord will perfect that which concerneth me" (Psalm 138:8). Or write down your own faith-filled thoughts about your problem, remembering that God is your partner through anything.

Every day, reread your notes and add new thoughts and prayers. They'll help you keep an expectant attitude.

In the next few months, I invite you to an experiment: When a problem comes up that feels monumental or even one that is just plain worrisome, try practicing the four steps of *C.O.P.E.* Keep a notebook or use the *Daily Guideposts* notes section in the back of each month to record your progress. Keep a steady record. Then in three months, on May 8 (we'll remind you), let's look back at the results. Write us and share your experience: Guideposts Books, Attn: *Daily Guideposts* Editor, 757 Third Avenue, New York, NY 10017.

Practice *C.O.P.E.*-ing and learn to process your problems instead of being immobilized by them!

Father, with Your help, I know I can C.O.P.E. *with anything.*

—Marilyn Morgan Helleberg

Friday

9

There is... a time to weep, and a time to laugh....

—Ecclesiastes 3:1,4

Last year at a conference a group of us were in a "storytelling" session in which people gathered in circles to tell stories from their lives. One of the participants had attended a "clowning" workshop just before the session and showed up wearing a white clown-face and a gigantic red smile painted ear to ear. When it came time for her to tell her story, I expected a happy tale to match her face. Instead she told about her husband's death seven years earlier and how she had been stuck in grief ever since.

It was such a contradiction to see her tell this story of pain while wearing a big red clown-smile, I couldn't help mentioning the irony to her.

She thought a moment, then said, "You know, maybe that's why I've been trapped in my grief. For seven years I've been crying on the inside and smiling on the outside. Creating the illusion of happiness was easier than facing the hurt."

Now when I ache inside with a problem, I think of that woman. She was a striking reminder that help and healing do not come when we pretend and mask our pain, but rather when we are honest and admit our need.

Father, do not let me hide my hurts so they fester in the dark, but help me find the courage to bring them into healing light.

—Sue Monk Kidd

Saturday

10

The Almighty...shall bless thee with blessings of heaven above, blessings of the deep that lieth under, blessings of the breasts, and of the womb.

—Genesis 49:25

As a child growing up in the fifties, I was a precocious worry wart. My mother, seeing my light on late at night, would come into my room sleepy-eyed, her hair set in bobby pins. "Worrying again?"

"Uh huh," I would nod.

"What about?"

"Well, I didn't do so well on the math test today," I would mumble. It wasn't true. But I didn't want to tell her the real reason. I had just changed from a public to a private school. Oh, how I longed to wear cashmere sweaters, just like the other girls! How I worried that they would laugh at my unstylish clothes!

My mother would perch on the edge of my bed, cuddling close. "What's number one on the *Hit Parade*?" she would ask and start singing the latest hit song without waiting for me to reply. "'When you're tired and you can't sleep,'" she crooned softly, just like the record, "'count your blessings instead of sheep....'"

Then she would say brightly, "Since you're up, you can do what the song says. Make a Bedtime Blessing List. Writing down all the good things God has given you will put your mind at ease."

It worked. I hadn't realized that my blessings far outnumbered all the material things I felt I lacked. My blessings snaked down one page and across another, and before long my hand was tired, my eyes heavy, and it was all I could do to ask mother to turn out the light.

How do You bless me, Lord? Let me count the ways, lest I forget:

1. ____________________________________

2. ____________________________________

3. ____________________________________

—Linda Ching Sledge

Sunday

11

So we know and believe the love God has for us.
—I John 4:16 (RSV)

When her much-loved bassett hound Buttercup died, my five-year-old granddaughter Jessica and I had a long talk. I told her how sorry I was and she responded with great feeling that it was the saddest day of her life. "But the good part is that Buttercup is no longer sick," I said.

"And that she is in Heaven," Jessica added.

"Yes, she was a good dog, and I'm sure God found a special place for her in Heaven."

"Where is Heaven?" Jessica wanted to know.

I paused to compose my answer, then told her, "It's where God is."

"And God is everywhere," she said emphatically.

"Yes, Jessica, He certainly is."

That conversation brought to mind Jesus' scolding of His disciples when they tried to bar children from flocking to Him. The passage ends with Christ blessing the children (one translation suggests "hugging them") and the admonition that "Whosoever shall not receive the kingdom of God as a little child, he shall not enter therein" (Mark 10:15). For adults that often means making a Grand Canyon leap of faith; for children it is only a baby step. Maybe the answer for those who have trouble bridging that chasm of intellect and skepticism is to find a believing child to lead them. Say a child who knows without any doubt that her beloved dog is with Jesus in Heaven—right now. How could it be any other way?

In You is found sure refuge and relief,
I believe, Lord, help Thou my unbelief.

—Fred Bauer

Monday

12

And whatsoever ye do, do it heartily, as to the Lord, and not unto men.
—Colossians 3:23

February is Black History Month. Last February our public library engaged a distinguished university professor to speak on W.E.B. Du

Bois, the educator and author. Du Bois was the first of our race to earn a Ph.D. from Harvard University.

After much preparation, the evening came. When the honored guest arrived, only nine people had shown up, including myself. But for two hours the speaker told us all about Du Bois, holding us spellbound! He had given his best to a nearly empty hall.

It made me remember the time I had been engaged to speak and found an overflowing audience. As it turned out, a choral group filled the entire program, which ended without my uttering a word! I left, kicking the snowdrifts, and when I got home I complained to my wife Ruby. She listened, then said, "You prepared, you were there, you kept your word. What more could you do?"

She was right. Yet there was something more I could have done—I could have acted more like that gracious university professor, who was not resentful that so few came out to hear him but gave enthusiastically and generously. The next opportunity I have, I pray that my attitude will be gracious and that God will be proud of my actions.

Is God looking upon you with pride and joy?

Dear God, help me to do my best with enthusiasm whether or not someone is there to watch, compliment or applaud. —Oscar Greene

Tuesday

13

Then Jesus took the loaves and gave thanks to God and passed them out to the people. Afterwards he did the same with the fish. And everyone ate until full!
—John 6:11 (TLB)

When I was a kid, whenever my Uncle Ralph visited, he'd end each meal by saying something at breakneck speed that he'd been required to say at military school years before: "My gastronomical satiety admonishes me that I have reached that state of deglutition consistent with dietetic integrity." After a few visits, he laughingly admitted that all it meant was, "I'm full."

When I was a parent, I started thinking about the formalized, memorized grace my family said before meals. We rattled it off without listening to the words as quickly as Uncle Ralph blurted out his "I'm full" message.

I decided to forego the memorized version and instead let the children take turns saying whatever came to mind. Sometimes it was thoughtful, as when Jeanne said, "God bless Grandma and help her to feel better. Thank You for this food, our home and each other." Sometimes it was quick and filled with teenage humor, like the time Michael blurted out, "Rub-a-dub-dub, thank You for the grub. Amen."

For the last few years now, just before the food is served, the children and I have been taking turns reading the *Daily Guideposts* selection for the day. Besides the inspirational message that reminds us of the Lord's goodness, we've all become better "out-loud" readers and the selections often lead to lively dinner conversations. Maybe before meals is the time you and your family could enjoy this book together.

Lord, thank You for this food and for my wonderful family. Thank You for giving us this time together each day to draw close to one another and to You. —Patricia Lorenz

Wednesday

14

Take heed therefore how ye hear.... —Luke 8:18

Valentine's Day. What a good time to share something my friend Jan taught me about developing emotionally close relationships. It's this: More than anything else, the one thing people want is to be heard. It's the magnet that draws people to one another, keeps them coming back and holds relationships together. Here are some things I've learned from Jan about listening:

- *Instead of small talk, share something personal about yourself.* Vulnerability opens the door to closeness.
- *When the other person shares, listen!* Show by facial expression, nodding or appropriate questions that you're really hearing. You don't have to agree. Just listen.
- *Don't steal the conversation by saying, "Oh, that happened to me, too."* Let the other person express all they need to say.
- *Try to share feelings instead of intellectual concepts or pat*

answers. "I understand. It makes me sad, too." Instead of, "The Bible says..." or, "All you have to do is...."

- *Never give advice unless asked, and maybe not even then!* Most people really don't want it and may avoid you in the future if they choose not to follow your advice.
- *Above all, don't judge.* Accept, and you will be accepted.
- *Finally, never betray a confidence.* Value and respect what was shared, and safekeep it in your heart and prayers.

Let's give our spouse, parent, child, sibling or friend the best valentine of all this year—the chance to be truly heard.

Lord, help me to listen with my heart! —Marilyn Morgan Helleberg

Thursday

15

And from him that would borrow of thee turn not thou away. —Matthew 5:42

Today, because it was his birthday, I find myself thinking of Glenn Kittler, the wonderful warmhearted man whose wit and wisdom cheered all of us who worked with him. Glenn has been gone for three years now, but I'm sure many readers of *Daily Guideposts* remember him and his cat Louie.

Glenn said something once that I've never forgotten. We were walking together along an avenue in New York City when we were approached by a wistful woman who said she needed money because her children were hungry. Glenn took out a handful of coins and gave them to her.

As we moved on I said disapprovingly, "That woman's here every day with that same story. She'll probably just buy a drink with that money you gave her."

"Perhaps she will," Glenn said. "But you know, I think God sometimes sends people like that just to test our sense of charity." We walked a little farther, and then he said, almost to himself, "The act of giving is more important than the merit of the receiver."

Jesus knew that, too.

Lord, use us to show Your love to others. —Arthur Gordon

Friday
16

WINDOWS INTO WONDER
The Impossible Made Possible

On that day the Lord made a covenant with Abram....
—Genesis 15:18 (RSV)

On a silent desert hillside, in the holy hush of evening, an old man named Abram stood thinking about his greatest disappointment: God had not given him a son to be his heir, and now it was too late. Suddenly, from out of the stillness, a Voice sounded, promising Abram the one thing he wanted more than anything else in the world—a son. The Lord also gave him a new name and promised to be the God of Abraham's people forever. Then, in a dream, God sealed this everlasting covenant by taking the form of "a smoking fire pot and a flaming torch," and passing between the pieces of the sacrifice. I wonder how many times, in the difficult days and months and years that followed, Abraham was about to give up when he happened to see a flaming torch, and it reminded him of God's promise. Surely he carried that image in his heart for the rest of his life, as an assurance that impossible things are made possible by God's grace.

Like Abraham, I know about disappointment. For more than a year my precious daughter Karen has been treated for depression at a clinic in Topeka. Karen's future is uncertain, and I can't help worrying about her. But since I've soaked myself in Abraham's vision, I've become more aware of the *flicker of flames*... in a fireplace, on the altar at church... wherever a shining light catches my eye. Somehow, these lights remind me that Abraham's God is my God, too, and that He is still quietly working His miracles in the lives of ordinary people like Karen and you and me.

Perhaps you, too, have a sadness or a disappointment. Maybe you'd like to join me in watching for God's flame, as we go through the month ahead. I don't know where you will see it next. Maybe the stars in the sky or the night-light in your hallway will be reminders for you. Or perhaps you'll be standing on a darkened city street and notice a single light in a high window... and suddenly you'll smile, remembering that your Friend is near. Last week, as I was dining out with my daughter, I noticed the reflection of a candle flame in her eyeglasses. It was like a secret wink from my heavenly Friend, reminding me that Karen is His... and so am I.

During the month ahead, Lord, let every flame I see remind me that You are my God, the One Who makes the impossible possible.
—Marilyn Morgan Helleberg

February Prayer List Reminder

Return to your Monthly Prayer List on the calendar opening page and review your requests. Give thanks for prayers answered, renew old prayers and add new concerns today. Then pray once again our *Family Prayer for February.*

Saturday

17

In Thee, O Lord, do I put my trust.... —Psalm 71:1

Years ago, in winter, a young man was traveling to the West. He came to a river, but no bridge was in sight. It became obvious to him that he would have to cross on the ice. He took a tentative step. He thought he heard the ice crack, so he pulled back. But there was no alternative. Then he remembered that if you distribute your weight over a larger area, you have a better chance on thin ice, so he got down on his hands and knees and crawled out on the ice. But even in this position, he was afraid, so he stretched himself out full length on the ice and inched himself along. When he was in the middle of the river, he heard someone whistling. Cautiously, he lifted his head to see a farmboy driving a team of horses pulling a wagonload of wood right across the river.

Have you ever felt like the fellow timidly stretched out on the ice? I have! I had come to a major turning point in my life—early retirement—and was not prepared for it. No more regular paycheck; living on a so-called fixed income. *What will we do if we run into a financial emergency? What will we do if the car breaks down? What will we do if our house is destroyed by an earthquake? What if...? What if...?*

But, I thought to myself, *what about the promises of God?* I could trust God when I was getting a paycheck; why couldn't I trust Him in retirement? Why was I so timid about the promises of God? My faith and confidence returned, and though I'm not like the farmboy driving a team of horses across the ice, I am walking confidently with a sure and steady step. And I'm whistling as I go!

Dear Lord, give me a faith strong enough to take that first steady step on the uncertain stretch of ice before me. —Lee Webber

Sunday

18

Fireside Friend

Let him become a fool, that he may be wise.

—I Corinthians 3:18

Our long Minnesota winters can be harsh—especially on the spirit. They start in November and get steadily colder. January brings below-zero temperatures and February sees fifty-below windchill factors.

In an attempt to cheer up her often housebound family, Mom fills our screened-in porch with dozens of bright, multicolored balloons. As they dance in the wind, they lift not only our spirits, but also those of the people waiting at the chilly bus stop just outside our door.

It was on such a gloomy day a few years back that my friend Kathy and I sat by our picture window, gazing a bit dolefully at those valiant little balloons cavorting joyfully out on the porch. Suddenly, inspiration came out of nowhere. We grabbed a handful of magic markers, donned hats, coats, gloves, scarves and boots and headed outside. We sat ourselves down on the snow-covered porch swing and began to draw the silliest, goofiest faces we could imagine on each of the balloons.

Our reward an hour later was dozens of silly smiling balloon faces plastered up against the window. I smiled, too. Our drawings weren't great art, but they showed how a little creativity could put a fun face on a dreary day.

Now, let me ask you on this cold, wintry February day—if I can use the creativity God gave me to brighten up my world, right here in frostbitten Minnesota, what can you do to brighten your corner of the world? Invent a new recipe, make up a song, write a funny poem? Whatever it is, be sure to enjoy!

Dear Lord, You gave all of us the gift of creativity. Help me to use mine by sharing it with others. —Tammy Rider

Monday

19

In the multitude of words there wanteth not sin: but he that refraineth his lips is wise. —Proverbs 10:19

A couple years ago while doing some research on the Constitution, I became intrigued by that enigmatic, larger-than-life figure, George Washington. At the Constitutional Convention in Philadelphia, he was the obvious leader of the young nation. A victorious general, the retired commander-in-chief, he was already "the father of our country," a man many thought should be king. He was elected president of the convention hands-down and with his customary modesty—calling on God's help, as always—he agreed to serve.

But all during that long, hot, stifling summer, he exercised his considerable authority in a surprising way. As the delegates argued back and forth about the power of the states versus the federal government, the power of the judicial branch over the legislative, the power of the president over the legislative, the general sat at their head—silent, impassive, austere. Sometimes with a slight nod he would indicate he was in favor of an idea or suggestion. At several crucial moments he spoke out, but never more than ten minutes at a time. No, it was by his respectful, courteous silence that he exerted the most influence. He would wait for tempers to subside, and then with a few words guide the delegates to the compromises that made the Constitution possible.

I admire that, envy it. In too many meetings at church or at work, I ramble on or interrupt, too enchanted with my own ideas to keep silent about them. Not Washington. He knew that sometimes the most effective way to persuade people is through forbearance, patience and caring.

On this Presidents' Day and every day, Lord, let my words be carefully chosen and spoken.
—Rick Hamlin

Tuesday

20

So overflowing is his kindness towards us that he took away all our sins through the blood of his Son, by whom we are saved.... —Ephesians 1:7 (TLB)

One day, darting off to a rehearsal, my teenage daughter exclaimed, "I don't want to be late. When I'm late I'm mad at myself, and I don't *like* to be mad at myself, it hurts my feelings!"

I laughed at the time, but behind those bright words lurks a spiritual truth: How much time we waste, and how much misery we cause ourselves, by being "mad at ourselves" over our failures. Current ones, as trivial as being late, or painful mistakes that still haunt us from the past.

Here are some things that have helped me overcome, or at least control, this very human dilemma.

1. If the self-scolding is about something fairly innocent, *laugh at yourself and talk back*: "Okay, okay, I goofed. What I did was stupid and silly, and I'm sorry, but this isn't worth worrying about. I'll do better next time."
2. If the mistake was a little more serious, *acknowledge your virtues as well as your faults:* "Yes, I've hurt and failed some people, but I never really meant to. I've helped a lot of people, too. And I intend to help even more, every day I can."
3. If the pains of remorse and self-accusations are sharpest over things that happened long ago, remember this: *You were a different person then*. Nobody stands still in life. Our very bodies shed their cells, rebuild, regroup. We are constantly being molded and shaped by time and people and circumstance.

The Lord said, "Behold, I will make all things new!" You are no longer the person you were even five or ten years ago. When you think of that person, let it be fondly, with compassion and understanding. Say to yourself, "I've changed. I'm a new person today, trying to grow into something much better and finer."

These thoughts have helped me a lot. I hope you'll find them useful, too.

Thank You, Lord, for Your guidance as I continue to grow into the person You want me to be. —Marjorie Holmes

Wednesday

21

How beautiful are the feet of them that preach the gospel of peace.... —Romans 10:15

A two-day blizzard closed roads in our part of Kansas, but on the third day, the sun peeked through the clouds. Despite radio warnings that "nonessential travel is discouraged," I decided to make the fifty-mile trip to my office. I had the road to myself until I hit Highway 83, where a string of vehicles stretched as far as I could see. There'd been an accident, and traffic was moving one lane at a time.

I couldn't pass. I couldn't do anything except fume! Half of the traffic was recreational vehicles with out-of-state plates. *They certainly aren't essential travel,* I thought. I glared and muttered at the motorists, leaning on my horn if the vehicle in front of me didn't keep up the pace.

Then a maroon car crept past mine. The woman beside the driver smiled and held up a handmade sign that said "Peace."

Know what? My tension faded and I stopped blaming the other drivers for my predicament. I could have worked at home one more day: I had no more right to the road than the other travelers. I decided to pass along the peace that had been shared with me. I didn't have a sign and needed both hands to drive, but I could smile... and did.

Stuck in traffic? Smile, and be at peace.

Lord, thank You for people whose actions remind me that You are the Prince of Peace. —Penney Schwab

Thursday

22

But if we hope for that we see not, then do we with patience wait for it. —Romans 8:25

Last night Lake Michigan dumped half a dozen inches of "lake-effect" snow on my town. Snowplows push through drifted streets; merchants snow-blow sidewalks. Nowhere is there a sign of spring—nowhere except at the Dairy Barn.

The Dairy Barn is one of those wonderful seasonal phenomena—opening in late April and closing just after Labor Day. All summer long kids (even old ones like me!) line up for sundaes and floats and sodas. When summer ends, the Dairy Barn boards up its windows with huge pieces of plywood. Depressing, right? Not really. In fact, those very pieces of plywood have become a symbol of hope for me all through the cold, blustery winters—because written on them in huge white letters are these words: OPEN SOON.

Soon. I remember that when my wheels spin on packed-down snow. I think about crocuses when I scrape ice off my windshield. I imagine hot fudge while I shovel out my mailbox. And that simple sign has taught me the importance of *expectant* waiting in other areas of my life, too. I visualize myself ten pounds thinner as I pick up the speed on my daily walk. I *see* a tranquil family meal, free from sibling squabbles, while I set the table. I imagine children listening and smiling when I give my next talk at middle school. I anticipate health and happiness filling up my life.

Why not join me? Close your eyes right now and *see* your hopes realized—a child healed or a problem solved or a promotion received. Now open your eyes and expect great things to happen—*soon!*

Thank You, Father, for the power of hope. On this wintry day I believe in spring; in the midst of my troubles, I believe in Your peace.

—Mary Lou Carney

Day Brightener

MEDICINE CHEST

For the blues, read Psalm 27.
For an empty purse, read Psalm 37.
If discouraged about work, Psalm 128.
If people seem unkind to you, John 15.
If you cannot have your own way, James 3.
If you are all out of sorts, Hebrews 12.
For a traveling companion, Psalm 121.
If you are losing confidence in people, I Corinthians 13.

Friday

23

But be ye doers of the word, and not hearers only....
—James 1:22

"Runway heading to eleven hundred feet," my flight instructor said. "Ninety degrees left—twenty degrees of bank for your crosswind." Each time Gary gave me an order, I would follow it exactly. "Left ninety degrees to downwind. When you reach fifteen hundred feet, level off."

This lesson was one I had done before. I knew that day I should be ready to make my first solo flight. I had all the maneuvers under control; all I had to do was follow Gary's instructions. He gave me step-by-step directions all the way to a good landing and then, "Give it the power." And we were off again for another circuit.

This happened repeatedly. However, with each circuit, Gary's instructions became less frequent. When finally I looked at him inquiringly, he burst out, "Why don't you fly like you know how to? Do I have to tell you everything over and over again?"

I was shocked. I had felt so comfortable just following his instructions. But he was right. The next three touch-and-go's I did without a word from Gary. And I did the following three without Gary in the plane. It was a simple lesson, but learning to take responsibility to do the things I know how to do is a lesson that never goes out of date.

Lord, let Your will be part of my life, not something I must always be reminded of. —Brian Miller

Saturday

24

And the Lord shall guide thee continually....
—Isaiah 58:11

Some days, I just wish life would leave me alone. I don't like change. I like to live a fairly structured life, serving dinner at a regular time, knowing where everyone in the family is, going down to pick up the mail at the same time every day. When I don't have that underlying structure in my life, I get irritable and feel slightly off balance all day.

This has been a notably unstructured week, and I'm feeling stressed out today, like a washing machine trying to cope with a comforter. So I'm calling a time-out. We'll have pizza for dinner, and I'll read a good book instead of trying to "be productive." You see, I've learned to give in to life now and then: If it's going to throw me an unstructured week, I'll ignore my desire to impose order and just go along for the ride. Who knows, it may take me somewhere wonderful that I never would have seen if I'd forced life back into its comfortable routine.

Father, give me the grace to enjoy the adventure of an unplanned day, letting You take me where You will, instead of where I will.
—Toni Sortor

Sunday

25

He casts forth his ice like morsels; who can stand before his cold? He sends forth his word, and melts them.... —Psalm 147:17–18 (RSV)

They're still calling it the "Alaska blast," this swath of frigid air originating in Siberia that swept across the nation via Alaska last winter. It was the largest high pressure system ever measured in North America. Let me rephrase that: It was one gigantic deep freeze. We felt like walking icicles in the "land of the midnight shivers."

In that kind of weather, as one lady stated so succinctly, "You hear the sound of cars not starting." A couple of nights we placed our car battery by the woodstove in a valiant attempt to keep it alive. Up the highway, where windchill plummeted to −120 degrees, oil turned to jelly and rubber tires became so brittle, they shattered. Emergency broadcasts urged travelers to stay off the roads.

Some of our friends had only a woodstove. They had to set an alarm clock every two hours to get up and stoke the fire at night. In the stores, everything that had anything to do with heating dwindled to nothing. But bless our TV news station. They ran clips from previous summers showing swimmers, bikers and sunbathers, reminding us all that this, too, shall pass. It seems impossible, in the grip of winter, to believe that the bud is bound up in the brittle branch or the rose lies in the frozen earth... but, as the Scriptures say, the Lord will "send forth His word" and melt the ice away.

Are you caught in the grip of a "cold spell"—depression, perhaps, or loneliness or grief? Have you asked the Lord to "send forth His word"—His comfort and hope and love—to warm the chill in your heart? Try it right now and see if joy and gladness are not hidden inside you just waiting to burst into bloom!

Almighty God, reassure me that my winter shall pass and the frozen earth once again shall bring forth the rose. —Carol Knapp

Monday

26

This is the victory that overcomes the world, our faith.
—I John 5:4 (RSV)

One bright, frozen day in downtown Atlanta, I stood outside a soup kitchen as a line of homeless and hungry people gathered. My husband and I had come to help serve the noon meal. As I neared the door, I noticed a woman wearing a thin coat, a ski cap and *one* glove. She clasped her cold, unprotected hand in her gloved hand, trying to rub some warmth into it.

"I see you lost a glove," I said to her.

"No," she replied, a smile lifting her face. "I *found* a glove."

That woman lives in my memory. She taught me that even in bleak moments, I should look with eyes of faith. The pessimist sees one glove missing; the optimist sees one glove found. The pessimist looks to the ground and sees the mud. The optimist looks to the sky, and sees the stars....

Which one are you today?

Father, in all circumstances help me not to assume the worst, but to expect the best. —Sue Monk Kidd

Tuesday

27

Even in old age they will still produce fruit and be vital and green. —Psalm 92:14 (TLB)

The winter before my dad's sixty-ninth birthday, he and his retired friend Fritz decided to clear away trees and brush along a canal, just a few blocks from Dad's house. Every morning, Dad and Fritz bundled up and with their gas-powered chain saws blasted away the overgrowth on the slope next to the water. By springtime, they'd cleared a mile-long stretch six to eight feet wide. The next winter they did 1.2 miles, completing the project.

Impressed with the canal's new look, the Rock River Development Authority widened and resurfaced the path along the canal for bikers, walkers and joggers, and in July organized raft and canoe races. Then the Department of Conservation did some landscaping and added a ramp for the handicapped to the path.

Because of the initiative of two retirees in their late sixties, a beautiful new state parkway was created for the whole town to enjoy. And Dad says the harder he worked those two winters, the better he felt and the more energy he had. "Doing something positive for the town makes me feel good about myself!" he added.

Is there a project that might improve your town? Cleaning up debris along a river or creek? Planting flowers downtown? Painting old park benches? All it takes is one person to get the project started. Could it be you?

Lord, get me started, keep me busy, and thanks for the added boost of energy that comes with the territory of doing for others.

—Patricia Lorenz

Wednesday

28

Fireside Friend

A man that hath friends must show himself friendly.... —Proverbs 18:24

When I first moved to California, I had a very difficult time adjusting. I'd heard that people here were so friendly. So I looked forward to daily morning strolls and having strangers say, "Hello!" But nothing like that happened. No one ever greeted me and as I searched for friendly faces, I got more and more dejected.

When I complained about this to my new coworker Cal, his forehead wrinkled. "That's odd," he said. "I've gone jogging many times on that very same path and every single person I pass says 'Hello.' Would you like me to show you?" I nodded, agreeing to meet him at seven the next morning.

The next day as I walked fast and Cal jogged, I was startled to hear an enthusiastic "Hello!" as we passed the very first person on our route—but it had come from Cal! Right away the man returned a cheery "Hello!" Another person came along: "Hello!" Cal called. "Hello!" the woman replied with a big smile. "Hey," I said to Cal, "that's cheating! *You* said hello first."

But then I laughed when I saw how I had been cheating—cheating myself! In the end, saying hello first could only make me the real winner. Not only the winner of good moods, a positive outlook and heightened confidence, but of cheerful people and potential friends.

Why not practice being a "winner" with every face you meet today?

Dear God, help me be the one to make the first friendly move.

—Linda Neukrug

Thank-You Notes to God

1 ______________________________

2 ______________________________

3 ______________________________

4 ______________________________

5 ______________________________

6 ______________________________

7 ______________________________

8 ______________________________

9 ______________________________

10 ______________________________

11 ______________________________

12 ______________________________

13 ______________________________

14 ______________________________

15 ______________________________

16 ____

17 ____

18 ____

19 ____

20 ____

21 ____

22 ____

23 ____

24 ____

25 ____

26 ____

27 ____

28 ____

MARCH

S	M	T	W	T	F	S
				1	2	3
4	5	6	7	8	9	10
11	12	13	14	15	16	17
18	19	20	21	22	23	24
25	26	27	28	29	30	31

SPIRITUAL TREASURE

Remove the Plank

"How can you say to your brother, 'Let me take the speck out of your eye,' when all the time there is a plank in your own eye? ...Take the plank out of your own eye...." —Matthew 7:4,5 (NIV)

The annual ritual of spring cleaning clears away cobwebs and creates bright, shiny spaces. Even God seems to be sprucing up His creation as clean March winds blow across the earth and sky.

What better month to give yourself a going over? Take a good look at the debris that has gathered in your life, the "planks in your own eye," as Jesus called them. And set to work removing them.

You'll feel a fresh wind blowing inside, as well as out.

My Monthly Prayer List

Family Prayer for March

Father, help me to be alert to the loneliness of those around me. Let me offer a prayer, an ear, a shoulder—or a hug.

Thursday
1

THROUGH AN OPEN WINDOW
Banish Fear

Perfect love casteth out fear.... —I John 4:18

I'm not the only one who enjoys the view from my open window. From her vantage point on top of my bed, my dachshund Heidi surveys the world outside our apartment. She barks at the various birds landing and taking off from the windowsill. And she's fascinated by the movement of the green leaves on the ivy vines that cling to the side of the building. It's fun to watch her.

Heidi and I have been together for sixteen years now. Sometimes, someone will ask me, "What do you plan to do when Heidi goes?" I realize they mean, "Will you get another dog?" But my answer is usually, "I don't want to think about it."

The truth is, I do think about it—a lot. Whenever I do, I'm filled with a sense of fear. *What will life for me be like without her?* I wonder. *How will I cope?*

One day, while talking to my minister, I told him about my fear. "Eleanor," he counseled me, "you must face the fact that Heidi's life *will* end someday. But, meanwhile, there's something you can do to banish fear." Then he suggested that I sit quietly with the palms of my hands facing upward. "Tell God that your fear of losing Heidi is in your hands," he instructed. "Then turn your palms over. Naturally, your fear will drop out. Now turn your palms upward again. They are empty, ready to receive God's perfect love."

Now, whenever I worry about Heidi I often perform this little exercise of casting out fear. In so doing, I'm reminded that God has been with me all these years. He will be with me even when I no longer have my dog. He will help me cope.

Is there a fear that keeps popping up in your life? Perhaps you should try this little exercise, because God's plan for you does *not* include fear.

Dear Father, every day this month I'll repeat Your reassuring words: "Perfect love casteth out fear." —Eleanor Sass

Friday
2

Make love your aim.... —I Corinthians 14:1 (RSV)

There's an old Carolina story about a man who whittled beautiful little dogs out of wood. One day he sat whittling on his front porch, when a woman stopped and admired his talent.

"That is the finest dog carving I've ever seen," she said. "What is your secret?"

The old man stopped working, gazed at his work and said, "Well, ma'am, I just get a block of wood and whittle away everything that doesn't look like a dog."

I wonder what would happen if I took this day, this block of twenty-four hours, and whittled away everything that didn't look like love. What sort of beautiful day could I carve?

Father, help me gently remove what is unloving from my life.

—Sue Monk Kidd

Saturday
3

And it shall come to pass, that before they call, I will answer; and while they are yet speaking, I will hear.

—Isaiah 65:24

"God has a private line, you know," a friend remarked during a discussion on prayer. Some people looked puzzled, but not I. When we moved to our Kansas farm home twenty-one years ago, we became the sixth family using the same telephone line. We quickly learned the different rings: one short, one long meant the call was for Buttons. Two longs was Gibson's ring. Ours was a short, a long and a short.

The constant ringing was annoying. Even more troublesome was the difficulty in getting the phone when we wanted to use it. All the neighbors would quickly relinquish it for emergencies, but did a call to the parts store to check on a three-point hitch for the tractor qualify? And while adults wouldn't think of "listening in," two preschoolers often eavesdropped. What a relief when the telephone company switched to private service!

Sometimes I act as if God were on a party line. I decide He's too busy to listen to my concerns. Or that my persistence on some matters might be annoying. Or even that someone can overhear the personal things I need to share with Him.

My friend's comment reminded me that God's line is always open, always private, and that He longs to hear from me each day. Won't you join me right now in a direct-dial prayer call to God?

Thank You, Father, for the wonderful privilege of my own private prayer line to You. —Penney Schwab

Sunday

4

What shall I render unto the Lord for all his benefits toward me? —Psalm 116:12

Church attendance was down because of the bone-chilling temperatures and heavy snow flurries. I needed someone to serve with me as an usher and noticed Frank, who years ago had been a Sunday school pupil of mine.

I was reluctant to ask him because of a near-fatal automobile accident that had left him in a coma for months. When he regained consciousness, his confidence was eroded and his memory impaired. He failed even to recognize me.

Out of a sense of urgency, however, I asked him anyway. To my surprise, Frank leaped eagerly from the pew and grasped my hand. He said, "Three years ago I was in a terrible accident, and the doctors didn't think I'd pull through. But here I am. Isn't it wonderful? All I can do is thank God!"

Frank ushered with quiet dignity, but there was a spiritual fervor about it. When the service ended, he said, "Thank you for asking me to help in this church I love so much."

But I was the one who should have been thanking Frank. He had completely changed my misconception of accident victims' capabilities. His body and mind might not have fully recovered from the accident, but his heart made up for it tenfold. Now if only I can live that way!

Dear Lord, if I have but one thing, I pray it may be a heart like Frank's. —Oscar Greene

Monday

5

Behold, I will kindle a fire in thee.... —Ezekiel 20:47

I think there are quite a few people in this world who have let the faith they had in childhood grow dim. Often they have been church members but have drifted away. They feel that it's too late to rekindle the flame, but I believe they are wrong because that flame never goes out completely. Some sparks are always there, as this little story shows.

It was early morning when a married couple came into the lunch counter with their little girl who was five or six. The seats at the counter had a few silent occupants: a pair of glum-looking teenagers, some tired nurses from the hospital's night shift, two or three tough truck drivers and one worried-looking businessman with a briefcase. The burly counterman with tattooed arms was handing out doughnuts and coffee. Nobody was saying anything.

All at once the little girl spoke up: "Mommy, don't they say the blessing in this place?" There was a moment of silence, then the big counterman said to her, "Sure we do! You get ready to say it, honey!" He glared up and down the counter and growled, "Bow your heads and shut your eyes!" And everyone did.

Then the sweet voice of the little girl said, "God is great, God is good, and we thank Him for our food. God bless everyone in Jesus' name." Heads were raised then, and everyone smiled at everyone else—all except the businessman who stood up quickly, paid his bill and left.

But outside, in his car, he put his forehead down against the wheel and wept like a child. After a while, when his sobbing ceased, he laughed aloud and said, "It's back! I've got it back!" He meant the faith he had been taught so long ago. All it took was the simple, pure prayer of a little girl to get him going again.

Are there times when you feel that the flame of your own faith is burning low? Ask God to breathe on the embers in some special way. When He does, that flame will leap higher than ever.

Thank You for never giving up on any of us, dear Lord.

—Norman Vincent Peale

Tuesday

6

So he carried me away in the spirit into the wilderness....
—Revelation 17:3

Ian Frazier, author of *My Life on the Plains*, writes, "The Great Plains are like a sheet Americans screened their dreams on."

Oh, yes! If you go a few miles off Interstate 80 anywhere in the midlands, you can sense the breath of God in the great, quiet expanse of rolling fields and gentle hills. Sometimes in the fall and winter, I stand on a country road, surrounded by the blankness of a land that is painted wheat-colored or untouched white. And in that blankness, I discover something about who I am. Often I'm overcome with a deep sense of all the unclaimed possibilities of my life as God's child. Why, I could learn to play the flute, or study astronomy, or reread *Walden*, or find a lonely child to hold. For me, the plains are a mirror, a blank slate, a sheet of white paper waiting for its poem.

I'm not suggesting that you move to the Great Plains. I only urge you to find your own open space for discovering yourself and for projecting your dreams. Perhaps the ocean can be your screen, or the moonlit sky viewed from a city rooftop, or your own living room when you close your eyes, open your heart and invite God to write on your inner screen.

Lord, help me to find an open place to screen my dreams on.
—Marilyn Morgan Helleberg

Wednesday

7

I will lead them in paths that they have not known: I will make darkness light before them....
—Isaiah 42:16

"I feel like I'm in a long black tunnel," the woman wrote. The word *tunnel* jumped out at me—and I knew why. My husband and I had recently spent several months in Austria. Wherever we drove in that mountainous land, the road led through tunnels, some of them stretching so many miles we'd begin to wonder if we'd ever see daylight again. But of course we would, bursting from the blackness into the sunshine of a brand-new landscape. And looking back we'd see the jagged outline of the formidable mountain through which we'd just passed.

There were other ways over the mountain, of course: We could have followed the old roads up precipices, across snow fields, along the narrow ledges. But skilled engineers had devised a better way.

As I pray for this woman, I'm picturing God as the Engineer and her dark tunnel as the way He has provided to speed her on her journey. I don't know what mountain of problems has plunged her into darkness. But I do know that the miles that seem so endless inside the tunnel are in fact the fastest way through: a marvel of road design through the barriers in our path.

Father, help me to believe that the tunnel in my life today is the way Your love has forged. —Elizabeth Sherrill

Thursday

8

[God] will bring to light the hidden things....
—I Corinthians 4:5

I'm thinking today about another kind of tunnel. Not the tunnels built for travelers that I talked about yesterday, but those that burrow deep into the earth in search of treasure.

I've been in this type of tunnel, too. I've dropped in a hydraulic cage into the blackness of a coal mine in Kentucky. I've crawled down into gold diggings in Colorado, salt mines in Germany. They're scary, these black, wet, claustrophobic holes in the ground. But for centuries men have accepted the challenge for the sake of what lies beneath the surface. Whether it's coal for power, salt for preservation or gold for beauty, men have known that some things of great value can be reached only by going deep.

Today, as I pray again for the woman who wrote of her "dark tunnel," I'm picturing hidden treasure deep within her: resources of joy she's never tapped. I see how frightening the journey inward is, at times how painful. In my prayers today I see her tunnel as a mine shaft, sunk patiently by God beneath the surface of her life, probing down inch by inch, in spite of the fear, bringing hidden things to light, uncovering treasure she does not dream is there.

Father, the tunneling hurts, but I trust the Miner.

—Elizabeth Sherrill

Friday

9

Seek him that maketh the seven stars and Orion....

—Amos 5:8

At five o'clock in the morning I am often standing out on the lawn in my bedroom slippers, my face unshaven and my hair tangled from sleep. I am getting in touch with God. In the clean, morning air, the ebony sky is ablaze with other worlds. With a pair of powerful binoculars I roam through the Milky Way, stop by the planets and finally peer into the moon's craters.

"You seem very happy," my wife notes at breakfast.

I smile like someone with a secret. "Yes, I am. I feel good. I just took a little trip." I glance at the binoculars on the counter, and she gets that knowing look in her eyes.

Are you dreading this day's confusion and complications? Perhaps you need to take a few minutes to look up at the God of Order. If He can keep the heavens untangled, then surely He can guide you through rush-hour traffic and a crowded agenda.

Dear God, my world is pretty small compared to Your creation, but it is important to me. Lead me through the maze of this day and make my life an orderly one. —Daniel Schantz

Saturday

10

Fireside Friend

O Lord, thou hast searched me, and known me.

—Psalm 139:1

It had been another harrowing day—one of many I had experienced since coming to England to nurse my father who was ill. One day I took the bus downtown to a restaurant to eat a solitary dinner. Preoccupied with longing for my family back in the States and the overwhelming sadness of my father's imminent passing, I had carelessly hung my handbag on the back of my chair. When the check came, I discovered my purse was gone.

Panic gripped me. In that bag was every shred of identification I had—my passport, driver's license and credit cards. I had lost all my proof of identity to the outside world. At that moment, I felt helpless, scared and lost, like a child deprived of a security blanket. Fortunately, my sister and other relatives came to my rescue, and after several days of exasperating explanations, transatlantic phone calls to my husband and a trip to the American Embassy in London, my passport was replaced.

But I will never forget that moment in the restaurant. As I reflected on it, I asked myself: Stripped of all my worldly labels—daughter, wife, mother, customer, citizen, licensed driver—just who would I be? I realized then that these many roles, however much they meant to me, are all transitory and subject to all kinds of documentation and obligation. But there is one identity that never changes, that needs no documents of proof, that has no strings attached, and that role is *child of God*. He knew me before I was born and He will know me when all my earthly identities cease to have any meaning. How supremely comforting it is to know that I am so loved and accepted!

Loving Father, help me to rejoice always in the knowledge that I am first, last and always Your precious, beloved child. Amen.

—Stephanie Oda

Sunday

11

Casting all your care upon him; for he careth for you.

—I Peter 5:7

In the wintertime I feed the birds, not only because I enjoy having them in my yard, but because by doing so I am cooperating with God's plan. In the Sermon on the Mount, Jesus said God feeds the birds and I become the means by which He does it. So when I feed the birds, I open my heart in a very special way to feel the Lord's presence and realize that through me, God is accomplishing His will.

But lately I have experienced something new. I was listening to the radio and heard a most unusual duet. Garrison Keillor and Willie Nelson were singing an old song that I had learned as a boy:

Just remember in His word
How He feeds the little bird;
Take your burden to the Lord
And leave it there.

The next time I fed the birds, this song began to ring in my mind: "Take your burden to the Lord and leave it there." I thought to myself, *I ought to do more than just sing the song. I ought to do what it says.*

I was carrying a burden. A friend had called to ask my help in his battle against discouragement and depression. I had tried to help, but it seemed so feeble. What could I do? *Take your burden to the Lord,* the song said, so I prayed, "Oh, Lord, You know the burden of my heart for my friend. Please do for him what I cannot do, and lift him by Your strong hand."

Then I remembered that the song also said, *Leave it there*. That was not so easy, but I knew that God never intended that I should go down under a load of concern. I had prayed in faith, now I had to trust God for the outcome. In time, my friend's period of darkness passed, and I learned the art of praying and letting go to God.

Now every time I walk outside to feed the birds, I am reminded to take my burden to the Lord... and leave it there.

Dear Lord, let Your care for the birds remind me that You care about my smallest concern today. —Lee Webber

Monday

12

Only, let every one lead the life which the Lord has assigned to him, and in which God has called him.
—I Corinthians 7:17 (RSV)

Near our home is a quiet lake where a beaver family has built a lodge on a secluded cove. I can lean over from my canoe and scoop in my hand stray, freshly peeled sticks floating in the water. God has created a fascinating design for these shy, industrious creatures. Behind a beaver's large front teeth are two flaps of skin that close, enabling it to gnaw wood and carry branches while swimming without swallowing splinters or taking in water. Its transparent eyelids close underwater, allowing unobstructed vision while keeping debris away from sensitive eyes.

A familiar display I delight in watching is tail-slapping. The beaver, signaling others of potential danger, lifts its wide flat tail and smacks it down hard on the water, making a sharp cracking sound. Then it dives for safety beneath a flurry of spray.

As the beaver paddles toward shore, I ponder nature's precisely laid pattern. Each animal is at home in its own setting. The beaver doesn't frustrate itself trying to fly like an eagle or scramble over peaks like a mountain goat. It doesn't strain to develop the strength of a bear or grow the coat of a musk ox. A beaver's instinct says, "Be a beaver."

There are some things I will never be: a soloist (even my "Amen" is flat), an artist (a salesman thought I had young children after glancing at my clumsy holiday drawings taped in the window), a skydiver (my hands go clammy at the top of a ladder). So I will applaud those who possess abilities I do not have, and proceed to do the things I can. My instinct tells me, "Be yourself!"

Father God, Who formed us after Your likeness, thank You for the unique expression that is myself. —Carol Knapp

Tuesday

13

Nevertheless I am continually with thee: thou hast holden me by my right hand. —Psalm 73:23

I missed my family when I remarried and moved to Oklahoma. It was always a joy to return to Georgia, which my husband and I did often. One day, while back in Georgia, my daughter Julie asked me to pick up four-year-old Katie at kindergarten. Sitting in the long line of cars waiting for my turn to drive by the school door, I recalled the countless times I had done the same thing for my four children.

Katie bounded out to the car, delighted to see me, and we drove off. I had to stop by the drugstore, and as Katie and I got out of the car, she immediately put her hand into mine. She seemed to do it without thinking or making a big deal of it. I'd forgotten what a wondrous thing it is to have a small, trusting hand thrust into your own. As we left the drugstore, once again her hand found mine. No words. Not even a glance. Just her hand securely nestled in mine.

Driving home I thought about the incident. *Why, God must feel exactly as I had!* What joy He must experience when with complete trust and without fanfare we simply slip our hand into His and walk alongside Him quietly and with absolute faith. It's a joy I want to extend this very day.

Right now, Father, I'll slip my hand into Yours as I go about my day.

—Marion Bond West

Wednesday

14

Put on the whole armour of God.... —Ephesians 6:11

It was almost 10 P.M. and the kids were revved up, wrestling on our bed (knocking over piles of folded laundry in the process), shrieking—everything but kneeling at the foot of the bed for prayers.

On an impulse, I barked, "All right, gang, man your battle stations!" hoping to bring them to their knees, literally. And, wonder of wonders, nine-year-old Nikki slid obediently into place between my husband Michael and me, and six-year-old Sean plopped down at my left.

"You know," I mused to Nikki later, "'battle stations' isn't inappropriate for describing prayer. The Bible calls us Christ's soldiers, and tells us to put on God's armor to stand against Satan's attacks."

"Yeah," she agreed. "Some people just say good night, but we're showing Satan we're on Jesus' side."

Are you feeling like anything but a "prayer warrior" in the Lord's army today? No particular urge to praise, thank or ask? Don't want to be a hypocrite "going through the motions"? How about going through the motions anyway, if for no other reason than to let the Holy Spirit empower you as one "on Jesus' side."

Lord, remind me that prayer is not passive, but active duty in Your service.

—B. J. Connor

March Prayer List Reminder

Return to your Monthly Prayer List on the calendar opening page and review your requests. Give thanks for prayers answered, renew old prayers and add new concerns today. Then pray once again our *Family Prayer for March.*

Thursday 15

WINDOWS INTO WONDER
Holy Ground

The place whereon thou standest is holy ground.

—Exodus 3:5

When I think of Moses, I think: *Great Holy Leader*, because it was he who brought the Israelites out of their bondage in Egypt into the Promised Land. Such grand achievement makes my little daily acts seem insignificant. He was special, chosen, outstanding. How can I, an ordinary person, relate to him? But I've been rereading Exodus 3, and I've seen that before he became great, Moses was simply a common shepherd caring for the flocks of his father-in-law. One day, while he rested near some desert shrubs, a nearby bush suddenly burst into flame! It was a brilliant light, a strange fire that burned without consuming. Then a voice from within the bush called, "Moses." Then again: "Moses!" For a few moments, the young shepherd stood there, aware only of his rapidly beating heart. Then, breathless with all the fear and hope of the centuries, he answered, "Here I am."

"Take off your shoes," said God. "You are standing on holy ground."

Oh, I see the connection now! It was only after Moses, in all of his ordinariness, became aware of the holy ground under his feet that God could begin truly to use him!

I wonder. What is holy ground, anyway? Could it be that piece of carpet you were standing on when you remembered to call your shut-in friend? Or maybe it's that grassy spot by the creek where you first became aware that the Holy Spirit moves within you like a river. Perhaps it's the mat your office chair rolls on when you're working overtime and an out-of-nowhere creative idea finds you. Or could it be the chunk of sidewalk under your feet that morning you said to your friend, "I'm sorry. Please forgive me"? Once, after I'd cooked all afternoon to celebrate a family birthday, everyone ate and ran, leaving me with a kitchen full of dirty dishes. About halfway through the stack, as my anger simmered down, I suddenly became aware that the square of tile on the floor in front of my kitchen sink is holy ground. It's there that I perform the drudgery tasks that are a living sign of my love. Perhaps holy ground is wherever I am when Love calls my name. What holy ground will you walk on today?

Here I am, Lord...in my bare feet. —Marilyn Morgan Helleberg

Friday

16

Fireside Friend

These things I have spoken unto you, that in me ye might have peace. In the world ye shall have tribulation: but be of good cheer; I have overcome the world.
—John 16:33

While I signed, the nurse held the paper giving my consent for a Caesarean section. I had spent eight difficult hours in hard labor, and things were not going well. Long hours in Lamaze classes and dreams of an easy childbirth had been shattered. I was in trouble, the baby was in trouble. What was to have been the well-planned spiritual highlight of my life was instead a painful, out-of-control nightmare. Waves of pain swept over my exhausted body...I could hear a doctor barking orders. After that, I remember nothing.

This isn't the way I had it planned, I thought hours later in my hospital bed. I hadn't held my newborn on the delivery table, seen the look in my husband's eyes, heard the first cry. Hours later I didn't even know if I'd had a boy or a girl....

Then I heard, "Mrs. Smoot, here is your son...." The nurse wheeled the bassinet into my room and placed a red-faced newborn in my arms. Suddenly it didn't matter how I had it planned—I was holding a beautiful, healthy baby boy and God in His wisdom had allowed me to deliver this baby in a modern, well-equipped hospital. He had placed me in the hands of people with the knowledge and skill to save our lives. All the things I had thought were important weren't important after all.

God, help me to trust Your contingency plans when my own plans are not enough.
—Debbi Smoot

Day Brightener

FOR TIMES OF FAILURE

Grant me, O God, the mind to see
The blessings which my sorrows bring;
And give me, in adversity,
The heart that still can trust and sing.
—Marion Franklin Ham

Saturday 17

Now the Lord had said unto Abram, Get thee out of thy country, and from thy kindred, and from thy father's house, unto a land that I will shew thee.
—Genesis 12:1

When I was growing up, St. Patrick's Day was a day of great celebration in our family, but not because of any Irish blood in our veins or of any fondness for leprechauns or four-leaf clovers. St. Patrick's Day was my grandfather's birthday.

In particular I remember a play we grandchildren put on for his eightieth birthday, acting out scenes from his long life. I don't know who I was supposed to be, but at one moment I turned to my brother (in the title role) and said, "Go west, young man." My grandfather did. He moved to Los Angeles when both he and the century were young and started out by opening a bicycle shop in an area that is now full of fifty-story skyscrapers. From bicycle shop to machine shop to a partnership in a construction company, his was a classic Horatio Alger story—from highschool dropout to self-made man. Yes, he was a success, but I think the success he would have been proudest of was that after he was gone, all of his grandchildren graduated from college, our education paid for by money he'd put aside years before.

I believe that God gives us dreams to follow—like the one that led Abram and his people to Canaan, or the one that led St. Patrick to Ireland to convert the pagans, or the dream of a better life that brought my grandfather west at the turn of the century. On this day dedicated to the patron saint of Ireland, I plan to make a special effort to listen to my dreams. You never know where they will lead.

Lord, I will follow Your lead. —Rick Hamlin

Sunday

18

Do ye look on things after the outward appearance?...
—II Corinthians 10:7

Ever since my older son was a little boy, I've harbored the hope that he would grow into a gentleman, in the finest sense of the word—caring, peace-loving, gentle. The years went by, and that hope faded into the background as others took precedence: hopes that he'd pass Spanish, get into college, say no to drugs, get a haircut, not get any more traffic tickets. These more immediate hopes made me forget about raising a gentleman. I was more concerned with seeing him survive!

Then yesterday he did something so unselfish and caring for a friend in need that I found myself telling my husband Bill, "He's a good kid." This morning I realized I was wrong. He's not a good kid; he's a good *man*—a gentle man. Somehow, while I worried about the more immediate problems of everyday life, my son had become just what I'd hoped he'd be.

I'm going to use that lesson as I deal with his younger brother. I will remember that a boy with torn jeans, long hair and a rotten driving record can still be a gentleman in the things that really count.

Lord, help me to see the real person living with me in the disguise of a teenager. —Toni Sortor

Monday

19

And all things, whatsoever ye shall ask in prayer, believing, ye shall receive. —Matthew 21:22

Some years ago I read about a single mother. Even though she had no money, she prayed that her children would someday attend college. She even went so far as to hang three empty frames on the wall. The frames, she decided, would one day hold her children's college diplomas. Many years later, that is exactly what happened. Her three children graduated, and their diplomas filled those very frames.

Hanging empty frames is what I call *praying with vision.* You hold a picture of the future in your mind, and you pray for its realization. Here are some steps that have brought greater vision to my prayers. Perhaps they can enhance your prayers, too.

1. When praying for someone, insert the name of the person you're praying for into specific verses. Example: *Kim can do all things through Christ which strengtheneth her* (Philippians 4:13).
2. Find something concrete that symbolizes your prayer (like the empty picture frames for the diplomas). I've made a prophetic plaque for a friend who has not yet reached her goal, and I've drawn hearts and rays of light around a picture of a grieving friend.
3. Whenever you pray, keep these visual pictures in mind. Then place them in God's hands so that He can bring about the highest good for all concerned.

It seems the more visual my prayers, the stronger my belief. Isn't there someone you would like to pray for today? If so, then why not get started. Your prayer, strongly visualized, might change a life!

Father, help us to pray... visualizing *and believing.*

—Terry Helwig

Tuesday

20

Fireside Friend

Thou shalt make them drink of the river of thy pleasures. For with thee is the fountain of life....

—Psalm 36:8–9

My mother is *O'odham* (Papago and Pima Indian) from Arizona. When we were growing up in Los Angeles County, Mama would tell us about the hot desert sun and the importance of water, a precious and valuable resource in the desert. "We would wrap the clay water *olla* (pot) in wet burlap to keep the water cool," she would begin, "and then set it in the shade of the *ramada* (an arbor made of branches)."

She would fill a large pan with tap water, pretending that it was the olla. "Close your eyes and imagine," she would say, as we dipped our cereal bowls, pretending they were gourds, into the cool water to drink. As we savored the water, Mama described the taste of wet clay and described the water-soaked edges of the gourd dipper. We drank deeply, feeling the distant, ancient land beneath our bare feet, and the hot sun and relentless desert beyond the shade of the ramada, and we knew that water was life.

Like the O'odham, the desert people of the Bible knew that without water there can be no life. Is it any wonder that water is used so often in the Bible as a symbol of God's grace and love and mercy? Sometimes my spiritual life feels like a desert—long stretches of dryness, feelings of emptiness. It is then that I seek an oasis. It could be a visit to a retreat house, or a walk along the beach or simply the privacy of my bedroom—any place where I can be still and take a long drink of God.

If you are in the desert right now, find an oasis. God will be there to quench your thirst.

O, Lord, You are the fountainhead of all life and goodness. Thank You for being the Living Water in my life. —Georgiana Sanchez

Wednesday

21

Not by might, nor by power, but by my spirit, saith the Lord of hosts. —Zechariah 4:6

At the boys' ranch where I've worked for the last twenty-three years, we used to run about fifty head of white-faced cows and one Angus bull. One year our herd contracted pink eye and since it was contagious, we had to treat all of the animals for the disease. Once we rounded up the cattle into the corral, one of us would grab a cow around the neck and another would pull up each eyelid and squirt in a little medicine. Sometimes we had to throw a cow down before we could treat it.

Things went smoothly until we got to the bull. His neck was like a sequoia tree trunk and the way his nostrils flared, he reminded me of an old-time locomotive blowing steam. I walked up cautiously and put my arms around his neck. He stood still until one of the other men came over to put in the medicine. As he reached for the bull's eyelid, the big Angus flicked its head and sent me sprawling. The idea of wrestling the bull down was out of the question. I knew if we tried, somebody would get hurt.

But if we didn't treat the bull, he would carry the disease back to the herd. So after a few more tries at holding his head, I asked the Lord to help us. It was no casual prayer. I really meant it.

On the next try, I put a rope around the bull's neck and tied him to a support post. All the Angus had to do was shake his head and he could tear out the post, maybe bringing the barn down. Another man reached for his eyelid. Amazingly, the bull didn't flinch. He stood rock steady while the ointment was put under both eyelids. When the job was done, I untied the bull and opened the gate to the pasture. He walked out as if nothing had happened.

There may be some scientific explanation for his cooperation, but as far as I'm concerned, that bull was subdued by the Lord. Since that day, I've done a lot of praying for some of the "bulls" I have had to face in life. Whether it be in business or working with delinquent boys, I've found that when you sincerely ask for it, the power of God can calm the most volatile situation.

Thank You, Lord, for Your power, which is greater than all of our problems. —Brian Miller

Thursday

22

Fireside Friend

Let all bitterness and wrath and anger…and slander be put away from you, with all malice….

—Ephesians 4:31 (RSV)

"I'm fifty-five," said the little man on the three-wheeled bicycle. "How old are you? Twenty-two? Boy, I wish I was twenty-two again." He stooped to pick a soda can out of the gutter, adding quietly, "You can bet I'd be doing some things different. I'd have me a real job."

For two weeks, I followed Bob around photographing his life for a newspaper story. Bob was a "canner" in my hometown. He made his living collecting and selling aluminum cans to be recycled. Every day Bob went out in the morning darkness, enduring all sorts of Missouri weather, and searched trash bins, alleys and curbs for cans.

When Bob was in the third grade, his mother got sick, and he stayed home to take care of her. He never went back to school; he never learned to read or write. Yet not once during the weeks that I photographed Bob did I see any bitterness on his part. On his rounds about town, he waved to everyone, his wrinkles creasing his face like a Cabbage Patch Doll. At the end of my project, I asked Bob what he wanted more than anything in the world. He said simply, "I'd just like to work."

Life has been much kinder for me than it has Bob. Yet the other day when I managed to lock my keys inside my car, I started to complain bitterly. Suddenly, I saw a flattened tin can lying in the street, and I remembered Bob. My frustrations were so little in comparison to his daily struggles to survive. As yet I have few wrinkles, and I've never had to save one can. When life starts showing on my face—and in my attitude—I hope it is as free of bitterness as the Can Man's.

Lord, let my face reflect the goodness of living for You each and every moment of each and every day. —Teresa Schantz

Friday
23

In everything God works for good....
—Romans 8:28 (RSV)

I came home with a new hairdo last week...a curly permanent like Orphan Annie's. When my husband got home, he took a long look. "I...like...it," he said slowly, which let me know he didn't because that's how he talks when he has to rehearse what he is saying. I didn't like it either, so I had a real problem on my hands—or rather, on my head. But I have this firm conviction that God tucks serendipity blessings into every problem. So I began to search for what I might learn from a bad hairdo that made me so self-conscious I didn't want to go out in public. I couldn't find an answer, which was frustrating because I'm not very good at waiting.

For days, I avoided people, but finally the curls seemed to relax a bit and so did I. When I told a friend about my curly hair and self-consciousness, she laughed, "Don't you know that getting used to a new permanent teaches us to have patience?"

Aha, that's it! I thought. Now you might assume I was grateful for her help in finding the lesson in my permanent (patience), but that isn't what caused my "Aha!" It was the tangible proof *again* that God tucks the lesson—serendipity blessings—into all our problems. Though sometimes, we need patience and help in finding them.

Are you in the middle of a problem that seems to have no blessings? Don't give up. You'll find them.

Lord, help us look at our problems with faith, patiently seeking the serendipity blessings You have tucked inside them.

—Carol Kuykendall

Saturday
24

They that go down to the sea in ships...see the works of the Lord....they cry unto the Lord in their trouble, and he bringeth them out of their distresses.
—Psalm 107:23, 24, 28

Every year, at Islamorada in the Florida Keys, a ceremony is performed at the beginning of Lent, called the Blessing of the Boats. We saw it one morning while vacationing there. A priest stood on a bridge with his microphone, waiting to bless the boats that were approaching, most of them trimmed with pennants, balloons or brightly colored flags—a kind of regatta, both serious and gay. We watched them as they sailed slowly toward the place where the crowds were gathering along the shore. We were close enough to see and hear the priest, lifting his arms and pronouncing the same few words over each craft as it passed before him. Asking the Lord to bless it, and keep it safe at sea.

A beautiful and touching sight, somehow. This parade of boats of all kinds, some of them cabin cruisers of various sizes, some of them yachts—like obedient children awaiting their turn. How wonderful and strange it seemed that no matter how sophisticated their owners, there is this human desire to draw near to God at this season, to pay homage, and be blessed and protected as you put out to sea.

My husband George and I pondered this, walking back past other, smaller boats still rocking at the docks, or parked by mobile homes or trailers. Suddenly, before a battered old houseboat, my husband paused to make the sign of the cross.

"Bless you, too," he told it. Turning to me, he gestured to include the rest. "They're just as deserving of a blessing, and probably need it more! Let's do it."

I laughed, but agreed. And as we proceeded, it warmed our hearts to sign each one with the cross—these humbler unadorned vessels—and echo, as best we could, the Blessing of the Boats: "God protect you and those you carry. God go with you and keep you safe."

Dear Lord, whoever we are, from whatever background, we are all at sea. And we all need You, wherever we go, or how far. Thank You that any of us can be Your priest to deliver this beautiful blessing to one another.
—Marjorie Holmes

Sunday

25

Therefore be imitators of God.... and walk in love, as Christ loved us.... —Ephesians 5:1–2 (RSV)

In mid-career, I suffered a failure of purpose. The joy and pain of teaching exhausted me. So on a trip back to Hawaii, my birthplace, I decided to capture the voices of my family on tape. I was looking for a way to measure the years, to test my idea of success and to feel less like a stranger to those I loved.

Uncle Dennis was one of the first people I wanted to speak to. He had risen from office boy to president of Hawaii's largest bank corporation, and possessed all the tokens of success: a beautiful home, cars and condominiums. It took me awhile to work up the nerve to call him, but he was glad to hear from me and immediately invited me to his office. After greeting me warmly, he urged me to begin.

Long after the tape ran out, we were still talking. He spoke not of his public successes but of his private tribulations. He described the shock of his young wife's fatal illness, the terror of being left a widower with small children, his love for his two daughters and two sons, and the hope that he had been a good enough parent over the years. Would he be the same if his wife had lived? he wondered. I sensed that he would have traded all he owned to have her by his side.

I gave him a hug and left, no longer feeling like a stranger.

Too often I expect vulnerability and doubt only from myself, not from others, especially those of prominence and wealth. What my uncle showed me is that time is not marked by years, but by joy and pain. And that success is not measured by what we own, but by how deeply we love.

How rich I am, Lord, when I love another as wholly as You love me!

—Linda Ching Sledge

Monday

26

Neither shall ye break a bone thereof. —Exodus 12:46

Part of my work as an orthopedic surgeon is to fix broken bones. We use all sorts of things to hold them together while they heal: old-fashioned plaster of paris, screws, plates, even a device that looks like a child's Erector set. But God heals each bone together in the same way, and it is a pretty good model for us to use when we set out to heal a broken relationship in our lives.

The first thing that happens when a bone fractures is muscles around it go into spasm, fluid builds up next to the break and that pain keeps us from moving. All this prevents further damage from happening.

Keep still—don't make matters worse.

Next the dead tissue is removed. This includes the tissue damaged by the injury and the ends of the bones so that fresh, good tissue is there when the healing starts.

Clean up the misunderstanding.

Only then does the body send in other cells to begin the healing. Notice it isn't the fracture that heals itself; it is the new cells that haven't gone through the damage that effect the cure.

Ask God to enter the relationship to help bring you together.

Finally, the pain and swelling abate to allow for more activity. And as we use the injured part more, it begins to heal faster. Then when it's all over, the bone is stronger than ever.

Use the reconciliation to do more together, to grow stronger together.

Lord, Your plan for us is to be whole, in our body and in Your body.

—Scott Harrison

Tuesday

27

Lift up now thine eyes, and look.... —Genesis 13:14

"Perdiddle!" my son Brett said.

"Per-what?"

"Perdiddle," he laughed. "That's what you say when you see a car with one headlight. I bet I can spot more than you!" And by the time we reached home, he had.

"I had no idea there were so many!"

"You have to look for them, that's all," Brett said.

Now I see perdiddles everywhere—because Brett has made me aware of them. And he's reminded me that I will, basically, find what I look for. If I expect other freeway drivers to be careless, they will. If I *know* my husband won't appreciate the extra time I spent on dinner, he probably won't. If I'm certain I can't learn to play golf, I can't. If I believe all teenagers are impolite, the ones I meet inevitably will be.

So today I'm going to look for good things—a flower blooming in an unexpected place, a turtle sunning himself on the banks of the nearby pond, a jogger with graceful stride, a group of laughing children kicking a soccer ball in a field. I'm going to search out laughter and optimism. You can, too.

Keep my eyes off the shadows, Lord. Today and throughout the new year ahead I'll walk in the brightness of Your love!

—Mary Lou Carney

Wednesday

28

Fireside Friend 

Thou hast granted me life and favour, and thy visitation hath preserved my spirit. —Job 10:12

"You dope," I muttered. "You numbskull." I had just muffed a presentation to a client, and was talking to myself in the mirror in the empty ladies' room at work. A coworker walked in, heard me and looked around, shocked. "Who are you talking to?"

"Just myself," I admitted sheepishly.

My friend was aghast. "Would you dream of talking to somebody else that way?" When I shook my head negatively, she reminded me, "Remember, it says in the Bible, 'love thy neighbor as thyself.' It doesn't say '*better* than thyself.' Never treat yourself any worse than you would treat another human being. Running yourself down is an insult to the One Who created you."

When she left, I thought about how often I put myself down, how often I mercilessly criticize the way I look or act. It sometimes seems as if I have a little scorekeeper in my head—who only keeps track of the things I do wrong!

Now I turned to my reflection in the mirror and prayed, "Dear God, what would I say if a friend made the mistakes I made on that presentation?" The answer came immediately. Turning to the mirror once again, I said firmly (and truthfully), "You tried very hard. You did the best you could. There's always a next time." My shoulders got a little straighter, and I resolved to give all my comments the "Would you say that to a friend?" test from then on.

Dear God, let me pay myself one compliment today—and let me believe it.

—Linda Neukrug

Thursday

29

O give thanks to the Lord... To him who alone doeth great wonders.... —Psalm 136:3–4

Has your life seemed lacking in miracles lately? Nothing to lift your heart? Nothing to make you glad you're alive?

When I feel that way, I think of my favorite poetry book title, *Who Tells the Crocuses It's Spring?* Then for ten minutes I list similar questions beginning with "*Who.*"

Who makes the trees turn all those beautiful colors in the autumn?
Who splashes silver rain in shining puddles?
Who makes the stars shimmer in the night?
Who gives me sight so I can delight in a cardinal's brilliant crimson against the sparkling snow?
Who puts the love in my beloved collie's soft brown eyes?

God does. That's Who. And I bet you, too, can find the *Who* in your life that makes it all worthwhile. Right now, look around and ask yourself:

Who ____*?*
Who ____*?*
Who ____*?*

Lord, may I never stop finding lovely things to wonder about in this world filled with Your miracles. —Aletha Jane Lindstrom

Friday

30

That we may be able to comfort them which are in any trouble, by the comfort wherewith we ourselves are comforted of God. —II Corinthians 1:4

Grief is something that all of us encounter from time to time. Most people eventually put it aside and go on with living. But some find that difficult to do. What's the remedy when long-held grief leaves a person shrouded in darkness?

Years ago, I was traveling in Spain with two other college students. In Malaga, we stayed in a *pensione,* a private home that took in guests. It was comfortable enough, but strangely somber. The owner never smiled. His wife wore black. In the living room was a grand piano, but it was always closed. The maid told us that the wife had been a concert pianist, but three years ago her teenage son had died. She had not touched the piano since.

We carefree youngsters gave little thought to this. One afternoon when we came home full of high spirits, one of my companions sat down at the piano and began to play, rather badly, a college song that we all began to sing. Almost at once, the maid rushed in looking distracted. Behind her came the husband frantically motioning to us to desist. At the same time, another door opened and there stood the *senora,* tall and pale and silent.

Our music died away. We were horribly embarrassed. We didn't know what to say or do. Then suddenly the *senora* smiled. She came forward, pushed my friend aside, sat down at the piano and began to play the triumphal march from *Aida,* wonderful, soaring music that seemed to fill the whole house and drive the shadows away. What had happened? She had felt sorry for *us,* not for herself, and that sudden warmth had melted the ice around her heart.

Concern for others. Perhaps that's the best prescription for grief. If we're wise enough to use it.

Father, give strength and courage to those who mourn.

—Arthur Gordon

Saturday

31

Fireside Friend 

Whatsoever thy hand findeth to do, do it with thy might.... —Ecclesiastes 9:10

When I was five and six years old I spent many afternoons with my great-aunt. During the time I stayed with her I often played underneath her large mahogany dining room table. I'd make up little imaginary sailors who braved great dangers in their attempt to get from one side of the table base to the other!

Once while I was in the dining room, I noticed a heavy wooden hanger by the closet. "Auntie, why do you have that big hanger there?" I asked, pointing to it.

"Oh, that hanger is for Bobie's coat," she said in her lilting Barbadian accent. Bobie, her brother, visited almost weekly. "He's a big man and he wears a heavy coat: I have to have a heavy hanger to support it."

When I recalled that incident the other day, it made me think about the way I sometimes handle my problems. *How often I've attempted to support "heavy" situations with "thin, wire hanger" efforts,* I thought, *like inadequate prayer or halfhearted commitment.* Today, instead of taking the easy way out, I'm resolving to approach my problems with determination. For instance, I'd like to get an A in a college course I'm taking. I can choose the easy way and get by with a passing grade, or I can choose to fall in love with my local library, meeting writers like Blake, Wordsworth and Shelley. And at my next class I can practice the fine art of taking notes!

Do you have a "heavy" problem to hang? Why not resolve to give it the support it needs—fervent prayer, full-bodied effort, sustained commitment. That's my resolution!

Father, help me to avoid yielding to the temptation of the easy way out. —Robin White Goode

Thank-You Notes to God

1 ______________________________

2 ______________________________

3 ______________________________

4 ______________________________

5 ______________________________

6 ______________________________

7 ______________________________

8 ______________________________

9 ______________________________

10 ______________________________

11 ______________________________

12 ______________________________

13 ______________________________

14 ______________________________

15 ______________________________

16 ____________________

17 ____________________

18 ____________________

19 ____________________

20 ____________________

21 ____________________

22 ____________________

23 ____________________

24 ____________________

25 ____________________

26 ____________________

27 ____________________

28 ____________________

29 ____________________

30 ____________________

31 ____________________

APRIL

S	M	T	W	T	F	S
1	2	3	4	5	6	7
8	9	10	11	12	13	14
15	16	17	18	19	20	21
22	23	24	25	26	27	28
29	30					

SPIRITUAL TREASURE

Lighten the Heart

Rejoice and be glad.... —Matthew 5:12 (NIV)

Question: Why do angels fly so high?

Answer: Because they take themselves so lightly.

So the old saying goes. April with its bright flowers and chirping birds seems to be God's way of urging you to put aside the bleakness of winter and experience a lighthearted joy.

This month make it a point to lighten up and create new gladness in your life. Look for the lighter side of circumstances. Laugh at yourself. Rejoice in life's small and simple blessings. And just watch how high you soar!

My Monthly Prayer List

Family Prayer for April

Dear God, help our local and world leaders to make decisions on the side of justice and right. Let Your will be accomplished everywhere—including right here!

THROUGH AN OPEN WINDOW
Share Your Life

And he said unto me, My grace is sufficient for thee: for my strength is made perfect in weakness.

—II Corinthians 12:9

The little calendar on my desk beside the open window tells me that today is April Fool's Day. It reminds me that there was a time when I worried about being thought a fool.

It happened many years ago while on a weekend retreat with a young adult group. We'd been discussing the importance of "total honesty" with God and with one another. I could manage this in most areas of my life, but there was one subject I never discussed—something many of you know about by now—my hearing impairment. I'd always tried to pretend it didn't exist, and because I was such a good lip-reader, I could bluff my way through most situations.

Now, I pondered talking about it in the Saturday evening sharing session. *I just hope they don't think I'm a fool,* I worried. *Some may even think I'm asking for special treatment.* But finally I decided that it was worth being thought a fool if that's what it takes to be totally honest.

I can still remember my nervousness, the tremor in my voice as I spoke to the sixty-five men and women gathered in a circle in the main room of the retreat house that evening. But once I'd started, all the barriers came down. I told them about growing up with two deaf parents, about lipreading, about my hearing aids. And when the session ended, I knew by their smiles and their hugs that my friends did not think I was a fool. In fact, several thanked me because they, too, had hearing and other physical problems that they had difficulty accepting.

Today, I know God's will for me is to be a completely honest person. He wants me to share my life with others. If it takes being thought a fool to accomplish that, why then in a way I'm being what St. Paul said, "a fool for Christ's sake" (I Corinthians 4:10).

Dear Lord, in this month as we celebrate Your Resurrection, give me the grace to share both my strengths and my weaknesses with others.

—Eleanor Sass

Monday

2

Being... a doer of the work, this man shall be blessed in his deed.
—James 1:25

Every spring out by our mailbox a bed of beautiful narcissus blooms. One day a neighbor boy wanted to know what kind of flowers they were. "They're called narcissus," I explained, "after a young man in a Greek myth." Then, I repeated the story about Narcissus, the youth who saw his image in a pond, fell in love with it and pined away until he was turned into a flower. That's why we sometimes call people who are in love with themselves narcissists.

People in love with themselves seldom put themselves out to help others. Remember the parable of the Good Samaritan who went to the aid of the man attacked by robbers? At the end of the story Jesus says to all of us: "Go, and do thou likewise" (Luke 10:37).

So what happens when we feign blindness in the face of need and "pass by on the other side of the road"? The answer is that we are guilty of a form of narcissism. By too much preoccupation with ourselves, we miss the great blessing God promises to those who willingly put themselves out for others.

Lord, give us hearts both warm and soulful,
Always willing to serve the woeful.

—Fred Bauer

Day Brightener

A DISCIPLE'S PRAYER

O God,
Help us to be masters of ourselves,
That we may become the servants of others.
—Alec Peterson

Tuesday

3

For there is no difference between the Jew and the Greek.... —Romans 10:12

Did you ever think eggs could bring people of different faiths together? Well, one year our friends, Ron and Cindy Bauman, invited my husband Vincent and me to their family's Passover seder. It so happened that this particular year Passover fell on Holy Saturday, the day before Easter. We accepted the invitation eagerly and looked forward to it. We knew that Passover commemorates the Exodus of the Israelites from Egypt and their safe flight across the Red Sea. And that this early spring festival is a happy time for Jews who celebrate their people's rebirth in freedom from bondage under the Pharaoh.

On Passover night, we were welcomed at the family table and encouraged to participate in the prayers, the Exodus narrative and songs. When it came time for the family to taste of the hard-boiled egg from the seder plate, I remarked to Cindy, "Why later I'll be going home to boil eggs just like these and color them for our own family's Easter celebration tomorrow."

Cindy smiled and went to the kitchen. "Here," she said when she came out and presented me with the extra eggs. "I made these for those who wanted more than just a taste of the egg from the seder plate."

Later, as I set out the Passover eggs on my kitchen counter, I thought that it was exceedingly appropriate that these eggs, which symbolize hope, life and rebirth for our Jewish friends, should now take their place in our Easter festivities as symbols of our own hope in Christ's Resurrection, and renewal in the life of our Christian faith.

Lord, teach me to see the similarities among people, not the differences. —Mary Tomaselli

Wednesday

4

But they constrained him, saying, Abide with us: for it is toward evening, and the day is far spent. And he went in to tarry with them. —Luke 24:29

It was a sunny early spring day several years ago and I was in a gray mood. I'd been turned down for a job I truly expected to get, and after several such disappointments, I was frustrated and discouraged. I called up my old friend Jim to discuss the situation. He would understand.

We met outside his apartment and started walking. We walked through the park, kicking stones, tossing a Frisbee, watching a baseball game. We walked over to the museum and saw a mime perform for the crowds waiting outside on the steps. We bought some hot dogs and sat on a bench, watching kids sail their model boats. We talked about the movies, his girlfriend, the weather, his job, some mutual friends and a bit about my disappointment, but not much. Still, when the day was over, my spirits were lifted and I could look at life with a more hopeful attitude. Just being with Jim had done that for me.

On Easter Day, on the road to Emmaus, two of the disciples were walking when a stranger joined them. They were grieving over what they believed was Christ's end and told the stranger all that had happened. He walked with them, he talked to them, he supped with them, and only when he took bread and broke it did they recognize their Savior. In their grief, He abided with them. Like Him (and like Jim), there are often people in our lives who stick with us in our times of sorrow. Lord, let me be one of them.

Lord, let me walk with those in distress, as You walked with Your disciples on the road to Emmaus. —Rick Hamlin

Thursday

5

Let thine hand help me.... —Psalm 119:173

Sometimes I have trouble finding God. I know He's not hiding, but it seems that I am distanced from Him. At times like that, prayer and Bible reading are helpful. But we have access to Him in another way, too. In ourselves—*in our bodies*, God has hidden shadows of Himself for us to see.

As a physician, I see these wonders constantly in my work. Just for a moment, look at the hands you are using to hold this book. For the rest of the day think about them as you use them. When you gently push your hair back from your forehead, marvel at the sensitivity that can differentiate each strand as it passes through your fingers. Or when that jar cap is stuck and you begin to twist it, sense the power just before the top grudgingly releases its hold.

Remember your hands today when you pause to think. Perhaps unconsciously your two hands meet, fingertips touching fingertips. You bring them to your face, tucking your thumbs beneath your chin, and your forefingers rest on your lips... waiting for that inspiration or that solution to a difficult problem. There is a name for that position of our hands... *prayer.* Reaching up to Him by folding our hands together so that they can no longer do anything but wait for the touch of His hand.

When we pay attention to them, our bodies can be a holy and prayerful connection to our loving Father, Who made them.

Great God Jehovah, Who upholds us in Your righteous hand, may our bodies be ever-present reminders of Your nearness. Amen.

—Scott Harrison

Friday

6

You meant evil against me; but God meant it for good.... —Genesis 50:20 (RSV)

One year as the children and I dyed Easter eggs, we dipped the ends of the eggs in different colors, creating two-toned combinations. Pink and green, red and blue, purple and yellow. "Oh, Mama, they're be-e-eautiful!" exclaimed my daughter Ann.

That night when the children were asleep, I tiptoed through the backyard with a flashlight, hiding the eggs for the children to find the next morning. At 5:00 A.M. I woke to the light pattering of rain outside. The eggs will be ruined, I groaned.

By the time the children woke, the rain had stopped. As they grabbed their Easter baskets, I explained about the rain, trying to prepare them for the worst.

Their little hands groped around flower borders and tree trunks. Finally Ann raced toward me displaying her eggs. "The rain made them more beautiful," she cried. I peered into her basket, startled to see that the rain had streaked the colors together, creating a lovely swirled effect we never could have achieved on our own.

As she skipped off, it occurred to me that in a tiny way I was witnessing the message of Easter in my own backyard. Just when you think a calamity has struck, God surprises you by transforming it into a blessing. No matter what befalls you, He can turn it around and make it beautiful.

Lord, help us create something beautiful out of the mishaps and tragedies in life. —Sue Monk Kidd

This Side of Easter
HIS FINAL GESTURES

Join Carol Kuykendall during Holy Week as she relives the Easter story (Matthew 18-28) and *ponders* the final words and actions of Jesus, seeking clues to what they have to say to us today in 1990. As we come to understand His purpose during His final days on earth, may we also learn by His example how to live more *purposefully* now and all our days on this side of Easter. —The Editors

Saturday 7

Day One—Living Purposefully

For I have given you an example, that ye should do as I have done to you. —John 13:15

The phone rang on a bright spring morning.

"I have inoperable lung cancer," my friend Lois told me simply. With that news she began the final steps of her forty-three-year journey, which ended one cloudless summer Sunday morning just before dawn. I had the privilege of walking beside her during those days... driving her to the doctor, pushing her wheelchair around the neighborhood, helping her up and down stairs.

Looking back, what I remember most are the powerful memories of how she lived *purposefully* during those last weeks, wasting none of her limited time or energy in self-pity or anger. Instead, she typed up her family history, wrote messages of loving motherly advice to her two children and spent unhurried time with people explaining that the source of her strength was Jesus—Who loved and cared for her. Walking with Lois left me wanting to live more *purposefully*, following her inspiring example.

Now, on the brink of Holy Week, I think about walking alongside Jesus with the same awareness. He was only thirty-three years old when He rode into Jerusalem that first Palm Sunday and saw the shadow of the cross looming on the horizon. He knew His time was short and He understood His *purpose*: He had come to die for us. Yet, this God-man had another purpose: He would show us how to live. In His humanness, He shared our problems. In His divinity, He gave us perfect solutions.

In the days ahead, let's step back into that first Easter, asking our searching questions of Jesus and seeking the deeper meaning of His final gestures. Then let's think about what His example means to us and how to follow it in our everyday lives. For instance, how did Jesus conquer His fear of the cross and how can we conquer our own fears of failure or inadequacy? And why, having been given Jesus' perfect example, do we sometimes still fall short in our own day-to-day living when we're quick-tempered, unforgiving or self-centered?

Let's look for these answers together... and maybe, by the end of our Holy Week journey, we'll have a fresher understanding of how Jesus lived and why He died.

Lord, open our eyes as we walk alongside You this week; enable us to hear and see the messages of Your final gestures. Amen.

—Carol Kuykendall

Palm Sunday

8

Day Two—He Rides a Donkey

Your attitude should be the kind that was shown us by Jesus Christ.... —Philippians 2:5 (TLB)

Jesus, why did You ride a donkey today?

A donkey seems so... lowly and common... *and You are a king, making Your triumphant entry into Jerusalem. Look how the people adore*

You, running before You, laying down their garments for You to walk upon, strewing Your path with palm branches and fresh flowers, jubilantly shouting, "Hosanna!" "Blessed be the King!" You are the hero of this ancient ticker tape parade.... Why then, Jesus, did You choose to ride a borrowed donkey? You could have ridden a magnificent, prancing steed ...or asked to be carried into town on a fancy litter.

Ah, I think I see, Jesus. You have chosen a manner completely in keeping with Who You are in God's eyes: the peaceful Redeemer, humbly sent to fulfill God's promise. Whatever others may have thought or wanted of You, You would not be persuaded to be Something or Someone You're not. You were Yourself. You were being REAL, *true to what God had called You to be.*

Is that why You rode a donkey that day, Jesus?

Sometimes I question who I am, liking myself one minute, other days wishing I were someone else. Sometimes I act like someone I'm not...or fail to act like the person I really am. Last night the phone rang as I was on my way to a church meeting. It was the mother of my daughter's new friend. "Where are you going?" she asked.

"To a *school* meeting," I answered. *Why did I say that?*

"Don't be a chameleon," my mother used to advise, which meant, "Don't be like one of those lizards that change colors to match their surroundings."

When Mother Teresa travels, she doesn't stay in fancy hotels or arrive in sleek limousines. She is true to her calling—helping the sick and poor by being her humble, charitable self.

When Jesus rode a donkey into Jerusalem, He wasn't swayed by temporary circumstances or the fickle adoration of others. He knew the same people shouting "Hail to the King" today would be shouting "Crucify Him!" by Friday. And He wasn't swayed by the fear of consequences either. He remained true to God's purpose for Him... and did not compromise that truth...even to save Himself from dying on the cross.

Could He be asking us *purposefully* to do the same in our own lives?

Lord, may Your gesture of riding a borrowed donkey into Jerusalem remind us always to be REAL, *true to ourselves, no matter the circumstances or consequences. Amen.* —Carol Kuykendall

Monday
9

Day Three—He Gets Angry

Be angry but do not sin.... —Ephesians 4:26 (RSV)

Jesus, why did You get angry in the temple today?

You stand for love and gentle kindness, but today You burst into the temple, raging with white-hot anger. You knock over tables, release the doves and shout at the vendors and money-changers. "It is written that 'My house shall be called a house of prayer.'" Your booming words bounce off the walls, "But you are making it a robber's den!" Matthew 21:13 (MLB). The place looks more like a souvenir shop than a holy place of worship. It was a defilement, a slur against God. And that blatant irreverence angered You.

But Your storm of anger disappeared as quickly as it appeared. Once You cleared the temple of the money-hungry scoundrels, You calmly went on with the business of teaching and healing.

Oh Lord, in this act then, are You telling us it's okay to get angry sometimes—if we get angry for the right *reasons and make changes in the* right *places?*

Is that why You got so angry in the temple today, Jesus?

Getting angry for the right reasons isn't always easy to do. Just the other day I called the doctor's office to confirm an appointment. "Hold please," the receptionist commanded, pushing a button and plugging me into the annoying sound of canned music before I could say anything. As the minutes ticked by, *I* got ticked. Later, in a hurry to get downtown, I let a car squeeze in front of me in a long line of traffic and the driver didn't even wave a "thank you." Inside my anger was building. Suddenly, the light in front of me turned red and I stopped abruptly. Catching my breath, I thought back to Jesus and His anger in the temple.

I wonder if the feeling of anger isn't like a red light signal in our lives, telling us to *Stop*...*Look*...and *Listen*. *Stop* at the feeling of anger. *Look* for the reason and name it. *Listen* to what God has to say about that reason and then take action. All too often, my reasons are impatience...pride...envy...and I know what God says about that kind of self-centeredness. Yes, perhaps anger demands action—something needs to be changed—but my anger usually demands change within *myself...within my temple.*

The light turned green and I proceeded calmly. Then I remembered how Jesus *finished* His anger. He didn't hold a grudge or grumble endlessly about those money-changers. He acted with *purpose*—and He forgot His anger. He had expressed His truth, and then went to His next task.

This third day of Holy Week, could Jesus be asking us to handle our own anger *purposefully*, in the same way?

Lord, help us put our anger to the "Red Light" test... to stop, look, listen. To act purposefully, *then to forget and move on to our next task.*

—Carol Kuykendall

Tuesday

10

Day Four—He Teaches

Come ye, and let us go up to the mountain of the Lord... and he will teach us of his ways.... —Isaiah 2:3

Lord, why did You spend so much time teaching this week?

As the shadow of the cross inched closer, surely You wanted to begin shutting out the noisy world and gather in Your strength by spending time alone with Your Father, family and close friends. Yet, it seems at every opportunity, You went to the multitudes to teach... in the temple, on a hillside. Is it because teaching is part of Your purpose? Did You become man so You could articulate God's thoughts in words we could all understand? Knowing Your time was near, did a sense of urgency compel You to teach incessantly this week?

Ah, Jesus, I also see that in this important last week You taught us which is the greatest commandment in the law: "You shall love the Lord your God with all your heart, and with all your soul, and with all your mind" (Matthew 22:37, NKJV*). And the second greatest commandment: "You shall love your neighbor as yourself," (Matthew 22:39,* NKJV*). So Your last days taught us that these two commandments are the sum of everything You wanted to say. How simple....*

Is that why You were teaching the multitudes so purposefully in Your final days, Lord?

Sometimes in my own stubbornness or willful pride, I forget these two great commandments. The other morning, for example, I noticed our neighbor had put up a "For Sale" sign... not on his home but on a tiny piece of property *between* his house and ours! Subdividing? My instinctive response was resentment. *How could he? What about our rights...our privacy...our property values? It's not fair!* Then, as sometimes happens at times like this, I heard a still, small voice inside my head: "Second commandment: Love your neighbor as yourself."

I *can't!* I rationalized, again adding up the reasons.

"You *can*—if you put the First Commandment *first*."

It was hard, but I knew I had to try. After all, I'd committed myself to aim more *purposefully* toward His examples. So I took myself to a quiet corner in the house and prayed. I told God how much I loved Him. And I asked for help in loving my neighbor. Pretty soon, a peace that passes understanding filled me and squeezed out my feelings of resentment.

But I've also learned that yesterday's supply of First Commandment love is not always sufficient for today's needs. Every morning when I walk out to our mailbox and see the sign, I feel that familiar pang of resentment that reminds me that taking time to love God wholeheartedly is a *daily, purposeful* commitment...and out of today's fresh supply flows today's love for others.

Do you think maybe that's what Jesus was trying to tell us this fourth day of Holy Week?

Lord, may we remember that loving You is what enables us to love others. Help us in that task, now and every day on this side of Easter. Amen. —Carol Kuykendall

Wednesday 11

Day Five—He Washes Feet

Wash me thoroughly from mine iniquity, and cleanse me from my sin. —Psalm 51:2

Lord, why did You wash the disciples' feet before the Last Supper?

Washing the feet of guests was a servant's job. Yet as You and the disciples assembled, no servants appeared and no one else volunteered. Surely You surprised the disciples when You took off Your robe, poured water into a basin and began gently to wash their dusty, dirty feet. Did You purposefully intend to make this gesture part of Your Last Supper message?

Earlier amongst themselves, the disciples had argued about who was the greatest, and now they were silent as they watched You perform the lowly task. Then Peter objected. "You shall never wash my feet," he exclaimed, pulling away.

"If I do not wash you, you have no part in Me," You told him firmly.

Ah, I think I see, Jesus. Were You telling us that loving You means recognizing our need to come to You and allow You to "wash our feet"—that is, to participate in a spiritual *cleansing? Was Your gesture telling us that we are capable of truly great servanthood only if we allow You to cleanse us of the daily accumulation of dust and dirt and sins in our lives?*

Is that why You washed the disciples' feet, Jesus?

I'm a lot like the disciples, assuming I should be great, and not recognizing my need to come to Jesus for cleansing when I fall short. Several years ago I remember sitting by my mother's bed, spooning pieces of grapefruit into her mouth. I'd always imagined that when she and I reached this point in our lives, I would lovingly take care of her with selfless joy. Instead, I was angry that she was dying of emphysema at age sixty-six, and exhausted with the emotional struggles of role reversals. As I stabbed at the grapefruit, I squirted myself in the eye with some juice. *"Oh!"* I cried out, dropping the spoon. And then the tears of frustration came.

"I'm sorry," my mother whispered weakly, and we both knew she wasn't talking about the sting of the grapefruit juice.

Later, I sat curled up in a ball on her living room couch, aching with guilt and pain. I felt like such a failure. A little girl still longing to be taken care of by her mother; an adult, impatient and angry that the aging parent had become like a child. Then I remembered the image of Jesus washing the disciples' feet. Like Peter, I don't want to appear helpless or needy; I expect to be great, serving and loving others with perfect, unfailing devotion. Ah, suddenly I see my real sin: *pride.* Because I expect to be perfect instead of accepting my imperfections and my need to allow Jesus to cleanse me.

Jesus is not surprised by my actions today. He understands, and waits, to wash my feet. So as I sat there on the couch, I deliberately stretched out my legs and visualized His gesture of washing my feet. That quiet, *purposeful* moment enabled me to get up and return to my mother with renewed energy and strength. I did not have to pretend greatness; I could serve her with a humbled, human heart.

Lord, may we purposefully *allow You to wash our dirty feet every day, because You alone can cleanse us. Amen.* —Carol Kuykendall

Maundy Thursday

12

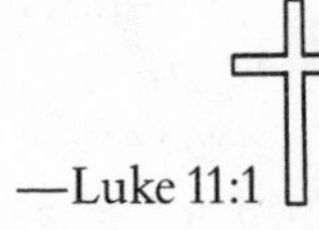

Day Six—He Prays

Lord, teach us to pray.... —Luke 11:1

Jesus, why did You lead the disciples to Gethsemane to pray so late at night?

It was nearly midnight when You finished the Passover celebration, and even though You must have been bone-tired, were You also wide awake, in lonely terror of what lay ahead? Even though You are God, in Your humanness, Jesus, You must have felt afraid.

"My soul is very sorrowful, even to death" (Mark 14:34, RSV), You confessed to Your disciples before asking Peter, James and John to go with You into the garden. Together you strolled among the gnarled olive trees and then You asked them to "watch with You" while You prayed. Moving a little apart, You fell to Your knees and began pouring out Your anguished heart to God. "My Father, if it be possible, let this cup pass from me" (Matthew 26:39, RSV), You prayed. Perhaps, at that moment, You were tempted to run away into the night and escape the cross altogether. But no, You surrendered, "Nevertheless, not as I will, but as thou wilt" (Matthew 26:39, RSV).

Ah, I think I understand, Jesus. In those hours of prayer, something miraculous happened. Your fear was transformed into unwavering strength and courage. Are You showing us, Jesus, that prayer prepares us to meet our challenges? That prayer is the most powerful possession we have and that when we seek "Thy will," our greatest fears in life—and death—can be swallowed up whole and transformed into purposeful *living?*

Is that why You went to Gethsemane late at night to pray?

Sometimes I feel afraid of risky challenges. Tomorrow at noon I have to give a speech in front of fifty people. That may not sound like much of a challenge, but I've read that most people fear public speaking more than death. Today I believe that statement. The clock ticks. I can't organize my thoughts, and I feel paralyzed with fears of failure, rejection and inadequacy. I'm tempted to call and say, "I can't."

How do I pray my way from fear to courage? I think of Jesus in Gethsemane. First, He sought the comfort of a familiar place and asked close friends to pray for Him. Then in prayer He spoke to God. Confessing His fears and desires, He then sought to *know* and *do* God's will over His own. In that act of surrender, Jesus received strength sufficient to meet the challenge. The process took not *one* prayer, but *three* separate sessions.

Did it work? Compare His results to Peter's. Jesus asked him to watch and pray. *Three times* Peter fell back to sleep. In foregoing prayer and clinging to "self will" instead of "Thy will," Peter *lost* his way from fear to courage...and before dawn, he denied knowing Jesus...*three times*.

Will praying for "Thy will" work for me...or for you? *Purposefully*, I'm going to give it a try.

Lord, Your prayers in Gethsemane turned fear into courage. Let me in all things seek Thy will. Amen. —Carol Kuykendall

Good Friday

13

Day Seven—He Forgives

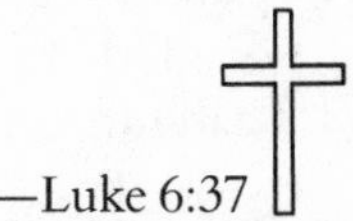

Forgive, and ye shall be forgiven. —Luke 6:37

Jesus, why did You forgive the soldiers who beat, mocked and crucified You today?

How could You forgive them as they pounded those sharp spikes into Your hands and feet, the thudding sound echoing eerily across the valley below Golgotha? Surely as they hoisted You up and plunked the crude cross into place on the barren hillside, the searing pain began suffocating You immediately. Yet as You gasped for breath, You cried out not for Yourself, but in a plea for them: "Father, forgive them; for they know not what they do" (Luke 23:34). Your words must have surprised the soldiers gathered at the foot of Your cross. There, in the face of suffering and injustice, with only enough life left to utter a few last words, You focused on forgiving. Why?

Ah, I think I see, Jesus. Are You telling us again what You taught

about forgiving in Your life? You said we must forgive others if we want God's forgiveness; and we must forgive "seventy times seven" or always *...no matter the circumstances (Matthew 18:22). And Jesus, did forgiving flow naturally from Your heart, even as You died on the cross for our sins, because that's how You* purposefully *lived, practicing forgiveness every day?*

Is that why You were able to forgive Your persecutors that Holy Friday, Jesus?

As a parent, the greatest pain I can imagine facing is the accidental death of a child, and the greatest example of forgiving is the *purposeful* choice to forgive the person responsible for that death. Some time ago I read about a mother who forgave the drunk driver for killing her only child—a college freshman—two days before Christmas.

At first she was filled with uncontrollable hate and anger, emotions that shocked her because she was a Christian. But in time, with Jesus' words "Father forgive them" echoing in her head, she began to see the twenty-four-year-old killer as a hurting person, imperfect and needful as she was, and she began to reach out to him with loving forgiveness. She visited him in jail, got permission to take him to church and eventually began to absorb him into their family life.

This mother's act of forgiveness reflects the same truths Jesus taught:

—Forgiving is not an instinctive reaction but a *purposeful* choice we make to reach above our feelings of hate or blameful resentment and allow God's forgiving love to flow through us.

—Forgiving comes from the realization that we all are sinners in God's eyes and we all stand on the same level ground at the foot of the cross.

—Forgiving brings healing because as we forgive others, God forgives us.

—Forgiving flows from a person's heart in difficult moments if forgiving love has been stored there through time, which comes from practicing forgiveness every day.

On this Good Friday when Jesus died to forgive our sins forever, could He be asking us *purposefully* to focus our lives on forgiving; that is, to practice forgiveness every day?

Jesus, may Your words, "Father, forgive them," continue to echo down to us from the cross, changing our lives as we aim for Your example.

—Carol Kuykendall

Saturday
14

Day Eight—He's Silent

Return, O my soul, to your rest.... —Psalm 116:7 (RSV)

Jesus, why were You silent?

It is the Sabbath and people have retreated behind closed doors to observe the tradition. The streets of Jerusalem are quiet and deserted, unlike the chaos and frenzied emotions displayed on Good Friday when You were crucified.

Even Your faithful followers are in seclusion somewhere, feeling physically and emotionally drained. John, the "disciple whom You loved," must be hurting deeply. He was with You until the end, standing at the foot of the cross with Your mother, watching You suffer. Just before You died, You asked him to take care of her. Later, as they carried Your body off to the tomb, John gently led Mary away...but where and to what? Ever since that life-altering day three years ago when he and his brother James dropped their fishing nets to go with You, John had a single purpose in life: to follow You. Now You are gone. In the silence, a question must ricochet loudly in John's mind: What next? *Is this day of silence merely a coincidence, Jesus, or a* purposeful *part of Your Plan?*

Ah, Jesus. I think I see. Could it have been that in John's tired and confused state he was too fragile and fatigued to think about the future? Did the silence of the day provide him with the much-needed rest he required to regain this physical and emotional strength? Enormous change was at hand. Did this time of aloneness give him the clarity he needed to begin facing the inevitable tomorrow? Could You be showing us that after a loss or crisis, we need a transitional period of rest before we can shift gears and face the future?

Is that why You were silent this day, Jesus?

Sometimes following a major loss or disappointment, I, too, feel confused about the future. I remember the day Kendall, our youngest, went off to her first day of kindergarten. I walked her out to the school bus, hugged her tight and snapped a picture as she climbed up the steps. I waved as the bus disappeared around the corner, but she didn't even look back. Later, as I wandered around a quiet, empty house, the throbbing realizations began to slowly sink in: Today marked the end of an era. Mothering is a temporary job description. The anchors of my identity are shifting. I have to find new challenges and set new goals because my children are growing up and needing me less. Surely God has something in mind for me in this next season of life. *But what? Where? How?* Suddenly I felt deeply tired—not muscle tired, but soul tired—and the questions seemed too overwhelming. That day I finally decided I would do nothing, and maybe tomorrow I would be able to think about the future.

Could these have been the very same questions John must have asked following the crucifixion? But Jesus probably knew he wasn't ready for the answers until he rested, so He planned a day of *purposeful* silence between His death and Resurrection. With that gesture, He also tells us that sometimes we have to come to a complete stop—and *purposefully* rest—before we're ready to change directions and take on the new challenges He has in store for us.

Lord, may we know when purposefully *to seek moments of silence—restful transitions—that restore and prepare us for Your new challenges.* —Carol Kuykendall

Easter Sunday

15

Day Nine—He's Alive!

And, behold, I send the promise of my Father upon you.... —Luke 24:49

Why did You rise from the dead at dawn, Jesus?

It must have been a long, dark night for Mary Magdalene who, like many others, faithfully followed You to Jerusalem from Galilee. Grief-stricken, she must have risen before dawn, gathered her assortment of oils and wrapped herself tightly in a cloak to warm her against the early morning chill. Now her heart is heavy, but she moves with purpose *on the way to the tomb to anoint Your body before Your permanent burial.*

Soon she reaches the tomb and shrinks back from the entrance in dismay. The stone is rolled way...the linen cloths remain in place, but like a deflated shell that has released new life. THE TOMB IS EMPTY...JESUS IS GONE! WHERE? HOW? Had Mary Magdalene forgotten what You had said, Jesus? Had her doubts grown so big during the darkness of the night that she is stunned to find Your tomb empty?

Slowly, the first fingers of dawn lighten the eastern sky. And with each ray of light, softly at first and then glowing in its full radiance, comes the truth... He's alive! He's ALIVE! HE'S ALIVE! The Easter morning promise bursts forth victoriously as the daylight overcomes the darkness. JESUS, YOU'RE ALIVE.... On the third day You rose again, Jesus, just as You promised.

Ah, Jesus, I see. Your Resurrection is a beautiful fulfillment of Your promise. As the dawn brought a new and glorious hope to Mary Magdalene, does the dawn of each of our days today bring us new hope? Did You mean to connect Your most awesome gesture with a daily occurrence so that each day we have a powerful reminder that You are alive... and that our faith overcomes the darkness of our doubts when we purposefully *remember and believe Your promises?*

Is that why You rose from the dead at dawn, Jesus?

Doubt sometimes wins over faith in my life, too... like the day my friend Lois died. The ringing telephone sliced through the early morning darkness and jolted me wide awake. I knew before I answered that Lois' struggle was finished. The day before, though she could no longer respond, I had sat by her bed and told her good-bye.

The digital clock said 4:22. "I'll be right there," I told her husband Don. But I took my time, dressing slowly, and reluctantly trying to connect the lifeless, stark word *death* with Lois. The two words still didn't go together as I got in the car and headed toward her house. By the time I reached her neighborhood, the first fringe of dawn glowed on the eastern horizon, and the promise of breaking day beckoned me so strongly that I pulled over to watch the sunrise. As the light overcame the darkness, I began to remember what Jesus said and did. He didn't promise that a good life was a long life—He was only thirty-three years old when He died. What matters is how we choose to live *purposefully* each day. And He didn't promise a life without suffering, but He promised to walk with us and give us strength sufficient to meet our challenges. And most importantly, He didn't say that death is an end, but a triumphant new beginning, because we have eternal life in Him. As I watched the night turn into day, death became a victorious new beginning.

Jesus. Resurrection. Dawn. He gave us this tangible, daily reminder that He is alive... His promises are real... and if ever our doubts grow bigger than our faith, we can get up before dawn and watch the sunrise, which helps us remember and believe, and choose to live *purposefully*.

Hallelujah, Lord, that Your Easter morning promise is reborn in each new dawn. Help us to live purposefully *each day, aiming toward the memory of Your gestures on this side of Easter.*

—Carol Kuykendall

Monday

16

WINDOWS INTO WONDER
The Impossible Stone

And they said among themselves, Who shall roll us away the stone from the door of the sepulchre?

—Mark 16:3

Darkness still blanketed the earth. The aroma of rich spices hovered in the air as Mary Magdalene and the other women walked in silence, their sandaled feet damp from the dew underfoot. Suddenly, one of them broke the silence. "Who will roll away the stone for us?" In their desire to express their love for their crucified Friend, they had forgotten all about that one big obstacle. Now the impossibility of it loomed before them. *But they kept going anyway.* When they got there, they found the stone already rolled away, and a shining angel waiting to tell them the most glorious news the world has ever heard: "He is risen." Think what they'd have missed if they had let the thought of the stone interfere with their faithfulness!

My friend Jan's mother is in a nursing home. Recently, in sorting through some of her mother's things, she came across a stack of letters that she had written to her mother many years ago during a time of alienation between the two of them. They were all unopened. At first, Jan felt the crushing rejection of that. Then she was flooded with thanksgiving for the fact that she and her mother had moved past that pain, that their loving relationship had been restored even though it had seemed so hopeless at the time of those letters. The thing that struck me as Jan told me about it was the amazing *faithfulness* of my friend, in continuing to write to her mother, even when her efforts to repair the relationship were met with stony silence.

What's the one big obstacle that's in your way? Perhaps this month you'd like to find a rock to place on your desk or in your kitchen windowsill, or wherever you'll see it often. It can remind you to go faithfully on, even in the darkness, not knowing how the obstruction will be removed. Like the women who went to the tomb, be faithful in expressing your love for Christ, and you may find that what was beyond your power has happened. The stone has been rolled away, revealing the shining presence of new strength, or surprising good news, or an opened way.

Jesus my Friend, I love You. —Marilyn Morgan Helleberg

April Prayer List Reminder

Return to your Monthly Prayer List on the calendar opening page and review your requests. Give thanks for prayers answered, renew old prayers and add new concerns today. Then pray once again our *Family Prayer for April.*

Tuesday

17

My ways [are] higher than your ways, and my thoughts than your thoughts. —Isaiah 55:9

When I worked in Jamaica helping underprivileged boys, one of my jobs was to teach welding. To help with expenses in our shop, we would do welding projects for people in the community. One day I received a call from a man who wanted me to make him a half-dozen decorative flower pot stands. He didn't know exactly what design he wanted, so I told him I would build one and bring it over for him to see.

I was in a hurry because we needed the money, so I slapped together what seemed like a good design of a flower pot stand. When I drove to the man's home, I was surprised to see that it was in a very nice residential neighborhood. I felt uncomfortable. I had on my work clothes and my hands were still grimy from the welding and painting. Holding the pot stand, I rang the doorbell and was met by a distinguished-looking man who ushered me into his office. "Let's see what you've come up with," he said pleasantly. I handed him the stand, which he set on his mahogany desk.

I was so ashamed. What hadn't looked too bad on my work bench had suddenly changed in its surroundings. At that moment my flower pot stand looked like something that belonged in the scrap pile.

"Mr. Miller," the man said, "I really like the design. But I'm sure this sample doesn't reflect what your final product will look like, does it?"

"Oh, no sir! This is only a quick job I did so you could see the design." (I had decided that when I walked in his door.)

"Good then. When can I expect delivery?"

When I returned with the stands he had ordered, he was pleased, but I had made sure this time that they were built right.

I've never forgotten that experience. All too often in my daily life I try to get by with thoughts or actions that seem adequate to me. It's only when I put God's high standards first that my life begins to reflect His perfect design.

Lord, let me always be able to see my life the way You see it.

—Brian Miller

Wednesday

18

O Lord, how great are thy works! —Psalm 92:5

Caught up in the excitement of Halley's Comet's return several years ago, I was impatient to see this famous visitor flashing across the horizon, never to return in my lifetime. The comet would be at its brightest in April, astronomers said, and would be seen best in the Southern Hemisphere. So where was I in April but deep below the Equator on safari in Africa's Kruger Park.

At a camp far out in the bush, where no city lights could intrude, I lay on the ground and pointed my binoculars expectantly at the night sky. First, a guide explained, I was to locate the four bright stars of the Southern Cross. In time I found them.

"Good," the guide said. "Now drop down from the top star." I did as instructed. "And move a little to the right." Done. "Can you make out a large kind of hazy blur?"

"Yes, I see that."

"Well, that's Halley's Comet."

That? No *whoosh* across the heavens? No extravagant tail? I had come thousands of miles for a hazy blur?

The next night, still hoping, I tried again. At two A.M., the recommended hour for comet-gazing, I got out of my cot and fumbled my way out into the darkness. There were no lights in the camp for its generator was off. Silence. No sound of people, not even of nocturnal creatures close by in the underbrush. Once again I lay on the ground and looked upward. *Maybe that spot up there could be said to have a tail*, I thought. But face it, this was not the comet I had come to see.

Sadly I put my binoculars down. Gradually my eyes began to scan the profusion of stars above me, millions, trillions of them. The sky swam around me, vast, wild with brilliant galaxies and jots of shimmering silver. Beautiful, but how chaotic it all seemed. Yet was this so? Hadn't even my fuzzy old comet returned on schedule, right on time? What seemed like chaos was really order, the order of an all-powerful God, and that little speck of humanity lying beneath the spectacle was just as much a part of the plan as the largest of celestial bodies.

Thank you, Mr. Halley, and your comet. Maybe it won't happen again in my lifetime, but I've had at least one moment in which I've known God's infinite majesty.

And thank You, Father, for the wonderful way You have of taking me by surprise.

—Van Varner

Thursday

19

The entrance of thy words giveth light....

—Psalm 119:130

Our words can have a tremendous impact on those whose lives touch ours. I thought seriously about this when I received a church bulletin recently. "When we speak words of love," it read, "we plant 'flower seeds.' Negative words beget 'weed seeds.'" Because I love flowers, this message appealed to me. I long to plant "flower seeds," but I often lack the proper words. The bulletin suggested using these "flower seed" phrases:

Good work!
Let me help you.
I forgive you.
Congratulations!
I'm sorry.
Thank you.
I love you.

I've copied this list on a card and glued a photo of one of my favorite flowers—a columbine—on the back. Each time I use one of these sentences, I put a check mark beside it. I hope this soon becomes a habit, producing flowers that seed and reseed in an endlessly widening garden.

Has your garden been overrun lately with weeds of anger or resentment, hurt or envy? Why not pluck them out and start planting "flower seeds" of hope, happiness, joy, contentment, peace. Water these "flower seeds" of yours and watch them grow tall.

Dear God, whenever I plant seeds of speech, let them reflect Your love. —Aletha Jane Lindstrom

Friday

20

Be not weary in well doing. —II Thessalonians 3:13

"I'm just burned out!" I announced to my friend Laura on the phone as I complained about feeling tugged in too many directions. Even as I used this blanket rationalization for weariness, I thought of a definition I'd seen recently: "Burnout is the stress and fatigue of the incorrectly committed."

I hung up the phone and gazed out the window toward the puffs of smoke rising above the irrigation ditch at the bottom of our hill. The sight is a familiar harbinger of spring in Colorado. Every year about this time, the ditch superintendent burns out the weeds that might suck up some of the precious water supply or impede its flow through the ditch to the farmland during the new growing season.

Burnout...a problem *and* a solution. Could God have placed the two together in a noncoincidental set of circumstances before my eyes today so I can see their connection? To alleviate the problem of burnout, I need to "burn out" the excesses to which I'm "incorrectly committed," because they drain my energy and clog the flow of God's power through me.

Immediately, I began to examine what was tugging me to see what could go. How about this committee where I have little input, and that drawer of unused recipes clipped from newspapers, and this sack of year-old magazines I keep meaning to get to? Surprise! Even these simple decisions gave me a new spurt of energy.

Why not try some "burning out" in your life this spring? Lord, show us where we are "incorrectly committed" so Your strength can flow more cleanly toward new growth. —Carol Kuykendall

Saturday

21

God...gives generously to all without finding fault....
—James 1:5 (NIV)

Once, interviewing a famous man for my column, I was amused but a little shocked by a sign he had posted in his vast library: *NO! YOU CANNOT BORROW A BOOK!* "Let people buy their own books," he declared, noticing my surprise. "Or patronize the public library. You know how careless people are about returning books. I love my books too much to risk losing them, even to friends."

I nodded, smiling to myself as I remembered two other true book lovers, who had a different way of showing it. One was Toppy Tull, my beloved English professor in college. Toppy left his personal bookcases unlocked, their contents available to anyone who wandered into his office. "I know I lose a lot of books," he admitted. But he felt more than compensated by making so many friends for *his* dearest friends, those books.

The other was Frank Foster, a young minister in our inner-city church. "I want our library to have as few rules as possible," he instructed. "No time limits on the return of books, and no fines. Let anybody take any book he wants and *keep* it as long as he wants. After a few weeks, if it hasn't come back, drop him a note, but no pressure ever. So what if you lose a book? Don't worry about it, bless it! Bless it to the good of the person who borrowed it, and to the others it may reach. After all, that's why these books are here!"

Neither of these men was rich or famous, but surely they were happier and more truly book lovers than the man with his selfishly guarded library.

Owning books was rarer when I was growing up. But today most of us have more books than we know what to do with. If this is your case, why not lend them freely, or give them away? There are children who have never owned a book; there are schools in poor sections that need books desperately. Church libraries welcome decent Christian books: so does the Salvation Army. Books are not to be hoarded, but shared. And even if a loaned book is lost, love it enough to bless it to the good of the one who has it! Isn't that the way God shares His love with us?

Dear Lord: Thank You for Your bountiful blessing of books. If we truly love them we will share them. —Marjorie Holmes

Editor's Note—*Tomorrow begins "Reading Is Fun Week" across the country. Why not join in on the celebration—support your local library; read to the handicapped, blind or elderly; gather the children and read a good book together. It's fun to read and learn. And last but not least, open the greatest book ever written, The Bible, and share your favorite passage with a friend or loved one!*

CELEBRATING EARTH

In the beginning God created the heaven and the earth.

—Genesis 1:1

So begins our Bible. So begins the history of the universe and humankind. Our very life, and that of future generations, depends on our love and care of our planet Earth. On this national Earth Day, join Elizabeth Sherrill for the next three days as we celebrate Earth and our God-appointed task for its care. —The Editors

Sunday

22

Day One—Become Faithful Stewards

It is required in stewards, that a man be found faithful.
—I Corinthians 4:2

They appeared in the early sixties, those first photographs from space. They changed forever the way we see the earth.

For the first time we beheld our planet whole: a blue and white jewel set in the blackness of the universe, lovely beyond imagining. Fragile beyond imagining, too—a shimmering dot in the yawning immensity of space. No longer the enormous earth men had struggled to explore and conquer: a mountain here, an ocean there, elsewhere a desert or a forest. Our portrait from space showed us a unity, a little ball, bound together and interconnected in every part.

But the revelation wasn't new, not really. That view of ourselves from beyond ourselves is God's view—the picture the Bible painted long before the camera caught it. God created the earth whole. He made it beautiful. He created Adam, "Earthman," to tend it in His name.

Over our kitchen table my husband and I have a magnetic board where we post prayer reminders. There since the sixties, among pictures of family and friends, we've kept a photograph of our planet, inspiring us to ask each day:

Lord, make us faithful stewards of the earth. —Elizabeth Sherrill

Monday

23

Day Two—Listen Carefully

Consider the lilies of the field.... —Matthew 6:28

The elderly Japanese gardener bent so close that his wisp of a beard stroked the needles of the tiny tree. The two-hundred-year-old pine was only eighteen inches high, an exquisite specimen of the art of bonsai.

The gardener moved on to a miniature maple, again lowering his head in what seemed an intimate communion. There was much more to see in San Francisco's Golden Gate Park, but I couldn't tear my eyes from this relationship between a man and the living things in his care.

Next he stooped over a small sturdy oak, then a two-foot-high cedar, product of nearly three hundred years of devoted care. What empathy with roots and soil, sap and bark, generation after generation, had gone into the nurturing of these trees!

I waited till the gardener straightened again. "Excuse me, sir," I said. "Would you tell me... when you bend down... are you speaking to the trees?"

The old man turned to me a face seemingly as full of age and wisdom as the trees themselves. "No," he answered. "I do not speak to the trees. I listen to them."

Lord, teach us the language of Your creation. —Elizabeth Sherrill

Tuesday

24

Day Three—Awaken to the World

The thief comes only to steal and kill and destroy....
—John 10:10 (RSV)

It's a parable of the world in balance. Deep within the scarlet flower of the trumpet vine lies the nectar on which the hummingbird depends to fuel his darting flight. And as the bird probes inside the trumpet, its feathers collect pollen, which it carries to neighboring vines. The stationary plant reproduces itself; the energy-hungry bird is fed.

On the slopes of the Andes Mountains, however, a different kind of bird is at work. Called a flower-piercer, this species has learned to circumvent nature's design. Instead of entering the mouth of the trumpet, as the flower's glory of color beckons it to do, the flower-piercer stabs a hole from outside directly into the nectar chamber... gorging itself on the sweet fluid, giving nothing in return.

No harm seems to be done in the teeming life of the Andean jungle. Hummingbirds outnumber flower-piercers. But a nightmare vision haunts me. What if the flower-piercers somehow became numerous enough and clever enough to eliminate the hummers? What if the robber-birds had it all their own way?

The vines would die out, of course... and so would the flower-piercers. In my nightmare the earth has become that glorious vine, mankind that short-sighted bird.

Lord, awaken us in this new decade to the harmony of Your world.
—Elizabeth Sherrill

Wednesday
25

Your Father knoweth what things ye have need of, before ye ask him. —Matthew 6:8

On the television series *M★A★S★H*, there was a character named Radar O'Riley, who acted as the colonel's secretary. His nickname was Radar because he had an uncanny knack for knowing what his boss needed even before he asked for it. Usually when the colonel said, "Bring me that file," Radar already had it in his hand.

Actually most secretaries possess a "secret" knowledge of the boss's needs. In fact, the word *secretary* is derived from the Latin word for secret. The word originally meant one entrusted with secrets or with that which is beyond general knowledge or understanding.

On this Secretaries Day, let's salute secretaries everywhere, especially that wonderful "radar" of theirs. Perhaps we can learn to use it in our own lives. For it is simply the caring ability to anticipate someone's need and meet it, usually before they even ask.

Thank You, Father, for knowing and meeting my needs even before I know them myself. —Sue Monk Kidd

Thursday
26

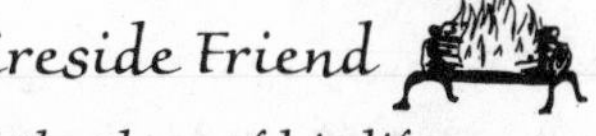

And he shall read therein all the days of his life....
—Deuteronomy 17:19

My library card expired today. I hadn't realized it until the librarian told me. "Do you have time for me to type up another one for you now?" she asked. "I'll make time!" I said. While I waited and she typed, I thought of all the hundreds of books I'd taken out over the past three years. I'd read novels that opened new worlds for me, non-fiction that made me think, romance novels that got me through dull stretches in my life and biographies that inspired me. I'd thumbed through the huge dictionary there, looked up recipes for peanut butter pie and beef stew, and helped my friend's child find out what *homesteading* meant in the encyclopedia. Books had eased my loneliness in moving to a new neighborhood and taught me how to make friends, too.

I thought about the librarians, and how they had helped me find a better job (by referring me to reference books showing companies in the Bay Area), aided me in learning about computers (by explaining how to use their new computerized system) and checked and rechecked books to find the correct spelling of an obscure word.

I thanked God, too, for the library itself, which I had used as an office when I began doing free-lance writing. I could nestle into a cubicle and concentrate in a way I could never concentrate at home, what with the ringing telephone and tempting television and refrigerator. So when the librarian came back with my freshly typed new card, and said, "Thank you for waiting," I sincerely said, "Thank *you* for being here."

Dear God, today, on this National Library Week, I thank You for libraries and librarians—and most of all for the gift of reading.

—Linda Neukrug

Friday

27

Have you not made distinctions among yourselves, and become judges with evil thoughts?

—James 2:4 (RSV)

We arrived in Alaska at the end of April and stepped right into "break-up" season. Break-up is a miserable, muddy mess. A kind of intermission between winter and spring, it is dingy snow, pothole-pitted roads, frozen lakes turning to mush, decomposed moose droppings and mud everywhere. One look and I was ready to return to my familiar paved streets and blooming lilacs.

As for the people, they were a motley crew—bearded men wearing untucked flannel shirttails, faded jeans and muddy boots; women slumped beneath old sweaters and muddy boots; runny-nosed children in crumpled, worn jackets and *more* muddy boots. I wondered, *How will I be able to stand it here? Why these people look barely human!*

But as the year unfolded and the glorious Alaskan summer arrived, I was awed by sparkling emerald lakes, wildflowers splashed across lush mountainsides and *no mud.* People were perky and alive, a bounce in their step. And as autumn and winter unlocked their own delights, I came to know my Alaskan neighbors and uncovered a generous, loyal company of friends, like Pete, who took my children ice-fishing and had a cookout with them on the lake; Charlie, who surprised us with a cord of firewood; and Granny, who taught all of us gentleness toward God's creatures. And as we weathered the long, cold winter, I admired these folks who had survived the months of brutal, sub-zero temperatures!

The next break-up season, when my husband Terry and I were out walking in our muddy boots, I remarked, "Remember that sorry-looking bunch we saw on our arrival? Well, I'm one of them now. And you know what? I love it!"

I guess there are other times in my life when a new challenge appears and I'm ready to hightail it back to safer and more familiar ground. It can be intimidating to meet new people, to rub elbows with someone whose life-style or attitudes are different from mine. Sometimes just facing a new day is scary, or entering a new phase of parenting or maybe switching jobs. But all I know is that I came to a strange place where my first steps got me and my cozy traditions ankle-deep in mud...and I fell in love.

Lord, calm my squeamishness by reminding me that plunging into the intimidating experiences You sometimes place in my path is the first step toward embracing them. —Carol Knapp

Saturday

28

Thou hast covered me in my mother's womb. I will praise thee.... —Psalm 139:13–14

A particular joy for my wife Cherry and me was the birth of our third baby girl. Even though Chelsy was our third, her birth was no less special than either of our first two children.

As I held Chelsy in my arms, her tiny dimpled hand reached out and grasped my forefinger. I felt as never before the total trust a newborn has in those who care for her; how, without any preconceived ideas or prejudices, she expects she will be loved and all will be well.

That evening I went home to my two active older daughters and to the cares of my farm. It was spring, a very busy and anxious time of year for a farmer. I not only had the ground to prepare and the corn to plant—a huge undertaking—but I also had the first cutting of alfalfa to mow and bale, as well as getting the heifers moved out to their summer pastures. But though I had just as many worries and tensions as I had a few days before Chelsy's birth, I now felt enveloped in a sense of wonder that no sisterly squabbles or planting problems could ruffle. Chelsy's little, loving face reminded me that although I had responsibilities and cares she knew nothing about, she knew something very essential that I need to remember always. My heavenly Father has an infinite amount of love and care for me—if I just reach out my small hand to grasp it.

Dear Lord, no matter how frantic my life gets, never let me forget to trust myself always to Your Fatherly love. —John Coen

Let us not therefore judge one another....
—Romans 14:13

My son John and his friend, whom I'll call Brent, have been buddies since they were in elementary school. One day John and I were sitting at the kitchen counter having a snack together when Brent's name came up. "He's certainly a loyal friend," I said. Then after a pause, I added, "*But* he's so loud and boisterous!"

John considered that for a minute and then came back with, "I think you've got it backwards, Mom. The way I see it is that Brent may be rambunctious, *but* he is a loyal friend."

Moving Brent's loyalty to the other side of the word *but* helped me to focus on what was really important about John's friend. It also made me rethink some of my own relationships. . . .

If there's someone you'd like to have as a friend, *but* he talks too much, or is too gloomy, or wears funny-looking clothes, why not try putting his good qualities on the other side of the word *but*. Just this little shift in perspective can make us more accepting of other people. I know. Brent is as noisy as ever, but he continues to be loyal to John. That's what counts.

Help me to focus on the good in others, Lord, and be *a loyal friend.*
—Marilyn Morgan Helleberg

Monday

30

For in him we live, and move, and have our being. . . .
—Acts 17:28

Last week while visiting a lodge in the mountains, my husband and I found a row of rocking chairs on the porch. We settled into a couple and started to rock. Soon more guests joined us until six chairs were rocking. I couldn't help but notice how out of sync the chairs were, like a row of pistons moving up and down, each at a different rhythm.

But something fascinating began to happen. Gradually the chairs fell into exactly the same rhythm. "Look how our chairs are all moving together now," I said to the man on my right, who happened to be a research scientist.

"If you hang several pendulums on a wall and give them enough time, they will do the same thing," he said. "Even insects that chirp or blink will eventually fall into unison. It's known as entrainment. It means that two or more rhythmic beings will gradually alter their movements until they are locked together in the same rhythm."

As we rocked on, I thought about this unusual scientific phenomenon that God designed into His universe, and I wondered. Hasn't God instilled the same mystery in the human heart? If I spend time rocking gently in God's presence, in time, won't my life-rhythm gradually fall into harmonious alignment with His?

Of course.

Teach me the art of spiritual entrainment, Lord. —Sue Monk Kidd

Thank-You Notes to God

1 ____________________

2 ____________________

3 ____________________

4 ____________________

5 ____________________

6 ____________________

7 ____________________

8 ____________________

9 ____________________

10 ____________________

11 ____________________

12 ____________________

13 ______________________________

14 ______________________________

15 ______________________________

16 ______________________________

17 ______________________________

18 ______________________________

19 ______________________________

20 ______________________________

21 ______________________________

22 ______________________________

23 ______________________________

24 ______________________________

25 ______________________________

26 ____

27 ____

28 ____

29 ____

30 ____

MAY

S	M	T	W	T	F	S
		1	2	3	4	5
6	7	8	9	10	11	12
13	14	15	16	17	18	19
20	21	22	23	24	25	26
27	28	29	30	31		

SPIRITUAL TREASURE

Go Two Miles

If any one forces you to go one mile, go with him two miles.

—Matthew 5:41 (RSV)

In May as the earth comes to life with fresh color and new growth, God seems to be going out of His way to touch us with beauty and wonder, pouring an extra helping of blessing into the world.

This month why not go out of your way and pour an extra helping of blessing into someone's life? Offer an extra portion of your time, money, concern or creativity. Jesus called bestowing such bonuses going two miles instead of one. He knew that being a two-miler makes the heart strong.

So during May, grow strong in heart!

My Monthly Prayer List

Family Prayer for May

Savior, help this month's new graduates discover that they need never stop learning, that they can keep becoming all that You've called them to be.

Tuesday

1

THROUGH AN OPEN WINDOW
Resist Temptation

God is faithful, who will not suffer you to be tempted above that ye are able.... —I Corinthians 10:13

Today, bright spring sunlight is streaming through my window. A great day for shopping. But if you're like me, you have too many charge cards in your wallet that you tend to use too often.

One day, while talking to a friend, I was bemoaning the fact that toward the end of each month I forget the number of times I've used each card. Then when the bills arrive, I'm shocked to see the amount I owe.

"I used to have that problem," my friend said.

"How did you overcome it?" I asked.

She told me that she started carrying her charge cards in a sealed envelope, instead of in her wallet. On the envelope, in bold letters, she wrote: *Pray Before Using*. "Before making a luncheon date or a purchase in a department store, I take out the envelope and pray, asking God if this expense is necessary, or if it will help someone. Often the answer is 'No.'"

I decided to do as my friend does. Sometimes it is hard to resist the temptation, but when the end of the month comes and the bills arrive, I'm always glad I did.

There are other forms of temptation, of course: stealing, overeating, gossiping, indulging in sensual thoughts. Whatever they are, it is important to acknowedge them and face up to them. During this month of May, why not begin each day with a prayer for your specific temptation? Visualize Jesus going forth with you. All during the day, whenever you feel tempted, imagine that He is by your side. Talk to Him. Thank Him in advance for helping you overcome your weakness. And remember: God's plan isn't for us to be immune from temptation. His plan gives us a way out.

Lord Jesus, You are my armor against temptation. Thank You!

—Eleanor Sass

Wednesday

2

As for me and my house, we will serve the Lord.
—Joshua 24:15

After fifteen years of living in my Manhattan apartment, it was high time for a little refurbishing. A workman was scraping paint from the door in the outside hallway when I caught sight of a tiny object on the jamb. I'd never noticed it before. "What do you think that is?" I asked the painter.

"A *mezuzah*," he said matter-of-factly.

"A *what*?"

"Guess you're not Jewish, are you?" he replied. "It's a blessing on your house."

"How'd it get there?"

"Don't know. Previous tenant, maybe."

Curious, I went right in to my dictionary: "mezuzah (mē-zōō′zä): a small metal case attached to the doorpost of the houses of devout Jews. It contains a parchment inscribed on one side with Deuteronomy 6:4-9 and 11:13-21, and on the other *Shaddai* (one of the names of God)."

Then on to my Bible. The two passages in Deuteronomy were similar. I was stirred as I read the words in which God commanded us to love Him and keep Him in mind and heart at all times. And each passage bore the same specific instruction about these commandments: "Thou shalt write them upon the door posts of thine house" (Deuteronomy 11:20).

No, I'm not Jewish, I said to myself, *but I like having this kind of reminder that God is here in this house, "when thou liest down, and when thou risest up"* as Deuteronomy 11:19 says.

"Mr. Varner," I heard the painter calling. "About the mezuzah. Do you want me to take it off?"

"No," I said. "It belongs here."

Bless this house, O Lord, as You have blessed me. —Van Varner

My prayer returned into mine own bosom.
—Psalm 35:13

One morning I began my day with an unusually long and intense session of prayer, hoping to make the day a special one. Instead, everything seemed to go wrong. The car stalled on me that morning; I was late for an important class I had to teach. A misunderstanding erupted between myself and a colleague—I was miserable the rest of the day. "I don't understand it," I said to my wife Sharon that evening. "I can't tell much difference between days when I pray and days when I don't. Why bother to pray if things are going to turn out like this?"

Her wise Irish eyes smiled at me. "I think it has to be that way. You know, God is not a vending machine, where you drop in a quarter and—"

"But I expect to see *some* results," I interrupted.

"And you will, but maybe not within a few hours."

"So I'm being impatient?"

"Maybe. But aren't we all?" She smiled that knowing smile, and I relaxed in the comfort of such a wise and understanding partner. I saw that it's not my prayers that are ineffective, it's that I often get in the way.

Today is a National Day of Prayer. At the end of this day the news will report crime, wars and natural disasters. Indeed, things may seem even worse than ever. Yet you can be confident that your prayers and mine are making a subtle but steady difference in the tone of the world. We have God's promise on that.

Lord, I am so impatient. Teach me to pray and then to trust You to answer in Your own good time. —Daniel Schantz

I have chosen the way of truth.... —Psalm 119:30

The grandchildren were having a discussion about truthfulness. "Is a lie badder than a fib?" the six-year-old wanted to know.

"Oh, yes!" said his older sister solemnly.

"Is even a *white* lie badder than a fib?"

His sister looked puzzled. "Well, um, maybe. I don't know. If you tell one to keep from hurting someone's feelings, is that so bad?" And she glanced questioningly at their Aunt Caroline.

"I think it's best to avoid all three," their Aunt Caroline said. "And I'll tell you why. When I was a young girl, I had a grandmother—your great-grandmother—who was very kind to me. On my sixteenth birthday, she gave me a book. I put it aside, meaning to read it, but I forgot all about it, until one day Grandmother asked me if I had enjoyed it. I was ashamed to say I hadn't read it, and I wanted to spare her feelings, so I said, 'Oh, yes, I enjoyed it very much!'

"Grandmother looked at me thoughtfully and didn't reply. Not long after that, she died. A few years later when I was cleaning out my bookcase and pulled that book down, out fell a check—a nice, fat birthday check that had been there all that time. Now of course I couldn't cash it because Grandmother was no longer living. So you see, you can never be sure when even a white lie is harmless. It's much better to stick to that old rule: 'Honesty is. . . .'" She looked at them quizzically.

"The best policy!" chorused all the grandchildren at once. So that took care of that.

Father, help us remember that truth tampered with is no longer truth. —Arthur Gordon

Saturday

5

God hath made me to laugh, so that all that hear will laugh with me. —Genesis 21:6

The night before, my son demonstrated a new wrestling move on his waterbed. The next night, I heard the sound of running water as I passed his room. Peering inside, my eyes came to rest on his water-bed (his 250-gallon, guaranteed-not-to-leak waterbed!). I bent down and looked underneath. Does the term Niagara Falls ring a bell?

The previous evening of gymnastics had caused the frame to crack underneath, tearing a hole in the mattress. My husband Sandy and I began throwing a few dozen towels onto the floor (which was useless), and soon we were shouting and running around like the Keystone Cops. Next we rigged the garden hose from the mattress to the bathtub, hoping to siphon off some of the water. That was futile, too.

Finally, we stood helplessly in the middle of this miniature lake and suddenly Sandy started to laugh. He bent double and bellowed. "Are you crazy?" I said angrily. "This is no laughing matter!"

"Why not? There's nothing else left to do!" he cried between guffaws. Funny thing about laughter—it's catching. A giggle escaped from my lips and spread into spasms of hilarity. It was a wonderful catharsis, and somehow it made the whole nightmare not so nightmarish.

Life is full of grand hassles (such as a non-reusable waterbed that we threw out), which I can do nothing about. But how I respond to these moments is strictly up to me. Laughter, I discovered, is sometimes healthier than anger and a whole lot more fun.

Lord, help me see the humor that lies buried within life's frustrating moments. —Sue Monk Kidd

Day Brightener

PRAYER

Give me a sense of humor, Lord;
Give me the grace to see a joke,
To get some happiness from life,
And pass it on to other folk.

—Chester Cathedral

Sunday **6**

Fireside Friend

Bear ye one another's burdens.... —Galatians 6:2

My sister Sue and I are best friends. Two years ago she was going through some very difficult times and began to withdraw from everyone. I tried to talk to her, but she enclosed herself in a dark, narrow world of emotional pain. "I can't talk about it," she'd say. I don't think I ever prayed for anyone as hard as I prayed for Sue.

One day, as I was shopping at a local department store, I saw a greeting card with a cartoon of a cat hanging onto a blank wall by her bare claws. Judging by the claw marks on the wall, she was slipping fast. "Hang in there!" the caption read. I sent the card to Sue. It was the first of many greeting cards, some funny, others spiritual. Sue later told me she was deeply moved by the latter and that some of the funny cards had actually made her laugh out loud. Imagine that! Despite her troubles, Sue laughing out loud. To this day, we still send each other cards. And we've extended the practice to other members of the family and to friends.

Is there someone you love who is hurting and needs to be reminded that God loves them? If it's difficult to reach out in person or by telephone, a greeting card just might help. A card allows a person the privacy they need, but it also reminds them that they are loved and opens the door to communication.

Father, help me reach out today to someone who is hurting.

—Georgiana Sanchez

Monday

7

Be not deceived; God is not mocked: for whatsoever a man soweth, that shall he also reap. —Galatians 6:7

Spring is a very important time of year for farmers; this is when we prepare the ground and plant the crops that will provide income and sustain our livestock for an entire year. First, the ground must be properly prepared to establish a good seed bed. Then correct amounts of fertilizer must be applied. Good viable seed, placed at exactly the right depth and spacing, comes next. This is followed with herbicides and insecticides to protect the young crop. It's a timely and very costly procedure, but if I want a bountiful harvest, there are no corners to cut.

One morning, as I was feeling the pressure of getting the planting done right, I snapped at the hired man for not going fast enough and I yelled at the kids for being in the way. When I tersely told my wife Cherry to hurry up and get lunch ready, she told me, "'As you sow, so shall you reap.' What kind of harvest do you expect with seeds of anger and impatience? Lunch will be ready in fifteen minutes."

I knew she was right. And I saw that for my life to be the type of "crop" God wants in His harvest, I must follow the same careful steps I use in my farming:

- *Prepare* the ground by opening my mind up to Him.
- *Fertilize* it with Bible reading.
- *Plant* the seeds of qualities like patience, love and generosity.
- *Cultivate* it with lots of prayer and churchgoing to keep it growing straight and strong.

Do you want your life to yield a bountiful harvest? There are no corners to cut! Why not join me today in establishing your "crop"?

God, as I establish my life, nurture me as I grow and produce a harvest for You. —John Coen

Put on the new man.... —Ephesians 4:24

Today I was leafing through a new book called the *The Dictionary of Cultural Literacy: What Every American Needs to Know*. In it the authors have produced a fascinating potpourri of information, beginning with a section on the Bible that will, if nothing else, serve as an intergenerational aid for Trivial Pursuit players.

Running down a list of entries in the English literature category, I tested the breadth of some family members. When "O. Henry" stumped a younger member, I explained that it was the pen name for William Sydney Porter, an American writer of short stories ("The Gift of the Magi" among them) that often featured a surprise conclusion or an "O. Henry ending." The writer's personal life story is a page turner. While working in a bank, some money came up missing and he was charged with embezzlement. Though O. Henry forever proclaimed his innocence, he was sentenced to prison and served three years.

What he did with himself while in jail is the part I like. He began writing and while still behind bars sold his first article to a national magazine. After his release, he became one of the most popular writers of his day—the best O. Henry twist of all.

The Bible is full of stories with "O. Henry" endings (maybe they should be called O. Zaccheus or O. Saul endings), which broadcast the good news that through Christ we can turn our lives around, that we can become new creatures. That truth may not be included in my book of things everyone should know. But it should be.

Lord, help us our bad habits to change,
Not just shuffle and rearrange. —Fred Bauer

Editor's Note: *If you participated in the* C.O.P.E. *prayer writing experiment, which was suggested on February 8, today's the day to return to your diary or notebook of prayers and see how you did. Then write us: Daily Guideposts Editor, Guideposts Books, 757 Third Avenue, New York, New York 10017. Tell us what this prayer experiment has meant to you. If you have not yet participated, but would like to try, begin the experiment now, and in three months write us and tell us about it.*

Wednesday

9

I was glad when they said unto me, Let us go into the house of the Lord. —Psalm 122:1

When I was a small girl, I didn't like to go into my house after school most days because my mother was at work. It was a friendly neighborhood and I was safe, but the house didn't feel right. Sometimes I went home with friends whose mothers were home cooking, rolling their hair or sitting on the porch. Their houses felt so good.

Wednesdays were my favorite days. It was Mother's day off. I would practically run home from school and there she'd be, working in the yard or talking with the neighbors. Some days, as I approached our house, I could hear music from the radio or I might smell a roast or ham cooking. I'd call out, "Mama!" and my heart would warm at her presence.

Many years later I felt that "Wednesday feeling" again. For so long I had attended church without really looking forward to it. I felt lonely in church. But one day, when I was in my early thirties, Jesus became a reality in my life. Old things passed away and all things became new—including going to church. I could hardly wait to get there. The One Who loved me would be there just for me! He'd talk to me and listen to me and have fellowship with me. I knew He'd be there waiting. I seemed to hurry up the steps like a child again, my heart shouting, *"Abba! Abba!"*—"Daddy! Daddy!"

Father, I'll never feel lonely with Your Presence always at home in my heart. Thank You for always being home for me.

—Marion Bond West

Thursday

10

I beseech you therefore, brethren, by the mercies of God, that ye present your bodies a living sacrifice....

—Romans 12:1

My favorite aspect of living in the desert out here in Arizona is the versatile plant life. Mesquite, for example, makes a perfect cooking fire, filling the autumn nights with a crisp, sweet aroma. A lost hiker can survive for days on the fruit of the prickly pear cactus.

But my favorite is the aloe. It rescued me again the other night. I burned my arm pulling a pan from the oven, so I rushed to the aloe just outside the kitchen door, cut off a leaf, sliced it open and began rubbing the soothing juice on my burn. Immediately it relieved my pain, and thanks to its healing properties, I knew I wouldn't have a blister or a scar.

As I nursed my wound, I realized I only pay attention to that plant when I need it. Yet when I'm hurting, I rely on it, and it's always right there, a living sacrifice. Can the same be said of me?

The aloe gives me a twofold challenge—maybe you, too:

1) *Appreciate the aloe, remembering its example of quiet sacri-*

fice. Do you know any "unsung heroes" who deserve recognition for their willingness to give? Praise them!

2) *Be more like the aloe, a living sacrifice*. Do you know someone in pain whose spirit might be healed through your gift of time or service? Give!

Strengthen me, Lord, to be willing to answer the cry of those in pain.
—Gina Bridgeman

Friday

11

Before he made the world, God chose us to be his very own...we who stand before him covered with his love.
—Ephesians 1:4 (TLB)

It's no secret that I didn't want my fourth child. I was in tears when our family doctor confirmed it. "But I already *have* three children—one of them ready for college. I thought I'd finally have more time for other things I enjoy!"

"Please don't take it like that," he tried to comfort me. "I'm sure this child will be a great blessing to you."

Oh, he says that to all his patients, I thought. *He's just being kind.* But Melanie was a joy and special treasure to all of us from the moment she arrived. And as she grew older she grew in grace, delight and beauty, with a wisdom that at times astonished me. Best of all, she loved the Lord.

I remember a time when she was barely five years old. We were walking past a church, and as she danced along beside me she was chanting a little made-up song: "Oh, oh, oh, I think you are the nicest mommy in the world. Oh, oh, oh, I love you, and you know why? When I was a baby angel in heaven God asked me: 'Look down and see which mother do you choose?' And I said, 'Eenie, meenie, miney-mo, catch a mommy by the toe. If she hollers let her go.' *But I choosed you*!"

It seemed funny at the time; only later did I feel its deeper significance. And even today I sometimes wonder: In the mysteries of creation, isn't it possible there are little souls somewhere just waiting to be born? Perhaps even choosing the parents God wants them to have?

Perhaps someone reading this today has a new life stirring within her. Unexpected, and yes, unwelcome. If you are such a someone, please remember this true story. Such a child can be a tremendous joy and comfort—beyond your wildest dreams. Perhaps there is a tiny angel somewhere who "choosed you" because God wanted it to, a child who will fill a special need in your life as it develops into a beautiful life of its own.

Accept this for the precious gift it is, and be thankful.

Dear Father, Who brings all life into being: Thank You for making me a woman, able to participate in the miracle of creation.

—Marjorie Holmes

Saturday

12

A cheerful heart has a continual feast.

—Proverbs 15:13 (RSV)

We were at a hotel for a banquet, which was a business obligation for my husband and me, but pure pleasure for our eight-year-old son Geoffrey, who had never been to one before. He has the gift of flinging himself joyfully into any new experience. And when our waiter put the first course, a beautiful fruit compote, in front of him, Geoffrey's face glowed with delight.

I watched him carefully spoon off the cherry at the top of the confection, put it into his mouth and savor its sweetness. Then he swallowed happily and pushed his dish away, ignoring the untouched mound of peaches, grapes, kiwifruit and pineapple.

"You shouldn't eat only the cherry," I chided.

"Why not?" he asked. "It was great!"

I had a host of stern, mommy-type reasons: Because the other perfectly good fruit is still uneaten. Because you only get one cherry per cup. Because you can't expect too much out of life. Because...because....But before I could begin my little lecture, our waiter appeared and with a flourish placed seven enormous fruit cups in front of my son.

"I see you like cherries," he said to Geoffrey with a grin. "These are extra. Enjoy!"

Geoffrey pulled the first bowl toward him and happily plucked the cherry from the top of the heap as the waiter stood by beaming. *Life may not always be a bowl of cherries,* I thought to myself as I watched the merry scene, *but what a blessing to be the kind of person who enjoys to the fullest the fruit that falls into his hands!*

Lord, give me a cheerful heart and all the fruit that it bestows.

—Linda Ching Sledge

Sunday

13

And Adam called his wife's name Eve; because she was the mother of all living. —Genesis 3:20

Have you ever seen a written contract of a mother's job description? If we hastily scraped one together it might look like this:

Keeper of all things. Homework papers, matching mittens, Blinky the Teddy Bear, permission slips, practice schedules... all available immediately upon request.

Knower of all things. When "I'm sick" is sick enough to call the doctor; when a difficult *no* is more important than an easy *yes*; when learning from a mistake is more important than "fixing it"; when to be quiet instead of speaking; the importance of birthdays; the names of all your children's friends.

Maker of all things. Chocolate chip cookies, forgetful mistakes (like names of your children's friends), Halloween costumes, dentist appointments, Christmas spirit, peace in the family, messy beds, brown bag lunches, children's smiles.

The position gives no sick leave, no days off, demands lots of overtime and no pay! Sound tough enough? On some days, it seems impossible, but take it from someone with seventeen years on the job: It's a position I wouldn't trade for any other in the whole wide world! That's why I'll take a moment on this Mother's Day to say:

Out of a universe of possibilities, You came up with the idea of mothers. Thank You, Lord. On this Mother's Day, please grant us the wisdom, strength and patience to meet the challenge of the job description.

—Carol Kuykendall

Monday
14

In thy presence is fullness of joy; at thy right hand there are pleasures for evermore. —Psalm 16:11

Have you heard about the many people who have been winning large amounts of money in state lotteries? A newspaper reporter wondered if this sudden, unexpected wealth made for happiness, so he interviewed a number of these people. He found that often the money did make them happy. For many of them, however, life's pleasures consisted of little things—talking with friends, having breakfast with their family, watching a favorite TV program. It was not the great wealth, nor the extravagances that money could buy that gave life meaning; it was the ordinary pleasures.

In my youth when I was brash and ambitious, I, too, sought material gain—a fancy car, electronic gadgets, a big house. It's not that these are unhealthy desires, but I learned very quickly what really mattered—a rest in the shade after mowing the lawn, an interesting book and some good music, my wife's reassuring touch after a disappointment, soup and a sandwich at our favorite restaurant, the joy after the birth of each of my children, and many other such things. These simple things have combined to make life truly rewarding and my family has given me true happiness. In such simple things, I can find a foretaste of heaven.

Dear Lord, I thank You for the many riches that surround me—simple everyday reminders of Your presence. —Lee Webber

Tuesday
15

WINDOWS INTO WONDER
A Quiet Voice

Speak, Lord; for thy servant heareth. —I Samuel 3:9

You remember Samuel, the little boy who lived with the old priest Eli, serving God in the Tabernacle. How *chosen* the child must have felt that night when he heard a voice calling his name. Three times, Samuel got out of bed and went to the priest, thinking he'd called him, but the old man kept telling him to go back to bed. *He* had not called! Then the priest realized that it was *God* Who called the boy, so he told him to answer, "Speak, Lord, for I am listening." And God did speak to Samuel—that night and for as long as he lived.

Just as God spoke to Samuel, could it be that He speaks to us too, but that His voice is drowned out by the TV, by small talk, by all the distractions of daily life and, most of all, by our own incessant thoughts? Perhaps we've heard His voice sometimes without realizing it.

Maybe it was God Who spoke to me in that slight tremor I noticed in the voice of my normally self-assured friend, alerting me to a hurt within her. Could it have been His voice that led my sister-in-law to phone me on that night I was feeling so lonely? I know that I have heard God's voice in the cry of a gull that calls my spirit upward, in the warm, haunting tones of a flute's song that tells me I am more than my senses, even in the glory and terror of a raging storm that wakes me up from dulling dailiness. Oh, yes. My God still speaks.

Where and when in your life have you heard His voice? Where will you hear it today? Let's listen this month for its gentle sound. It's a matter of *attentiveness.*

Speak, Lord, for I am listening. —Marilyn Morgan Helleberg

May Prayer List Reminder

Return to your Monthly Prayer List on the calendar opening page and review your requests. Give thanks for prayers answered, renew old prayers and add new concerns today. Then pray once again our *Family Prayer for May.*

Wednesday

16

The God of all grace... will himself restore, establish, and strengthen you. —I Peter 5:10 (RSV)

One day, at the post office, I overheard a woman talking about a stray dog with three pups hiding out in a culvert near her home. Just that morning I'd prayed, "Lord, please send us the right dog." Our border collie had died just a few months before.

The woman and I climbed into her pickup to go look at the strays. Sure enough, a trio of puppies huddled together inside a pipe beneath the gravel road, while an anxious mother ran around outside. It was clear she didn't know quite whom to trust.

The next day, hoping to rescue the mother and at least one of the pups, I returned only to discover the animal control officer had arrived first. I learned we could adopt the dogs by waiting a seventy-two-hour claim period, driving thirty miles to the facility where they were being housed and paying sixty dollars for the cost of their care. We did exactly that.

At last we brought home cream-colored Taffy and her black-and-white pup Dandy. Taffy, especially, bore signs of real neglect. Scavenging for food that went mainly to produce milk for her puppies had left her rail thin, with coarse hair that fell out in clumps. We began right away to feed her hearty meals, bathe and brush her and shower her with loving attention.

A year has gone by since we found our dogs. Now I look at Taffy frolicking—her body strong, her coat soft and shiny, her eyes unafraid—and I believe in the restoring power of love. Today, if you should happen across someone bearing "signs of neglect," will you apply a touch of love…God's love? Its restorative powers are marvelous!

Father God, Your love puts the frolic in our days. Alert us to others with whom we can share Your restoring love. —Carol Knapp

Thursday

17

The priests made repairs [to the wall], each in front of his own house. —Nehemiah 3:28 (NIV)

One of Grandma's evening rituals was sweeping. She'd begin in the kitchen, careful to capture every crumb, and end on the front porch, sweeping our welcome mat with vigor. Once I asked her why she swept the porch every day, even when it didn't need it. She leaned on the handle of her broom and winked at me, as though she were sharing a secret. "If everyone would sweep in front of his own door, the whole world would be clean."

I was much older when I realized Grandma wasn't just talking about stray leaves and tracked-in sand. And now I remember her simple adage when I'm tempted to repeat what I heard about that single lady on the next block. Or when I complain about the neighbor's dandelions. I recall it when I begin a rampage on "other people's" kids. Or when I want to blame my mistakes on someone else. That's when I check for crumbs at my front door. And taking my broom, I get back to the full-time job of keeping my own porch clean.

Forgive me, Father, for the times I've meddled in other people's lives. With Your help, I'll tend to my own affairs.

—Mary Lou Carney

Friday

18

Be... children of light. —John 12:36

I hadn't been home to Hawaii in more than eight years. I was living and working in New York City, far away from my mother, six sisters and their children, some of whom I'd never met or were just tiny infants when I left. I was reluctant to return home. Would I be a strange outsider from the mainland, more like a tourist than a beloved *kamaaiina* (old-timer)?

My anxiety rose as the small inter-island jet touched down onto the newly built runway. A fancy, concrete structure greeted me, instead of the old, run-down wooden shack that was once the island's only commuter airport. *This homey little island has changed*, I thought uneasily to myself. I followed the signs through unfamiliar corridors to the baggage claim area and waited alone in silence until my luggage arrived. This did not feel like a welcome home at all.

Then a honk from the road, the patter of bare feet, and suddenly tiny arms wrapped around me, squeezing so hard I almost fell over. Small round faces with shiny black eyes and smiling mouths shouted in unison, "Auntie Tes! Auntie Tes!" They jumped up and down, garlanding my neck with sweet-smelling *leis*, strung by their tiny hands the night before. "We knew it was you! We've seen your pictures!" one of them cried.

"Yeah," his sister agreed, "you're so pretty!" They grabbed for my attention: Two of the girls wanted me to admire their cartwheels; my youngest niece yelled a cheerleader's cheer; two nephews demonstrated a karate sequence; and another showed me his fancy football moves.

As I embraced my island family, the feeling of strangeness disappeared. I hadn't really been gone. Letters, phone calls, exchanged photographs had linked us to one another over the years. The children showed me how to make strangers feel welcomed—just bombard them with love.

I walked to the car, all my fears and hesitancies gone. "Now, Rico, I want to see one of your football games. And, girls, I want to attend your soccer meet. And the secret swimming hole, you'll take me there, won't you?..."

Father, let me be like a child in this world of strangers, and share my gifts of enthusiasm, excitement and encouragement with those around me.

—Terri Castillo

Saturday

19

Fireside Friend

For I know whom I have believed, and am persuaded that he is able to keep that which I have committed unto him against that day. —II Timothy 1:12

"Why, that would be chaos!" my friend exclaimed.

She referred to our plans for a local interdenominational retreat. Nevertheless, six of us from different church backgrounds had been meeting together, praying and seeking God's will about a retreat for women in our Walla Walla Valley.

That was twelve years ago, and each year I am amazed and delighted at the response to this twenty-four-hour "time apart with God." There are differences, to be sure. Some of the women attend worship services on Saturday, others on Sunday. Not all would agree on methods of baptism, the Lord's Supper or other practices. On the surface, it should be utter chaos.

But during those early planning days, a lovely woman from India made a remark that the retreat has adopted as a motto: "*What* we believe divides us; *Whom* we believe unites us."

So once a year, the women in our valley come together, not in chaos, but comradeship; not in havoc, but in harmony; for when Christ is at the center, all differences melt away.

Lord, may I join hands with my sisters and brothers who are united in our worship of You today. —Shirley Pope Waite

Sunday

20

He that is slow to anger is better than the mighty; and he that ruleth his spirit than he that taketh a city.

—Proverbs 16:32

When our Tim was little, story-time followed his nap. Winnie-the-Pooh books were his—and my—favorites.

I'm a self-taught typist and I make many frustrating mistakes. I'm also totally disorganized—forever misplacing pens, clippings, letters and scribbled notes. Frequently I end up discouraged, disgusted with myself, and unfit company for family and friends. Despite countless resolutions, I've failed to change my ways. But, thanks to Pooh Bear, I *have* changed my attitude.

One day, when I had hopelessly misplaced an important address I needed, I looked everywhere, even leafing through a book about this Lovable Bear of Very Little Brain. Pooh was constantly blundering, too, but did he rant and rave and hate himself? No. He just said, "Silly old bear. So like me," and went cheerfully about his business.

Now that book, with Pooh on its cover, is on my desk. When I get uptight and start berating myself, I glance at Pooh, smile, and say to myself, "Silly old me. So like me." Then I relax and, like Pooh, go cheerfully about my business.

Things get found, things get done—only calmly.

Father, help me to be kind and gentle, starting with myself.

—Aletha Jane Lindstrom

Monday

21

For I am poor and needy. —Psalm 109:22

When our daughter Teresa turned sixteen, she asked me to teach her to drive. I did, and the lessons went very well. Spurred by this success, the teacher in me went a step further. I lifted the hood of the car and said, "Now, I'll show you how to change the oil and check the fluids." At this point her eyes glazed over and her face disappeared behind a cavernous yawn. I could tell she was thinking, *I'll never need to know this stuff.*

She's in college now, and has her own '76 station wagon she calls "The Golden Barge." Now when I lift the hood to show her how to change the air filter or check the battery, she watches alertly and even asks questions. Sometimes she actually takes notes.

Why the difference? It's an old law of learning called "readiness." Teresa knows now that she needs to know. She doesn't want to break down on the freeway!

Is it possible that there is something God will try to teach you today, but that you will miss unless you are aware of your great need? It may be a lesson in patience or some other form of guidance, but you will receive it only if you are ready to learn. Perhaps, like me, you need to begin this day by praying:

Lord, make me ready to hear You. Don't let me miss out on the lessons You have planned for me this day. —Daniel Schantz

Tuesday

22

And do not... be of anxious mind. For... your Father knows [what] you need.... —Luke 12:29–30 (RSV)

How big a worrier are you? One measurement is how well you sleep.

Next time you get to tossing and turning over money, your kids, a health concern, a sour relationship or any other problem, I have a suggestion that makes more sense than counting sheep. It begins with the spiritual conviction that God is in charge of everything, including your life. Having affirmed that, take ten deep breaths, saying as you inhale, "Thy will," and as you exhale, "be done." You know the rest... *on earth as it is in Heaven*.

If you want a little more of Heaven's peace and a little less of this world's turmoil, turn your worries over to the Lord and rest on Him.

Lord, when our fear is earthly harms,
Take us in Your everlasting arms.

—Fred Bauer

Wednesday

23

Fireside Friend 

My peace I give you. I do not give to you as the world gives. Do not let your hearts be troubled and do not be afraid. —John 14:27 (NIV)

Myocardial infarction. E.K.G. Angiogram. Coronary Care Unit. Frightening new words in a frightening, alien world. Words and a world that were exciting to watch on a movie or TV screen—terrifying in reality. My forty-eight-year-old husband was having a heart attack.

I looked around—at Dennis hooked up to tubes and wires, at the room filled with bottles, machines and unfamiliar sounds. I floated somewhere between faith and fatigue. My thoughts drifted back to the contrasting calm of the past weekend where I had spent a private retreat at a convent. After a year of two major moves and my first full-time job, I had needed a break. Time to be quiet. To abide. Just to listen. I took my Bible, a pen and notebook. My room was simple: bed, desk, chair and a crucifix on the wall. Friday night the Catholic crucifix seemed strange and unfamiliar to Evangelical me. But by Sunday it had become a focus of my devotional time and a source of comfort.

The sound of Dennis' heart monitor interrupted my reverie and rudely brought me back from the peace of my retreat to the terror of C.C.U. As I glanced around the room, I remembered that this was a Catholic hospital. There on the wall across from Dennis was a crucifix, identical to the one at the convent. An object that a few days before had seemed almost alien now brought both present and remembered peace. God was with us even in the midst of the unknown and frightening.

That was two years ago. Dennis was released from the hospital, and it was touch-and-go at first. But with changes in diet and exercise, and cardiac rehabilitation, his life is back to normal...and our world is filled with one more reminder of God's presence.

Father, thank You for transcending the gap between the known and the unknown. Thank You for using the unfamiliar to bring Your peace and comfort. —Bonnie Wheeler

Thursday

24

Simon Peter saith unto them, I go a fishing. They say unto him, We also go with thee. They went forth, and entered into a ship immediately.... —John 21:3

The old wisdom for actors "between jobs" is to stay busy. In my days working as an actor I found this out the hard way. I had just come back to New York from my first job in summer stock, and quite frankly, now that I had some good experience under my belt, I expected the phones to be ringing off the hook. They didn't. Even worse, the rare auditions I went to only became opportunities for more discouragement. Finally, I had to be reminded by a friend, "Get busy. Do all those things you want to do but never have the time to do. Sign up for some classes, send your résumé out, start writing a one-man show. It's when you're busy that creative things start happening."

Sure enough, I got myself so busy I forgot my momentary lapse of confidence. And sure enough, in a couple of months, the phone *did* ring with the right opportunity—and of course, by then I'd stopped waiting for it.

Even to this day that friend's advice holds true: If I'm stymied on one office project, I get busy on another. If I'm depressed, anxious or bewildered, I get busy washing the windows, balancing my checkbook or cleaning out my closet (I'm sure to be rid of my blues before I get to the bottom of that mess!). If my wife Carol and I aren't communicating too well, we might give ourselves a break—take a walk through the park, go to a movie, eat out at a nice restaurant. Being together in a new surrounding gives us a new perspective on our problems.

After the Resurrection, we know that the disciples were confused, frightened, bewildered. And what did they do? They went fishing on the Lake of Tiberias, where Christ appeared to them once again. The point is well-taken: It's often when we're busy doing everyday things that we find what we're really looking for.

Lord, as I go about my day, don't let me miss Your face.

—Rick Hamlin

Friday

25

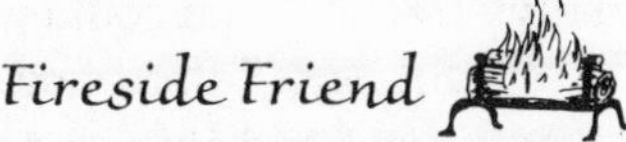

Thou shalt forget thy misery.... —Job 11:16

Although my Grandma Rae was housebound because of severe arthritis, she never let it get her down. She was well-read, informed on news events and through TV was up on all the latest trends. Visitors dropped by daily, myself included. One time a friend came to spend an hour cheering up Grandma. But it seemed that all she wanted to do was complain—about the weather, about a lazy husband, about a son who didn't visit often, about....

Grandma listened patiently, but when the woman began listing *Grandma's* troubles ("Oh, you poor dear, you can't walk"), Grandma put a stop to that right away. "I make it a point," she said firmly, "to forget my troubles as easily as most folks forget their blessings."

I remember being shocked at Grandma's blunt words and wondering how her friend would take them. But after a short pause, the woman laughed and began talking about the pleasure she got from her gardening and other hobbies!

I've always remembered these words. They come to me whenever I'm tempted to let my troubles cloud out a clear and sunny day. And so I pray:

Dear God, let me be as quick to forget my troubles as I tend to be at forgetting my blessings. And help me to remember Your goodness always.

—Linda Neukrug

Saturday

26

The way of a fool is right in his own eyes: but he that hearkeneth unto counsel is wise. —Proverbs 12:15

Zing! Whoosh! Cabs, cars and trucks zipped by on this busy New York street. People were everywhere, too—vendors with their wares crouched on sidewalks, pedestrians jaywalked through the streets, parents pushed baby carriages on crosswalks. There was barely any room left for my friend and me as we rode our ten-speeds.

"Be careful," Nancy warned me as we maneuvered through the heavy traffic. "You could get killed out here—keep your eyes out!"

"Yeah, yeah," I brushed her off. I had been riding in the city for a month now and I was an expert at bobbing and weaving through traffic.

Soon we hit a bottleneck and I noticed Nancy slow down behind me. But I thought to myself, *I can get out of this mess, no problem.* So I pedaled as fast as I could when....

Wham! A cab door swung open and hit me on my left leg, brushing me against a van on my right. But I kept on pedaling, even though I was in pain. When we got to our destination, my leg ached and a large bruise covered my thigh. If only I hadn't been so hard-headed and "kept my eyes out" as my friend had suggested.

I saw now how often I push and plod through life in my headstrong way, as when I drilled holes into my bedroom wall without waiting for my mother's supervision; or the time I took apart my car's engine before my father could help me; and in Home Economics, when I cut the material for a shirt before consulting my teacher—ruining everything.

My independent ways could sometimes get me in a lot of hot water. This bike lesson reminded me that I'm an adult now in this big, new city, but that doesn't mean I don't need God and others. Being an adult, I'm learning, is being big enough to receive another's help, and to ask for it, too.

God, help me to grow up so that I am sensitive enough to know when I need others and their help in my life. —Stephanie Samoy

Sunday

27

Fireside Friend

Launch out into the deep.... —Luke 5:4

As I sat in church at a healing service one morning, I could hear the guest minister saying, "You can be healed if you're willing. God is willing. Are you?"

I watched as a few people made their way to the front. Among them was Laura.

"I was healed," I heard Laura say, her face beaming. "God healed me as I sat in my seat, simply believing Him."

Later I cornered Laura, eager to hear more. She told me she'd suffered for three years with calcium deposits in her elbow. "I'd been willing to live with a limited range of movement," she said as she now flexed her arm easily. "Now I felt the Lord asking me if I was willing to be healed, and He healed me."

As I listened to Laura and saw her bright smile and arm raised up high without pain, there seemed to be a message for me in her miracle: *How am I limiting myself? Am I moving within a limited range? Shying away from challenges, restricting myself to certain friendships, avoiding certain people because they're too old or too young—or just different?* And the answer came: If the Lord can restore full range of movement to a stiffened elbow, can't He heal any "limits" in my life!

How is your range? Are there areas in your life that are stifled or restrained? Are you willing to break out of your limits? Bring them to the Lord and let Him give you "full range of movement."

Lord, I bring this limitation to You today. Free me to trust You to help me move beyond my problem. —Robin White Goode

Monday

28

Let no one seek his own good, but the good of his neighbor. —I Corinthians 10:24 (RSV)

Strange, the little things that encourage us and give us hope. My mother was to have surgery by an eminent specialist on the following day. Tests were still being done on her. I sat alone in the hospital hall while she was in X-ray. It was not yet seven in the morning. I watched the hospital come to life as all the people who made it run came to work in full force. I began to think about my mother's doctor. He had the finest reputation in the southeast. He was booked solid. We'd waited two weeks to fit into his schedule. He was unquestionably the best. But all his credentials and fine reputation, his thoroughness, didn't satisfy something deep inside me. I didn't even know what to call this feeling... sort of a gray area of discouragement.

While I was sitting there, the elevator door opened and out stepped my mother's doctor on the way to surgery. He was carrying a perfect pink rose. I didn't expect him to speak or even recognize me. He barely knew me. But *the rose*... the rose spoke volumes to me. The man inside the doctor *cared*, above and beyond his medical skill; he cared deeply. I imagined him out in his garden, before the sun was fully up, searching for the one perfect rose that bloomed to bring to... I didn't know who. It didn't really matter.

Just then the doctor saw me, smiled, and lifted his hand to wave, hurrying on his way. Even after he disappeared down the hall, I kept smiling too.

Oh, Father, could I also be an encourager today through some quiet, simple act? —Marion Bond West

Tuesday

29

Be strong in the Lord, and in the power of his might.
—Ephesians 6:10

For years, Sojourner Truth, the remarkable black woman from New York, born in slavery, trod the roads of America, preaching and singing of God's truth. Her life continues to be an inspiration to me, chiefly because, despite poverty, cruelty, sorrow and sickness, her faith never wavered.

One night in the 1840s at a huge religious camp meeting in Massachusetts, this faith was put to the supreme test. A mob of white youths stormed the campgrounds. "Burn the buildings!" they shouted. "Fire the tents!" Terrified people scattered, seeking safety. Sojourner, the only black person there, had the most to fear. She'd witnessed white gangs take fiendish delight in tormenting—even killing—Negroes. Shaking with fear, she, too, fled. Then she thought, *Why should I hide? I, a servant of God?*

Turning, she walked tall and unhurried to the crest of a small hill. Raising her arms and lifting her face to the moonlit heavens, she began singing the hymns she loved. Her rich, lovely voice soared serenely above the tumult.

The rioters raced toward her, armed with torches and clubs. But they stopped, overpowered by her singing. For a long time they listened, spellbound, as Sojourner sang hymns and talked of the cruelty of slavery. When she grew tired, they left quietly—some in tears—and the meeting continued.

Lord, help me, also, face my fears bravely and turn them into victories for You. —Aletha Jane Lindstrom

Wednesday

30

Fireside Friend

Greater love hath no man than this, that a man lay down his life for his friends. —John 15:13

It was a beautiful Memorial Day. Pear Tree Beach here in Darien, Connecticut, had come alive again after the long New England winter. The sun sprinkled diamonds of light on the waves and warmed the pale sun-worshipers. The air was filled with the happy sounds of children and the aroma of roasting hamburgers and hot dogs. As my husband and I spread our blanket on our favorite spot near the gazebo, our son Jason ran off to play on the rocks that jutted out into the sound. *What a perfect day,* I thought. *What a day for picnics, parades and parties!*

Then, we heard Jason call, "Mom! Dad! Come see what I found!"

We ambled down to the rocks and there, placed at about five-foot intervals for the entire length of the jetty, were laurel wreaths, their red, white and blue ribbons fluttering in the breeze.

Right then and there, tears welled in my eyes as I thought of all the men and women who were not there to share this beautiful day with their loved ones. We stood together—a fortunate, intact family—and said a prayer for those who had died to preserve our way of life.

I don't know who placed those wreaths on the rocks, but I thank them. It reminded me that Memorial Day means more than a day at the beach. It is a day to give thanks that we live in a land of freedom, peace and prosperity, and it is a day to cherish the memory of those who died defending it.

Prince of Peace, enfold our beloved war dead in Your arms; comfort those who mourn them; and help us, and all the nations of the world, live in peace. Amen. —Stephanie Oda

Thursday

31

The heavens are thine, the earth also is thine: as for the world and the fullness thereof, thou hast founded them. —Psalm 89:11

Only people who respect nature have loons on their lakes. Only those who play by nature's rules will hear the haunting cry that sets the hackles of your neck up and reminds you that you are an intruder in God's wilderness.

A loon can't stop you from building cabins around her lake and bringing in your powerboats, but if you do, she'll leave. If you want loons on your lake, you play by loon rules.

Maybe that's part of our fascination with loons. We can't control them; their presence is a blessing we have to earn. So if you're ever fortunate enough to hear a loon's cry rising out of the early morning mist over the lake, what you'll be hearing is God's voice, saying, "Congratulations. You know your place in My world. You have a loon on your lake."

Lord, teach us not to conquer, not to subdue, but to live in harmony with everything in Your world. Give us loons on our lakes.

—Toni Sortor

Thank-You Notes to God

1 ______________________________

2 ______________________________

3 ______________________________

4 ______________________________

5 ______________________________

6 ______________________________

7 ______________________________

8 ______________________________

9 ______________________________

10 ______________________________

11 ______________________________

12 ______________________________

13 ______________________________

14 ______________________________

15 ______________________________

16 ______________________________

17 ______________________________

18 ______________________________

19 ______________________________

20 ______________________________

21 ______________________________

22 ______________________________

23 ______________________________

24 ______________________________

25 ______________________________

26 ______________________________

27 ______________________________

28 ______________________________

29 ______________________________

30 ______________________________

31 ______________________________

JUNE

S	*M*	*T*	*W*	*T*	*F*	*S*
					1	2
3	4	5	6	7	8	9
10	11	12	13	14	15	16
17	18	19	20	21	22	23
24	25	26	27	28	29	30

SPIRITUAL TREASURE

Seek and Knock

Seek and you will find; knock and the door will be opened to you.
—Matthew 7:7 (NIV)

June is a seek-and-knock month, a time of setting forth on new challenges. Think of the newlyweds seeking a future together, of graduates knocking on the doors of new dreams.

This month set out to reach a new goal. Go after a worthy dream you didn't think you could reach. Challenge yourself to use your talents in a greater way to make the world better. Then roll up your sleeves and start knocking. Jesus said doors will swing open if you do.

My Monthly Prayer List

Family Prayer for June

Lord, anoint every marriage with the "oil of gladness"—humor—and the gift of not taking everything to heart, except the good things.

THROUGH AN OPEN WINDOW
Be Loving

Charity [love]...is kind...doth not behave itself unseemly.... —I Corinthians 13:4-5

Across my bed, in the room with the view, is a rose and gray afghan, knitted for me many years ago by my Grandmother Parry. Grandma Parry was a very proper British lady who lived with my parents and me for a while during my teenage years. One morning, feeling a little youthfully mischievous, I decided to "get a rise" out of my grandmother. So I wrote a letter to a handsome film star of the day, promising him my undying devotion and vowing to do away with myself if he didn't respond to me. I left the letter in an unsealed envelope, propped up on top of a dresser in the room that Grandma and I shared. Then I went off to school.

As I anticipated, Grandma read the letter. That evening, in front of my parents, she voiced her dismay. "Oh, I'm so mortified!" she cried. "I never thought my granddaughter could write such a shameless letter!"

I giggled, then confessed. It was just a childish prank. After dinner, Daddy took me aside. "Do you love your grandmother?" he asked me.

"Oh, yes, I love her dearly," I replied.

"Well, I don't think you showed it today. Your little joke caused your grandmother a lot of pain." I hung my head. Now it was my turn to be ashamed because I knew my thoughtless trick had unintentionally hurt someone and was not in accordance with God's plan for my life.

This month, before I tell an amusing story, or play a joke, or catch myself about to make a thoughtless remark, I'm going to make an effort to ask myself two simple questions:

Is it loving? Is it kind?

Maybe you can do the same.

Father, help me to behave in a loving manner...always.

—Eleanor Sass

The First Pentecost
THE COMING OF THE SPIRIT

The first six months of the church calendar are behind us; on Sunday, the second half of the year—the Season of Pentecost—begins.

Join writer Elizabeth Sherrill as she helps us prepare our hearts for the coming of the Holy Spirit where we will learn what this first Pentecost means in our daily lives. —The Editors

Saturday
2

Day One—Something Better

It is to your advantage that I go away....
—John 16:7 (RSV)

Tomorrow is the big day! Pentecost itself! Have you mailed your Pentecost cards? Baked? Decorated your home?

Neither have I. Even in many churches, tomorrow, there will be only token observance of this first and greatest anniversary in Christian history. Early Christians, were they to join us at church tomorrow, would be baffled by our lack of excitement. For the first few centuries there were only two dates on the Christian calendar: Easter and Pentecost. Advent, Christmas, Epiphany, Lent and all the rest were not yet celebrated. Christians honored just the two fundamental facts of our faith.

Jesus rose from the dead.

Jesus sent His Spirit to be with us.

The day the Spirit came—the day of Pentecost—was forever afterward observed not only as "the birthday of the Church," but as a day of rejoicing for each individual believer. "It is *for your good* that I am leaving you," Jesus told His disciples (John 16:7, NEB).

Could there be anything better, those first followers of His must have asked, than to have Jesus with them? His actual physical presence in their midst?

Yes, Jesus insisted. "For if I do not go away," He explained, "the Counselor will not come to you; but if I go, I will send him to you" (John 16:7, RSV).

Pentecost is the day the Counselor came. And ever since, Christians have affirmed Jesus' words: It *is* to our advantage. In hundreds of hymns across the centuries they've acclaimed the day that brought us something better...

Spirit of mercy, truth and love,
O shed thine influence from above;
And still from age to age convey
The wonders of this sacred day.
[Author unknown, 1774]

Holy Spirit, thank You for coming not only on this date in history but in my life today. —Elizabeth Sherrill

Sunday
3

Day Two—He Gives Courage

When the day of Pentecost had come, they were all together in one place. —Acts 2:1 (RSV)

All of them together—Jesus' mother, the eleven remaining disciples, an assortment of other men and women—120 people in all. A mere remnant of the throngs who had flocked to see Jesus during His earthly lifetime.

The "one place" was probably that same upper room in Jerusalem where Jesus had eaten the Last Supper with His friends. In the seven weeks since that fateful night they'd been rocked by events almost too momentous to grasp: their Leader's death...His resurrection... finally His ascension into heaven, leaving them alone now and afraid.

Jerusalem was a dangerous place for followers of the executed rabbi. The city swarmed with government spies and Temple informers. But Jesus had given His followers an order before He left them: "He charged them not to depart from Jerusalem, but to wait for the promise of the Father" (Acts 1:4, RSV). And so they stayed on in the risky city, clustering together in the upper room, waiting for they scarcely knew what.

Then it happened. It was a festive holy day in Jerusalem, the great Jewish feast of Pentecost. *"And they were all filled with the Holy Spirit"* (Acts 2:4, RSV).

All. Not just Peter and John and the other leaders, but all 120. Filled with joy, peace, love...and a strange new confidence. They burst from the room where they'd been hiding, into the crowded streets of the city. Instead of speaking of Jesus among themselves in whispers, they buttonholed everyone they met, shouting aloud their love for Him. Peter, who a few weeks earlier had tried to placate a mob by pretending he'd never heard of Jesus, delivered a no-holds-barred oration. "This Man *you* killed," he told the astonished crowd, "was the Messiah sent by God! You saw the amazing things He did, so don't try to excuse yourselves!"

Hard-hitting words. Effective words. By the end of that Day of Pentecost, those original 120 Christians had become more than three thousand...

What had turned weak people into strong ones? The same Spirit Who can take our self-centered, fear-filled lives today, and make them glorious.

Hail this joyful day's return,
Hail the Pentecostal morn,
Morn when our ascended Lord
On his Church his Spirit poured!

[Hilary of Poitiers, fourth century]

Holy Spirit, this Season of Pentecost let me take my faith out of hiding.

—Elizabeth Sherrill

Monday 4

Day Three—He Gives Grace

For the law was given through Moses; grace and truth came through Jesus Christ. —John 1:17 (RSV)

The streets of Jerusalem onto which those 120 new-minted evangelists erupted were even more packed than usual. From all over the known world pilgrims had thronged to the holy city for the ancient feast of Pentecost. Observed fifty days after Passover (*pente* means "fifty" in Greek), this was the day when Jews celebrated the giving of the Law on Mt. Sinai.

What a momentous event that had been! The most significant in their long history: the point at which a frightened group of runaway slaves had become a nation. And so the faithful had come, on this day of Pentecost twelve hundred years later—from Egypt, from Persia, from Rome—filling the narrow streets with their varied costumes.

It was the Law that drew these diverse races and cultures to Jerusalem that day. The Law that gave them their common identity and their strength.

But now, here in Jerusalem on this particular Pentecost, an even greater event had occurred. The giving, not of the Law, but of the Spirit. The forging, not of a nation, but of a Church that would include all nations. The transforming of a timid group of followers into the leaders of a world revolution.

The Law had laid down a set of rules that showed people how to live. "The law was our custodian," St. Paul would put it, "until Christ came" (Galatians 3:24, RSV).

Now, with the coming of the Spirit at Pentecost, those rules were henceforth to be inscribed not on tablets of stone, but on the human heart. The Spirit was to achieve what the Law could never in fact accomplish: implant Jesus' own mind and will in you and in me.

Breathe on me, Breath of God,
Fill me with life anew,
That I may love what Thou dost love,
And do what Thou wouldst do.
[Edwin Hatch, 1866]

Holy Spirit, what will You have me do today? —Elizabeth Sherrill

Tuesday

5

Day Four—He Gives Us Ears to Hear

Each one heard them speaking in his own language.
—Acts 2:6 (RSV)

It was the first thing the crowd in the Jerusalem streets noticed about these Christians on whom the Spirit had fallen. They made sense! These people speaking with such conviction about Jesus were, most of them, from Galilee. Yet their hearers—speakers of Aramaic, Greek, Latin, Persian, all of that polyglot throng—heard them "telling in our own tongues the mighty works of God" (Acts 2:11, RSV).

Whether the miracle occurred in the mouths of the speakers or in the ears of the hearers, scholars debate to this day. Perhaps it was a miracle both of speaking and of hearing... the miracle that occurs every time two people communicate. Every time we hear, really *hear,* what someone else is saying. Every time we get across what we mean, leaping out of our isolation to touch soul to soul.

It's most dramatic when the leap is made, as it was on that day of Pentecost, across foreign cultures. But it's no less marvelous when a bridge is built across generations or social custom...to the teenager at the breakfast table, or the woman at the office.

How often I forget to ask the Spirit's aid at these times! How frequently I "witness" to others and get a blank stare in return. How often I close my ears when others speak! For years I was deaf to the words "Are you saved?" Maybe I'd heard them too often, or maybe I'd formed judgments about the people speaking them, but those syllables never got past my outer ear. Until one day I listened to the meaning behind the words...and stepped into a whole new dimension of God's love.

Just as, on that day of Pentecost, the anniversary of the Giving of the Law became for Christians the anniversary of the Giving of the Spirit, so another Old Testament memory—the breakdown of mutual understanding at the Tower of Babel—was transformed by the Spirit into the marvel of comprehension.

In Salem's street was gathered
a crowd from many a land,
And all in their own tongues
did the Gospel understand;
For by the triumph of the Son
the curse of Babel was undone.
[George Timms, 1910-]

Holy Spirit, let me hear You in the words of others today...and they in mine.
—Elizabeth Sherrill

Wednesday 6

Day Five—He Guides Us

They attempted to go into Bithynia, but the Spirit of Jesus did not allow them. —Acts 16:7 (RSV)

Paul and Timothy are on a missionary journey, bringing the good news of salvation. But not hit or miss. They don't blunder from place to place simply in the hope that they'll find listeners. Jesus Himself is with them. Day by day, moment by moment, He instructs them. *Go* here. *Speak* there. *Keep silent* somewhere else. He points out the people He wants to reach, the words He wants spoken, the resting places He has chosen for them.

But—something extraordinary is going on! Paul and Timothy have never laid eyes on Jesus. They never knew the young Galilean carpenter whose ministry they had been carrying forward. This is more than twenty years *after* that Man was executed, probably before Timothy was born.

And yet...*Jesus is with them.* Encouraging, correcting, guiding. And at the same moment back in Jerusalem, down in Cyprus, in a hundred other villages and towns, other Christians are experiencing the same reality. *Jesus is with us!* He is *here,* close as a heartbeat, leading each of us step by step on our separate paths.

How is this possible? How can He be in so many places at once, attending so individually to each need? The answer, of course, is His Spirit, no longer confined to a single body, no longer bound by the physics of earthly existence.

For time is no more a barrier to the Spirit than space. All over the world in 1990, Christians know the same inner nudge, the same silent Voice that guided Paul and Timothy. Some years ago my husband and I set out on our own small missionary journey. We chose Africa because we knew so little about it: For an entire year we'd experiment to see if the Spirit still guides today.

He does! He led us to the countries, the people, the needs that we could never have contacted on our own. Because we were in strange settings, we asked Him about everything—what to eat, whom to speak to, where to stop for the night—and learned that nothing is too small or mundane for His involvement.

"It is to your advantage that I go away" (John 16:7, RSV), Jesus told His disciples. For by going away in physical form, He came to be with us in Spirit always and everywhere.

Come, gracious Spirit, heavenly Dove,
With light and comfort from above;
Be Thou our guardian, Thou our guide,
O'er every thought and step preside.
[Simon Browne, 1680-1732]

Holy Spirit, forgive me for the steps I take without asking the way of You. —Elizabeth Sherrill

Thursday

7

Day Six—He Loves Through Us

This is my commandment, that you love one another....
—John 15:12 (RSV)

It sounds so simple; it turns out to be so hard! To love *some* others, sure: Some people are easy to love. But if you knew a certain individual in *my* family...*my* office...*my* neighborhood! To treat all people decently, to be civil, to accord them their rights—that, with great self-control, I may manage. But to *love* them? The selfish, the arrogant? God alone could love some of the people I have to deal with!

And God alone does—His Spirit within me—making me capable of what I myself could never do. This is what drew the multitudes to those first Christians: their love for one another. "Now the company of those who believed were of one heart and soul, and no one said that any of the things which he possessed was his own" (Acts 4:32, RSV).

Were those first Christians perhaps naturally sweeter, more generous, than people in the twentieth century? It certainly didn't sound that way during Jesus' lifetime, as they bickered over who would take first place in the coming kingdom! But here they were, putting others' interests ahead of their own. "There was not a needy person among them" (Acts 4:34, RSV), onlookers wonderingly reported.

And not only poverty began to disappear among this little band of faith-filled believers, but disease as well! Wherever these first Christians went, healing followed, both for themselves and for everyone they met. But these Christians praying so willingly for the well-being of total strangers—these were the same men who not so long ago had wanted to call down fire from heaven to consume those who didn't belong to their circle.

What had happened to the cantankerous little group who had followed the rabbi from Nazareth?

Pentecost had happened. The coming of Jesus' Spirit, not as an external presence issuing commandments too hard for ordinary humans to follow, but as the power to keep those commandments, welling up from deep inside. From the time of that first Pentecost, Christians have made the wondrous discovery: not that we have become more loving, but that we have made room for Him.

Come, Holy Spirit, heavenly Dove,
With all Thy quickening powers;

Kindle a flame of sacred love
In these cold hearts of ours.
[Isaac Watts, 1707]

Holy Spirit, use my feet and hands and voice to love the people You bring to me today. —Elizabeth Sherrill

Friday

8

Day Seven—He Shows Us Jesus

When the Counselor comes...he will bear witness to me. —John 15:26 (RSV)

How the writers of the Bible struggle to convey their experience of the Spirit! Writing about the day of Pentecost, Luke can only say the Spirit came "like the rush of a mighty wind" (Acts 2:2, RSV).

Wind. Image of immense power, and yet...elusive, too. Strong... but invisible, unpredictable.

Of the three Persons of the Trinity, people have always had the hardest time describing this one. His very name, Holy Spirit, Holy Ghost, suggests something formless, ineffable. God the Father fills the mind with concrete pictures—the earthly father we had or would like to have had. God the Son has a human form, a thousand physical settings where we meet Him, from the manger in Bethlehem to the Cross of Calvary.

But God the Spirit? Artists most often portray Him as a dove, the form in which John the Baptist saw Him descend upon Jesus. A shy and gentle bird that flutters out of reach when you try to grasp it? A strange image of Almighty God!

The titles the Bible gives Him—Counselor, Helper, Advocate, Comforter—tell what He does, not Who He is. It's as though, when God comes to us as Spirit, He wants to remain out of sight, an inward experience rather than an entity we can focus on. It's as though He wants our attention somewhere else.

Which, of course, He does. "When the Counselor comes..." Jesus told His followers, "He will bear witness to *me*."

That is the Spirit's first and most constant function: to show us Jesus. He wants us to know Jesus as the One Who strengthens and guides and lets us do the Father's will. The Spirit comes to us not as an addition to our faith in Christ, but as its source. "No one can say 'Jesus is Lord,'" says St. Paul, "except by the Holy Spirit" (I Corinthians 12:3, RSV).

O Spirit of Life, O Spirit of God,
Increase our faith in our dear Lord;
Unless Thy grace the power should give,
None can believe in Christ and live.
[Johann Niedling, 1602-1668]

Holy Spirit, show me Jesus today... and each day throughout this Season of Pentecost. —Elizabeth Sherrill

Saturday

9

Now he that ministereth seed to the sower both minister bread for your food, and multiply your seed sown, and increase the fruits of your righteousness.
—II Corinthians 9:10

Stop by my house at 5:00 P.M. any day and you'll hear something like this: "Laura has aerobics today and won't be home until seven. Jim's at college. Did he say he'd be home tonight? Steve—where's he? Bill's bringing him home from wrestling practice at 6:15. Okay, let's cook four chops for 6:30 and hope for the best." Of course, Laura won't be hungry, Jim will arrive with two friends, and I'll be one chop short, unless I cook two packages and end up three chops over.

Mothers feed their families. It's one of the few clearcut role definitions left to us. One chop short or three chops over, we get it done, night after night. It's a drag, but one I'd hate to be relieved of. Because eventually everyone present sits down and I rediscover something: It's not the food that counts. What counts is that Steve made the varsity team, Jim got an A on a project, Laura has a great job offer, and we're all (more or less) there to provide the deserved pats on the back or make the needed sounds of sympathy. The chops are incidental—it's the company that counts.

Father, don't let me get so upset by the incidentals that I forget what my family really needs at dinnertime. —Toni Sortor

Sunday

10

For the Son of man is Lord even of the sabbath day.
—Matthew 12:8

The room smelled of disinfectant. Miss Heinke sighed as I walked over to the window and pulled back the drapes. "Good morning!" I said, my cheerfulness sounding forced even to me. Usually I enjoyed my work at the nursing home, but I hated working on occasional Sunday mornings. I missed the worship and communion I enjoyed at church.

I rolled Miss Heinke to one side of the bed and began the difficult job of changing sheets. She had been bedridden for as long as most of the aides could remember. I tried to block out the sounds coming from the dayroom—blurred television dialogue, the clack of checkers jumping, the drone of voices. I imagined I was in church, the rich sounds of organ music filling the sanctuary, tall white gladiolus gracing the altar.... Suddenly, I noticed Miss Heinke was humming. What was that tune? It sounded so familiar. Of course! "Amazing Grace." I began to hum along, and by the time I had finished changing the bed, I was singing. From down the hall came other voices, wonderful harmonies at home with the familiar words. All morning we sang—old hymns and Sunday school choruses. And when the last bed was made, I knew we all had, somehow, been to church.

I still don't like to miss church. But there are times when I can't be in God's house on Sunday—when I'm traveling; when the flu bug bites; when I *must* work; when the car won't start or the snow drifts are too deep. That's when I remember that lesson I learned so long ago: Worship is communing with God. Anywhere. He understands those times I'm unable to be in my pew on Sunday. So when I can't come to Him, well, He comes to me! And that makes every Sabbath special.

Thank You, Father, for Sundays. Remind me that, wherever I am, the day is still a time for sacred praise. —Mary Lou Carney

Monday
11

I have loved thee with an everlasting love....
—Jeremiah 31:3

Whenever I back out of my driveway, the words *I LOVE YOU* appear in the rear window of my car in bold, white letters. Actually, the words are chalked on the back of our neighbor's brick garage. A teen-aged girl put them there, hoping her boyfriend would see them on his walk home from school.

Most of the time I don't even notice the words, but sometimes they seem to glow like a message from God, written with an angel's hand.

When I am depressed, the message is "I LOVE YOU."

When I am angry, the message reads, "I LOVE YOU."

When I am torn with guilt, the words are "I LOVE YOU."

When I am terrified of the future, He whispers, "I LOVE YOU."

Those three words have taught me a lesson about the unconditional love of God. No, God does not love all the things I do, and He would like me to change. But *always* He *loves me*, no matter what.

I love you. The chalky words are growing dim from recent rains and I plan to renew them. Perhaps you would like to write those words on a card and post them where you will see them every day and be reminded that God loves you no matter what your mood or deeds.

I know I'm not always worthy of Your love, Father, but I am so glad You love me just as I am.
—Daniel Schantz

Tuesday
12

I will trust, and not be afraid.... —Isaiah 12:2

A letter came today from our friend George who lives in the shadow of the Whitestone Bridge on the edge of New York City. In one paragraph he talks about his friend Co-co.

Co-co is a big chocolate-colored poodle, the most remarkable dog I've ever met. Whenever we'd come to visit, Co-co would astonish us by seeming to understand every word George said to her. If he wanted his shoes from upstairs, she'd go and get them. If they were the wrong pair, she'd take them back and bring the right one. If George said, "Robber!" or "Crook!" she'd go tearing around the house to make sure there were no intruders. Now and then I'd see Co-co and George looking at each other with affectionate amusement, as if they shared a joke that none of the rest of us could understand.

But the years go by, and now George's letter says—and I know it was painful for him to write—that Co-co has gone blind. "We've evolved a way of looping her leash (which she hasn't worn in years) loosely around her shoulders, and with this she walks confidently by my side. I can steer her either way with the slightest pressure. So here I am, a seeing-eye person for a blind dog."

Now on afternoons like today with so many angry headlines in the paper and so many small problems crowding in, I somehow find it both touching and heartening to think of my friend George and his friend Co-co walking along tranquilly and trustfully, side by side. And I know the leash is only a symbol of the real bond between them.

The real bond is love.

Dear Lord, thank You for this wonderful world and all its creatures, great and small. —Arthur Gordon

Wednesday

13

He that findeth his life shall lose it: and he that loseth his life for my sake shall find it. —Matthew 10:39

A sinking realization sets in for new parents in about the third month. The initial excitement has worn off, a gentle routine of diapers, bottles, burps and baths has set in and you suddenly realize the freedom to do what you want *when* you want is gone. You are not going anywhere for the next twenty years—or more—without thinking about him. Even going out to dinner with your wife involves getting a baby-sitter, leaving a list of phone numbers behind "in case of emergency" and resisting a nagging desire all evening to call home "just to be sure things are all right."

I was trying to explain this to a friend of mine, a father who is a generation older and wiser. He smiled and said, "Wait until you're my age." His children were grown and out of college. He found he had plenty of peace and quiet in the house, but he missed being depended on. "It happens all your life," he said, trying to explain. "You lose something familiar and gain something new."

I kept thinking of his words. I can remember how exciting it was to go to school for the first time—and yet terrifying to leave the security of home. Going off to college, I felt so grown up to be living on my own—and yet how much I missed my family two thousand miles away. When I graduated, it was exhilarating to be free of tests, essays and grades—and yet frightening suddenly to face the prospect of supporting myself. At each step I lost something and also found a new part of myself.

Maybe that's what Christ meant by the paradox, "He that finds his life shall lose it." I know that by the time I started introducing myself as "Willy's daddy," I was hooked. Freedom or no, being a father is now a part of me.

Lord, help me change gracefully through the years, at each bend, embracing the new life You give. —Rick Hamlin

Thursday

14

Now there are diversities of gifts, but the same Spirit.
—I Corinthians 12:4

This Flag Day, my thoughts reach back to America's first moon landing during the Apollo space program... a day when I felt great joy and a tinge of sadness.

On Sunday, July 20, 1969, Air Force Lt. Col. Edwin Aldrin, Jr., and civilian Neil A. Armstrong eased onto the surface of the moon at 4:17:45 P.M., Eastern time. At 11:45 P.M., Armstrong planted an American flag on the moon. In all its 192-year history, this was by far the greatest distance the flag had ever been carried—240,000 miles from Earth! My joy and patriotism swelled.

But I was sad, too. Years earlier, I had been a technician on the Gemini space program that was terminated. I had hopes of working on the Apollo contract, but that didn't happen. Now I felt deprived, somehow, of sharing in this special moment.

But the years since then have made me realize that many people in America contributed to the moon landing in some way: Adm. Richard E. Byrd and Floyd Bennett's flight over the North Pole on May 9, 1926; Charles A. Lindbergh's solo flight over the Atlantic Ocean on May 21, 1927; and the Gemini space program itself.

I like to think that you and I played a part in this moon adventure, too. How? The American flag placed on the moon had fifty stars, each representing our own home states and therefore representing us! See how brightly it shines over our combined efforts!

Dear God, no matter how small or insignificant my contribution may seem, I'll remember that a combined effort with You is a most awesome thing. —Oscar Greene

Friday

15

WINDOWS INTO WONDER
A Wrestled Blessing

I will not let thee go, except thou bless me.
—Genesis 32:26

Jacob, who had cheated his brother Esau out of his birthright, had made the tough decision to face the brother he had wronged. Now he was all alone by the River Jabbok in the dark of the night. Tomorrow was the day, and Jacob was just plain *scared* because he knew he deserved to be punished. Can you imagine how he felt, all alone there by the river, when he was pounced on by an unknown being in the darkness? Yet Jacob did not run away. He wrestled with the man all night long, refusing to give up even after his hip was thrown out of joint. In fact, near morning when the stranger wanted to leave, Jacob said, "I will not let you go unless you bless me." It turned out that the "man" was really God, and the blessing He gave Jacob was a new name, *Israel,* "because you have striven with God and men and have prevailed" (Genesis 32:28). Jacob's courage in facing his struggle head-on won him not only a new name but also his brother's forgiveness, a new house and a fresh start in the land of Canaan. *He got his blessing!*

I need the lesson of Jacob's struggle. A longtime friend and I have had a falling out, and I've put off doing anything about it because I'm afraid of being hurt. When the pain of the broken relationship stabs at me, I try to get busy so I won't have to face it. Yet I know I must. With Jacob as my model, I can confront my problem squarely. I'll go to my friend, admit my own part in the stand-off, and tell her I want to mend our relationship. It's a risk. I want to avoid it. But I won't. I'll do it today, knowing that, *no matter what her response*, there is a gift waiting in the heart of the faced pain. Is there some issue you've been running from? Perhaps you'll step out with Jacob and with me, and boldly pray:

I will face this problem, Lord, and engage in whatever struggle it brings, knowing that a blessing waits at the end.

—Marilyn Morgan Helleberg

June Prayer List Reminder

Return to your Monthly Prayer List on the calendar opening page and review your requests. Give thanks for prayers answered, renew old prayers and add new concerns today. Then pray once again our *Family Prayer for June.*

Saturday

16

Fireside Friend

Her husband...he praiseth her. —Proverbs 31:28

We'd had a wonderful honeymoon and a smooth plane ride home, but instead of feeling happy, I felt slightly depressed. As we walked the jetway and looked through the glass wall at the crowd waiting to greet the passengers, my bleak mood intensified. My husband Paul asked, "Why so quiet?" After a moment's hesitation, I gestured toward the waiting crowd and confessed that I always felt a little bleak when I returned from a trip and no family or friends were waiting to greet me. (We'd driven to the airport and would be picking up our car at the parking lot.)

Suddenly Paul plopped his suitcase down and started walking away from me very quickly, leaving me standing there alone. I was aghast. Had my complaining angered him? I scanned the crowd frantically. Then I saw him standing in the throng of people, a big smile on his face, both his arms flung open wide to welcome me.

That was a good indication to me that the man I had married would be both family *and* friend.

Father, help me to remember to hold out welcoming arms to some person today, and be both family and *friend to them.*

—Linda Neukrug

Sunday

17

For our gospel did not come to you in word only....

—I Thessalonians 1:5 (NAS)

My father doesn't talk much.

My mother and I, however, spill over with words. We are never at a loss to describe our feelings, to tell stories, to offer advice. I often felt sorry for my father for not having the natural eloquence that we women did.

My last visit home to Hawaii, my birthplace, showed me how wrong about him I was. I was sitting talking with my mother in my grandfather's living room one afternoon. From where we sat, I could see into the bedroom where my grandfather, who is ninety-five, spends his days.

My eyes fell on my father, who was rubbing lotion onto my grandfather's arms. My grandfather lay on the bed, looking up at his eldest son. I had seen my father do this scores of times, but this time I saw the care with which he touched his father's gnarled fingers. I marveled at the tenderness with which he laid his hands on the age-spotted shoulders. Finally, I noticed the light shining in the old man's face as he drew strength from his son's fierce, protective love.

My father inarticulate? Not at all. Neither my mother nor I could convey so well in words what my father did through the touch of his hands.

God, on this Father's Day, we thank You for fathers everywhere. And in observing them, may we learn to be doers of Your word and not speakers only. —Linda Ching Sledge

Monday

18

From everyone who has been given much, much will be demanded.... —Luke 12:48 (NIV)

It was a sickening feeling to have our family car go slower and slower as I pressed the gas pedal farther and farther to the floor. Finally, our three-year-old "faithful workhorse" settled in at a maximum speed of twenty-five miles per hour—downhill!

An hour later the knot in my stomach melted as we finished the eighteen miles home. I still didn't know why our car was acting so badly, but a trip to the dealer revealed two things. First, at 52,000 miles, we were over the warranty period. Second, the problem was either in the fuel pump or the carburetor. The first would cost about fifty-five dollars; the second about nine hundred dollars. (Unbelievable!) I turned to another mechanic for a second opinion. He diagnosed the problem as the fuel pump. "It's forcing gas in faster than the engine can properly burn it up, and that floods the engine and you lose power," he said.

That comment reminded me of a bad spiritual habit I tend to have. When faced with a difficulty or a hard decision, I tend to saturate myself with prayer, Scripture and the advice of godly friends. Sometimes it's too much—and I feel spiritually "flooded." I'm like the fuel pump: Fuel comes in faster than I can burn it. I end up going nowhere slowly, wasting precious energy that could be directed toward others. I could be spending a day with the kids giving them free, uninterrupted attention. Or calling my brother and planning our next family gathering, which is important since we're separated by long distance.

So instead of flooding my prayers with a focus on me, I'm going to pray and give it to God. Then I'll focus my attention on others, riding along on the fuel and power that He provides.

Lord, make me aware of when I need to pull back from actively seeking Your counsel and hand over my prayers to You completely, freeing me to concentrate on others. —Eric Fellman

Tuesday

19

The highest heavens belong to the Lord, but the earth he has given to man. —Psalm 115:16 (NIV)

Last summer, my husband Paul and I visited St. Louis, where my parents grew up. My Uncle Mickey and Aunt Dell showed us all the places that had been part of their lives. Yet many of them were rundown, if they were there at all. As in many cities, no one cared for the buildings and parks as they aged, and they withered and died.

But then we visited the church where my parents were married more than forty years ago. It seemed untouched by time. I could almost see my mother walking down the aisle on her father's arm, past the huge marble columns near the altar. As God's house, people have cared for it through the years, preserving it for future generations.

Since then I've been thinking: *How can I care for something today, to extend its life and show my respect for God's world?* Here's one idea I'll start on today: Create a simple family tree for my children. I'll write down the names of as many relatives as I can and attach a story or photograph that tells something memorable about that person. I can contact other relatives to get their remembrances. Then I'll paste all my findings in a big scrapbook and give it to my children.

What can you do today to preserve a piece of the world God has given you? Preserve your own family history? Organize a neighborhood cleanup drive? Pray for world peace? Support an organization dedicated to saving the whales or other endangered species?

Lord, You've given us so much to enjoy. May we do our part to ensure that Your gifts will be part of our children's future.

—Gina Bridgeman

Wednesday

20

For since the creation of the world God's invisible qualities—his eternal power and divine nature—have been clearly seen.... —Romans 1:20 (NIV)

Victoria Falls in Africa is one of the seven wonders of the natural world. It's a mile-wide cascade of water that falls three hundred feet and then rises silently as a mist six or seven hundred feet above the vast Zambian plateau. The sun stacks rainbow upon rainbow into that mist. On special nights with a full moon, an iridescent "moonbow" sparkles, declaring the glory of God.

As I stood at those great falls, marveling at the wonder of His handiwork, I became aware of another great thing. Billions and billions of unique nerve cells were sending messages across a quadrillion interconnections within my brain, allowing me to view this beauty. They were also sending warnings to my center of balance, so I might safely stand on this precipice. And millions of other centers all interacting together created not only a conscious awareness of this breathtaking sight, but an awareness of Him Who created it.

As I walked away, still in awe of what I had just seen and felt, I gave my wife Sally a little extra squeeze. We had gone out of our way on this trip so that we could see the falls. "Thanks for bringing me," she said, drawing closer under my arm. That's when I sensed God's greatest wonder. Not the mighty falls, or even our powerful and intricate brains, but God's greatest miracle of love.

So I don't have to go to Victoria Falls or learn the hidden mysteries of the mind to see God at work, for it's there when I hug my grandson CJ and feel him snuggle against my neck. Or when I embrace my son Chris and feel the exchange of strength in our grasps. And one other very special time: when, my head bowed, He draws me close and floods me with His warmth.

Yes, the heavens do declare Your glory, Lord, but Your love for us proclaims it even more. —Scott Harrison

Thursday

21

Fireside Friend 

For the Lord seeth not as man seeth; for man looketh on the outward appearance, but the Lord looketh on the heart. —I Samuel 16:7

I was bored with the routes I'd been following for my morning strolls. One day I decided to walk down the alleys.

Alleys are not romantic; they are strewn with garbage cans and trash piles. As I matched backyards with homes I'd walked by, I noticed something interesting. The back of one unpretentious dwelling resembled a fairy wonderland. A riot of flowers neatly bordered the fence, a birdbath stood in the center of a terraced rock garden. Then I came to the backyard of a beautiful home I'd admired from the street. Six-foot thistles grew close to the alley. Debris was scattered everywhere—broken toys, untended flower beds, automobile parts—visible only to the owner and the garbage collector.

As I walked home, I thought of my own bodily house. My outward or "up front" appearance may pass the world's inspection, but what about my "backyard"? It's hidden from all but One Who knows its contents. He promises to collect the garbage in my life. But He expects me to pull the weeds from my thought life, put into His hands the broken dreams, dig deep to uproot thistles of resentment and unforgivenesss and to clean out the rusty wheels of procrastination.

Long ago, God looked into David's "backyard" and found a man "after my own heart" (I Samuel 13:14; Acts 13:22). Could He say the same of you and me?

Lord, I want my inner life to please You. Will You help me remove the sins, bad habits, hurt feelings, jealousies and resentments from my "backyard"? Then lead me to the sunshine of Your forgiveness. Amen. —Shirley Pope Waite

Friday

22

O Lord, I know that the way of man is not in himself: it is not in man that walketh to direct his steps.
—Jeremiah 10:23

The summer I was twelve, I came up with the grandiose idea that our family needed a swimming pool. "Mother, is it all right if I build us a swimming pool?" I asked, with shovel in hand. I was sure that a pool full of blue water would delight her.

My mother smiled and said, "Okay. Why don't you build it right over there." She pointed to the back corner of our half-acre yard. I grabbed a hammer and four wooden stakes, driving each one into the ground to set up my boundaries. Then I stepped back. I could visualize our pool with all the neighborhood kids splashing water at one another.

I was excited when I started to dig, but the ground was hard. I jumped on the shovel to drive it into the dirt. I strained my back, my arms and my legs for every clod of dirt I moved. Thirty minutes later, I had accomplished so little that the man next door asked if I was digging for worms. I worked a while longer, all the time looking at those stakes that seemed miles away. Then I decided that I had miscalculated the size of the pool. I moved the stakes in to about half the original distance.

In another half hour, I was moving my stakes closer again. By sundown I had dug a hole three feet by two feet and eighteen inches deep. I decided that it didn't need to be an inch bigger and dragged the hose to my pool. When my mother came to check on me, I was sitting in my mud hole with only one ambition left: to rest my aching muscles.

"When will our pool be finished?" my mother asked.

"It is finished," I said glumly.

As I think back on that experience, I realize that my personal ambitions have often been much like that pool. I start out with fantastic ideas of what my life will be like. Then after I've been digging for a short time, I start moving in my stakes.

Our dreams for life will tarnish if we're too unrealistic. We need to let the Lord direct us before we start hammering in our stakes.

Lord, let my life's plans and dreams be guided by You.

—Brian Miller

Day Brightener

God, give me sympathy and sense,
And help me keep my courage high;
God, give me calm and confidence,
And—please—a twinkle in my eye. Amen.

—Margaret Bailey

Saturday

23

Know ye not that they which run in a race run all, but one receiveth the prize? So run, that ye may obtain.

—I Corinthians 9:24

"Our strategy is to start slow, go slow and finish slow," my friend Nancy said to me with a laugh before the five-mile race in New York's Central Park. This was the first race we'd ever entered, along with eight hundred other racers from around the country.

At the starting line, I prayed that we'd at least finish the race and possibly place. What was supposed to be a "fun run" had turned into serious business for me. I wanted to leave my competitors in the dust.

The gun went off, and so did we. We were in the back of the pack, but then I remembered Nancy's words about starting slow, going slow and finishing slow. *Was she serious? Did she truly mean just to have a good time?* I got my answer right from the start when she began to tell jokes and stories as we ran side by side, and had me laughing uncontrollably. Even those racers who were walking started to pass us.

By the first-mile marker, I knew my goal of placing was shattered, and by the second-mile marker, Nancy had me stop for drinks of water and to tighten shoe laces. Soon the finish line was in sight, and we decided to run our hardest.

Nancy beat me by a fraction of a second, but my disappointment was minimal. That was because she'd made me achieve our original goal of enjoying ourselves. Plus, God did answer my prayers; we placed 651st and 652nd.

God, when I run for the finish line, I pray that I'll do so with a strong faith, a kind heart and a jolly soul. What a winning combination that will be! —Stephanie Samoy

Sunday

24

Stay, and I will tell thee what the Lord hath said....

—I Samuel 15:16

My sister Steff left her home in Hawaii and spent a summer in Washington, D.C., interning as a journalist for one of the national newspapers. "I want to leave my island job and work for a larger, more prominent newspaper," she told me upon her arrival.

During the next three months, Steff made inquiries and sent out résumés, but by summer's end there were no offers. Discouraged, she began a reevaluation of her goals.

A few days later, she called me. "I've been praying for guidance," she said, "and I think I know what God wants me to do."

"What do you mean?" I asked.

"First, I saw that my friends and my family are important to me and if I want to live near them, I should stay in Hawaii. Then I decided that I wanted to specialize in Pacific and Asian news, and what better place to do that? God seems to be telling me to 'stay put.'"

So Steff returned to her small, island reporter's job. Amazingly, a few months later, the national paper where she had interned invited her on a three-month journalists' tour of Asia. By staying put, she was available when new opportunities she could not have even imagined were opened to her. Some may call this coincidence, but couldn't it be, too, a wonderful example of what can happen when we seek God's guidance and follow it?

Do you have a grand dream that for whatever reason is unattainable? Perhaps God wants you to "stay put" for now. For the next few days, be still and open your eyes to the wonders and opportunities surrounding you in your own little island of living. Maybe there will be new steps to take—sooner or later—but they may need to begin first with a prayer and a change of heart.

God, give me the patience to "stay put" for now and to trust You to open my view to new windows of possibilities. —Terri Castillo

Monday

25

And those who are peacemakers will plant seeds of peace and reap a harvest of goodness.

—James 3:18 (TLB)

I wasn't meaning to eavesdrop, but one day Helen, our office manager, and I picked up the telephone at the same moment. "Where's my wife?" an angry voice bellowed, nearly shattering my eardrum. "She had a ten o'clock appointment at your clinic. Now it's noon and she's still not home. I'm sick of baby-sitting these fussy kids, and it's past time for their lunch."

My blood pressure went up about fifty points. How dare he complain? His wife was getting excellent, low-cost health care! I was about to shout back when Helen's merry laugh stopped me short. "You sound like my husband when he's hungry," she said. "We're really sorry appointments are running late, but the doctor had two emergencies. Why don't you make peanut butter sandwiches for the kids and eat a sandwich yourself. Then try reading stories. Your wife will be home before you know it."

The man forgot his anger and even thanked Helen for helping!

If you sometimes encounter "unreasonable" people, Helen's "Four-Point Peace Plan" will help:

1. *Use humor.* Shared laughter is contagious.
2. *Be understanding.* Put yourself in the other person's place.
3. *Speak softly.* Proverbs 15:1 reminds us, "A soft answer turneth away wrath: but grievous words stir up anger."
4. *Offer specific suggestions* for handling the situation. Like sandwiches and stories.

Lord, thank You for this lesson in peacemaking. Help me put it into practice. —Penney Schwab

Tuesday 26

He that is of a merry heart hath a continual feast.
—Proverbs 15:15

Several months ago I happened upon a letter in an old farm magazine. A wife wrote that at supper her family constantly argued or dwelt upon unpleasant experiences from the day. One morning she suggested, "Let's each watch for the nicest thing that happens today. Write it down and we'll share at supper."

The nicest things? Here are some of the things they recorded: sunlight making rainbows on dewdrops in a spider web; an unexpected shower when the fields needed it most; a woman in the laundromat quickly emptying her dryer and saying, "Use this one. It's still going"; a tiny red flower in the lane.

Simple, everyday things. Yet they were such day-brighteners that the family decided to continue the game. The farm wife reported increased awareness of God's gifts and happier days for everyone.

Poet Sara Teasdale wrote: "Life has loveliness to sell, All beautiful and splendid things...." And the price is simply awareness. We find what we're looking for. And when we're looking for lovely things, including kindness, we find them all around us.

Have you or your family been seeing only ugliness? Why not try the farm wife's system? It could easily become a happy habit.

Dear God, keep us always alert for the wonders of Your world.

—Aletha Jane Lindstrom

Wednesday

27

The Lord make his face shine upon thee, and be gracious unto thee. —Numbers 6:25

A six-ton block of Carrara marble, from Mount Altissimo in Italy, stands in Christus Gardens in Gatlinburg, Tennessee. Carved within the flecked marble is a concave sculpture of the face of Christ. (A concave sculpture looks as though the image has been pressed into the marble, like a handprint pressed into wet cement.) Beneath the face, these words have been carved: "The eyes of the Lord are in every place keeping watch upon the evil and the good."

As I moved to the left of the sculpture, and then to the right, I understood why the artist had chosen those words. Christ's whole face seemed to move with me. Not just His eyes, but His entire face turned to follow me, wherever I went—left, right or straight ahead. Even though it was an optical illusion, I was deeply moved. It seemed so fitting that a sculpture of Christ should possess such a mystical quality.

As I look at my own life, I wonder if I have done as good a job as the Italian artist. I have attempted to carve the face of God's Son into my humanity, but what kind of face have I carved? How do others see Christ in me? The sculpture has given me something to strive for.

I pray that Christ's image is pressed deeply into me, in a concave fashion,. so when others move to the left of me or to the right, they will see Christ turn and gaze out upon them...from all angles of my life.

Dear Father, help me to carve the face of Your Son within my heart. And let me give His face the freedom to turn lovingly toward others—no matter where they walk. —Terry Helwig

Thursday

28

Thy will be done. —Matthew 26:42

When I was in college, I often prayed that God would allow me to marry the girl I was then dating. I prayed and prayed, but it didn't happen. A few years after I finished college, however, and was farming back home, I met a girl named Cherry. A year later she became my bride. It was the right answer at the right time.

I learned a lesson from this that helped me through the mean summer drought we Midwesterners experienced a few years ago. It wasn't easy to watch my crops sizzle in the hot Kansas sun. Like so many farmers, I prayed for God to send rain and felt very discouraged when it didn't come. Finally, I had to accept that no matter how much I prayed for rain to come, maybe it wasn't time. And when I'd look over at Cherry's dear head bent next to mine in prayer, somehow it seemed okay. I felt ready to face whatever was to be.

As a matter of fact, the drought didn't turn out as badly as I'd feared. Some of our crops were saved by late summer rains. But the change in me had already taken place once I made the decision to see things from God's perspective instead of my own.

Have you prayed and prayed for something, and it just hasn't happened? You might want to try what worked for me: Pray, instead, to accept the lessons in what has been put before you and for the strength to accept the consequences. Then wait—for the right time.

Dear God, teach me to see the world through Your wide vision, instead of trying to make You see it from my narrow one. —John Coen

Friday
29

Fireside Friend

God hath not given us the spirit of fear....

—II Timothy 1:7

It was great to be a child growing up in Maine! The ocean almost surrounded our little village; its blue bigness was seldom out of sight. Except when the fog rolled in. Sometimes we couldn't even see the neighbors' houses, the cloud was so thick. The wet atmosphere amplified sounds, too, making far-off voices seem very close. As children, we felt the magic of the fog; and as grownups, we still talk about the tiger behind the playhouse.

We first heard it growl one foggy day during a pause in our play. Soon we heard it again, closer than before! We just *knew* that it was a fierce animal—probably a tiger! After some discussion, the other children chose *me* to go for help. I still remember the horror of being pushed out into the fog, alone with the tiger! As the door slammed shut behind me they yelled, "Run!" And I did.

A few minutes later, Dad and I returned. I was feeling better already, with my small hand safe in his great big one! Then the tiger growled again, and Dad started to chuckle. "So *that's* what you heard!" He told us about the "growler buoy," far out in the bay. Placed there to guide ships safely toward home, it has an odd growling sound, activated by the motion of the waves. It is seldom heard ashore, but the thick fog had brought its fearsome noise right to our playhouse door!

Are you quivering at a "growler"? Afraid of failure at a new job or business venture, perhaps? Worried about a doctor's report, or doubtful about your ability to handle changes in your family? Run to Jesus! He'll take your hand and help you face your situation. And if He chooses, He can show you how even the things we fear, when seen from His perspective, can "work together for good" (Romans 8:28).

Lord, quiet my fears. Banish the tigers that crouch at my door.

—Vicki Schad

Saturday

30

In that day you will know that I am in my Father, and you in me, and I in you. —John 14:20 (RSV)

You may recall reading here two years ago about my four-year-old friend Michael, with dancing dark eyes and insatiable curiosity, who had a remarkable culinary inspiration. Why not stir his bag of spice drops into my apple cake mixture? We did, and drew from the oven the first ever "Michael Surprise Cake" (*Daily Guideposts, 1988;* May 18).

Last summer, my cooking partner, now six, joined me in the kitchen once again to concoct his famous recipe. Busily we measured and poured, adding the chopped peeled apples and finally, the bag of bright spice drops. It was then that Michael noticed the sunlight streaming through the window and splashing across our mixing bowl, catching the candy pieces and turning them into sugary gems. "Oh, let's stir in some sun!" he squealed. Round and round his wooden spoon plowed through the sticky dough, the yellow light shining in.

Later, as I set the golden brown cake on the counter, Michael saw the pale slivers of peeled apple dotting its surface. His eyes grew round and he cried, "Look, there's the sunshine I mixed in!"

I was so taken by his acceptance of bits of the sun baked in his cake (now renamed the Michael Sunshine Surprise Cake!). Michael doesn't know it, but he mixed a little sun into my life that afternoon, too. In his own homespun way, he taught me to look for glimmers of another kind... the "Sonlight" of God stirring inside of me each new day.

Look closely. Do you see His Sonlight splashing over *you* right now? Isn't it wonderful!

Jesus, Light in my life, I see You now... here... and here... and over here. Oh, Lord, let's stir some more Son into my day, all day... every day. —Carol Knapp

Thank-You Notes to God

1 ________________________________

2 ________________________________

3 ________________________________

4 ________________________________

5 ________________________________

6 ________________________________

7 ________________________________

8 ________________________________

9 ________________________________

10 ________________________________

11 ________________________________

12 ________________________________

13 ________________________________

14 ________________________________

15 ________________________________

16 ____________________

17 ____________________

18 ____________________

19 ____________________

20 ____________________

21 ____________________

22 ____________________

23 ____________________

24 ____________________

25 ____________________

26 ____________________

27 ____________________

28 ____________________

29 ____________________

30 ____________________

JULY

S	M	T	W	T	F	S
1	2	3	4	5	6	7
8	9	10	11	12	13	14
15	16	17	18	19	20	21
22	23	24	25	26	27	28
29	30	31				

SPIRITUAL TREASURE

Shine Your Light

Let your light so shine before men, that they may see your good works, and glorify your Father which is in heaven. —Matthew 5:16

In July the sun shines brightest, pouring its blessings on Fourth of July parades, sunbathers and country picnics.

This month practice letting God's light shine through you. Offer an unexpected compliment, squeeze a trembling hand, pray for an enemy. In your own radiant way you'll beam a special blessing on those around you. And it will warm your own heart as well.

My Monthly Prayer List

Family Prayer for July

Dear God, bless this land of ours and help me to bless it, too—perhaps by planting a tree, recycling my "recyclables" or by simple, everyday kindnesses to my neighbor.

THROUGH AN OPEN WINDOW
Yield to God's Rhythm

And God called the light Day, and the darkness he called Night.... And God saw every thing that he had made, and behold, it was very good. —Genesis 1:5,31

As I stand in front of my open window this morning I notice the Christmas cactus. The plant won't bloom this time of the year because there are too many daylight hours. But shortly before Thanksgiving, when the nights lengthen, tiny buds begin to appear and by Christmas the plant is a mass of gorgeous, deep red blossoms that dance in the breeze coming through my open window. People often ask me how I get my cactus to bloom. The secret, I tell them, lies in the darkness. Starting in the fall, the plant must have deep darkness for about twelve of the twenty-four hours. The plant needs darkness to fulfill itself.

Sometimes darkness throws light into human lives, too. It certainly did in mine. I remember the time well. Neva, my roommate and best friend, had married and left the apartment we'd shared. Because she was older and wiser in the ways of the big city, I'd come to depend on her for everything. I seldom made a decision without consulting her first. Now I was alone. It was a dark time for me.

But then, as months passed, I began to make my own decisions and learn from my own mistakes. I panicked about whether to renew the lease on the apartment. But when I finally did, it turned out to be a wise and economical move. Poor planning caused me to order a couch that was too big for my cramped apartment. The store did take it back and the two-seater I got did nicely for the few years I ended up living there. Reaching down for strength within myself, I found my independence being tested, but learned I could accept this time of darkness as part of God's rhythm. It helped me grow... and then blossom... as He intended me to.

Today when dark periods come, as they sometimes do, I try to remember not to pray for them to disappear. Rather, I yield to God's rhythm and trust the darkness to bring me new light.

Do you have such dark periods in *your* life? Are you in one right now? Ask God to help you grow through it. I know He will. You'll blossom. Or, like the blooms on my cactus plant, you might even dance!

Father, during the evening hours this month, let me think on You and the goodness that darkness can bring. —Eleanor Sass

Monday

2

I was a stranger, and ye took me in. —Matthew 25:35

My seatmate on the airplane turned out to be a young Methodist minister. I forget now which of us spoke first, but I do remember something he said.

"The most fascinating hobby in the world," he said, "is also the most available. You don't need money. You don't need equipment. You can indulge in it any time. It will always bring you pleasure and sometimes profit. And what is this hobby? It's people. Other people. A steady, sustained, genuine interest in other people.

"Most of us never fully realize this. We have our friends and acquaintances, and we settle for that. But if we'd just look up from this narrow little circle, we'd see an endless procession of faces, each one different, each one fascinating, passing by on the fringes of our lives.

"We ignore them because we think of them as strangers. But what is so strange about them, really? Aren't they all children of God, just as we are? In that 'stranger,' for all you know, may be the answer to some problem that's troubling you, just as you may be an answer to something that's bothering him.

"But somebody has to take the initiative. So why not make the effort, perhaps just once a day, to reach out to some person who until now has been outside the circle of your life? God has given us a tremendous potential for friendship, for fellowship. Why not use it?"

"Why not, indeed," I replied. "Is this next Sunday's sermon?"

He laughed. "It might be. How do you think they'd like it?"

"I think they'd like it fine," I said.

I'm sure they did.

Help us to remember, Lord, that the failure to make friends is to turn our backs on the goodness of life. —Arthur Gordon

Tuesday

3

Give thanks in all circumstances....
—I Thessalonians 5:18 (NIV)

A man who felt that his home was too small asked a wise man what to do about it. The wise man told him to bring a succession of animals into the house. Soon the cottage was bursting at the seams. Then the wise man said to remove the animals one at a time. When the house was back to its original state, the man rejoiced at how spacious it seemed.

I think of that story sometimes when I find myself complaining about an everyday routine that I've taken for granted. Then a problem comes up to disturb it and shows me how much worse things could be. Suddenly, I'm appreciative of my "normal" routine. For instance, I've complained about the usual homemaker tasks of cooking, cleaning and chauffeuring. But after recently spraining my right wrist, I have a new appreciation for being able to rotate the crank of our hand-held can opener, to push the vacuum cleaner handle, and to turn the ignition key and steering wheel. Likewise, I grumble about getting up after a "normal" night's sleep, until those exceptions when I have to rouse several times before dawn for a hungry baby or a sick child. Then those commonplace nights of uninterrupted rest seem made of gold!

Can you think of an imperfect aspect of your day that, compared to how much worse it could be, is really pretty good?

Lord, thank You for how surprisingly good "normal" can be.
—B.J. Connor

Wednesday

4

Be very careful, then, how you live...making the most of every opportunity.... —Ephesians 5:15–16 (NIV)

Several years ago, around the Fourth of July, my allergies were particularly troublesome. So my husband Gary took the children to see the fireworks, leaving me with my antihistamines and tissues. As the evening darkened, sounds of firecrackers and distant laughter floated through the open window. I stepped out on the back patio, hoping for a glimpse of the grand display going on down at the park. Occasionally a burst of color split the sky and seemed to scatter the stars.

But as twilight deepened, I noticed another light show close at hand. Fireflies. They flickered in the dusk, flitting among the alfalfa in the field next door. Like neon specks of dust—so tiny, but so bright! And sitting there in that humid July darkness, I found myself mesmerized by the fireflies and indifferent, suddenly, to the fireworks. But why? I wasn't offended by the loud noise of the fireworks; I didn't mind their flamboyant glare. Then it made sense to me why I preferred the fireflies—consistency. Fireworks danced in the skies one night a year; fireflies made a habit of brightening all my summer evenings.

Sometimes my patriotism is like those fireworks—big and bright and brief. I put red, white and blue bows on my mailbox. I fly the flag. I applaud the speeches. And then I pack my patriotism away until the next big celebration.

So this year I'm going to work harder on being a day-to-day good American. I'll vote in the local elections and read those bulletins from my state representative. I'll remember the principles that founded this country—honesty and discipline and respect of individual rights. I'll put them into practice when I want to park in the "handicap" space at the post office or I disagree with a fellow worker. I'll remind myself that my children Amy Jo and Brett are individuals—and have some inherent rights of their own. I'll keep the pink almond bush in my yard well-trimmed and offer my services at my church. And like those fireflies, I'll make the world a little brighter. Day by day by day.

And you can, too—day by day. . . .

Thank You for my freedom, Lord. I accept the daily responsibilities that come with this great gift. —Mary Lou Carney

Thursday

5

He giveth his beloved sleep. —Psalm 127:2

Though I have seen many llamas in zoos, I had never observed them as working beasts of burden until a recent trip to South America.

Outside of Lima, Peru, I remember in particular one farmer leading several of these camellike animals to market. That is, until the lead llama decided his load of produce was too heavy and he needed a rest. In protest, he slid to the ground and refused to go on. The others in the herd reacted like dominoes, and the farmer resignedly sat down beside them.

The incident reminded me of the summer our family spent hiking on the Appalachian Trail with two Sardinian donkeys (named Pinocchio and Figaro). Like the llamas, when they grew weary, they would fall to the ground as if shot, and no amount of prodding could get them to their feet. They knew their limits and until refreshed they would not continue.

In this respect, donkeys and llamas may be wiser than many humans. I suggested as much not long ago to a friend who was making light of my habit of afternoon siestas. "A fifteen- or twenty-minute nap after lunch will make a new person out of you," I offered. He was not convinced. Today, from my newspaper, I got more ammunition. Dr. David Dinges, a sleep researcher at the University of Pennsylvania, says that adult nappers are sharper, healthier and happier. Next to Christ's invitation, "Come unto me, all ye that labor and are heavy laden, and I will give you rest" (Matthew 11:28), I can't think of any better midday rejuvenator for the weary.

Thank You, Lord, for Your gift of sleep,
Soul mender, mind healer, our bodies' keep.

—Fred Bauer

Friday

6

Let there be light: and there was light. —Genesis 1:3

In October 1879, Thomas Edison sat alone in his laboratory at Menlo Park, New Jersey. His "boys," as he called his helpers, were home exhausted after working days without sleep. For thirteen months they had searched for a metal filament that when sealed in a glass bulb and electrically charged would give off light. All their experiments failed. Funds were depleted, and financial backers were clamoring for results. Foreign newspapers called Edison a dreamer. Noted mathematicians said he was attempting the impossible.

Then Edison recalled a Scripture verse on light, the one from Genesis (above) he had read as a youngster. Hesitantly, his hand went to a mixture of lampblack and tar. He rolled the substance, sought a spoon of cotton thread and carbonized a strand. Would this frail substance withstand an electrical current that melted the hardest of metals? He would try.

For thirty-two hours, he and his helpers once again strove to produce one, unbroken, carbonized thread. Finally, one strand was sealed in a glass bulb and electric current was applied. The filament glowed and soft light crept across the laboratory. Victory at last! The electric light bulb was invented.

Is there some dream that you're holding on to? Your own unique invention maybe? Paying off the house mortgage? Or getting financing for a college degree? Hold fast to your dream, work toward it and, with God's blessing, you'll reach the light.

Lord, I ask You to put a dream in my heart and then give me the grace and persistence to work hard until it becomes a reality.

—Oscar Greene

Saturday

7

Cleanse thou me from secret faults. —Psalm 19:12

If you had come to visit me last summer, there would have been areas of the house I'd not have shown you—the storage room with its twenty-year accumulation of things we might use someday, the furnace room that rarely gets cleaned unless the repair person is coming, the family room closet where we pile all the things we can't decide what to do with.

Well, we decided, twenty years held enough unchecked accumulation, so we began working on those places that no one sees. It felt so good to be rid of the hidden clutter! My neighbor once told me, "I keep the living room in order for the sake of appearances. The basement and closets I keep in order for the sake of God."

Ah, yes! I need to apply that to the disorderly areas of my life as well as my house. I have to admit that I try to present my best self to the world, while hiding my inner disorder and chaos. Angry feelings often get stuck in some closet of my mind, where they accumulate like hidden trash. Little dishonesties, such as pretending to agree when I really don't, get stacked up in my inner storage room until they begin to tarnish my self-esteem.

Today, I'm going to invite Jesus into one of those secret places (my anger closet, I think), and ask Him to help me clean it out.

Lord, I want to keep my soul in order—for Your sake!

—Marilyn Morgan Helleberg

Sunday

8

Fireside Friend

And this is the promise that he hath promised us, even eternal life. —I John 2:25

For years my husband carried an insurance policy that provided him income protection from, among other things, disability through a heart attack. Twenty years of coverage later, he developed heart problems that resulted in a six-bypass surgery.

When his claim was submitted, it was denied on the basis that he was not *totally* disabled! That's when I learned about false security. I didn't know whom to blame: the insurance company for not honoring the policy, ourselves for being so naive, or God for not answering my prayer that the insurance company would pay the liability I so firmly believed they owed.

My search for a solution, any solution, to our dilemma revealed certain resolute truths about God and prayer: God answers prayer in His own time (in this case, several long months), and in His own way (by the complete return of my husband's health, a much better answer than my limited prayer deserved). And, while I was waiting with as much patience as the Lord afforded me, my new prayer focus uncovered the best insurance ever offered to humankind: the assurance of eternal life. And that's *not* false security.

Best of all, His offer is open to people of all ages, of all colors, at a premium we can all afford—and with a local agent! If you're not among the insured, won't you attend the church of your choice and check into it soon?

Father, thank You for the assurance of life eternal, purchased through the love of Your Son, Jesus Christ, Who is only a prayer away. Amen.

—Mary Jane Meyer

A FAMILY ADVENTURE

Join us for the next three days as we visit Eric Fellman and his sons on a camping-canoeing adventure in northern Minnesota. Discover how fun, excitement, shared experiences and faith in the wilderness strengthen the special bond between these family members.

—The Editors

Monday
9

Day One—A Special Closeness

A friend loves at all times, and a brother is born for adversity.

—Proverbs 17:17 (NIV)

Last summer, three generations of Fellman men took a trip into the Waters Canoe area of northern Minnesota. I was twelve when my dad first took me into that magical land of lakes, rivers, pine trees and walleyed pike. The years have never weakened the memories and bonds we shared camping and fishing together. My brother Greg and I wanted our sons (ages four to eleven) to share that same bond with us and their grandfather, so we loaded two tents, three cookstoves, a hundred pounds of food and two-hundred-fifty paper plates into three canoes, and started off on five days and four nights of adventure.

The first day it rained continuously for twenty-one hours. You can only guess what it was like being in an eight-by-ten-foot tent with five grade-schoolers for that long. And after a while, even the best tent can't hold back the ground water. Everything and everyone got wet, and then cold. Through thunder, lightning and crashing tree branches, my brother Greg and I kept the peace with stories, then games, then candy, and finally dire threats of bodily harm.

In the end, God restored order with sunshine. I had fretted all night about wet clothes, missed hours of fishing and cold meals, not realizing how frightening the night had been for the boys. The first one up was the youngest, my nephew John. He popped out of the tent, took one look at the clearing sky and hugged me around the legs, crying out, "Wow, Uncle Eric, we're still alive!" Before I could respond, he jumped back into the tent, crawled all over his brother and cousins, and woke them up hollering, "We're alive, we're alive!"

Peeking inside the tent, I saw everyone tumbling and giggling with the giddiness of unexpected survival. In that moment, it hit me that the trip wasn't about dry clothes, fishing and warm meals; it was about building relationships. Greg and I wanted our sons and our father to share a special closeness. Nothing could do that better or faster than holding together to survive a storm.

Dear Lord, when storms come, let me always see the strength they build, not the threats they bring. —Eric Fellman

Tuesday

10

Day Two—A Fishy Lesson

Let all bitterness and wrath and anger and clamor and slander be put away from you....

—Ephesians 4:31 (NAS)

Since my grandfather's time, there's been no debate about two things: the primary avocation of every Fellman—fishing; and the best fish to catch and eat—walleyed pike. Almost nothing can compare with gliding across a lake (so pure you can dip a cup into it for a drink) in early dawn, hooking a walleye and returning to camp to fry it for breakfast.

One day we took a canoe trip and my dad taught my sons and nephews how to fish. By afternoon all of us were out on the lake in three canoes, fishing the bottom with nightcrawlers. All of a sudden, Dad's rod bent double and his line sang as it spun off the reel. The grandkids started hollering with excitement. My brother and I backed our canoes away to give Dad room. With my oldest boy Jason manning the large dip net, Dad was slowly bringing the fish in when it suddenly shot up and broke the surface. The fourteen-inch walleye was clutched in the jaws of a thirty-five-inch northern pike! Jason scooped the net under them. As he did, the northern let go, and the walleye popped out of its mouth, but both were in the net.

For several minutes, the northern had fought the line, but had never been hooked. As Dad held the big fish up for everyone to see, he said, "Boys, he was just too mean to let go, and now we'll have him for supper."

That phrase of Dad's keeps coming back to me now and then. From time to time I find myself holding onto something out of stubborn pride and have been brought close to ruin because of it.

Why as a teenager in this very wilderness I'd learned that lesson the hard way. A group of us went canoeing and instead of unloading our goods at shore near where our next campsite was to be, I tried to "shoot" the rapids.

My canoe carried everyone's food, but despite their protests, I headed into the channel. Soon the force of rushing water drew the canoe forward. I lurched into one rock, swung sideways and hit a log. Right then I could have headed for shore and safety. But the others were watching and pride wouldn't let me stop. The next rock punched a hole in the aluminum skin of the canoe; I swirled sideways and everything dumped into the stream. I managed to save the main box of food, but all the extras, my clothes and fishing gear went to the bottom and were lost. Hanging on to pride almost ruined the trip.

That experience taught me well about the danger of being "too mean to let go!"

Lord, help me today to let go of those feelings and thoughts that only drag myself and others down. —Eric Fellman

Wednesday

11

Day Three—The Comfort of One Another

Therefore comfort one another with these words.
—I Thessalonians 4:18 (NAS)

As we paddled back to the canoe landing on the last day of our fishing trip, Dad got out first and went for the car. A message was on the windshield, and Dad drove hurriedly past the beach, calling to us that he had to make a phone call.

I was busy unpacking the canoes when he came back, and my six-year-old nephew Zackery ran to me asking, "Why are Daddy and Grandpa crying?" Running up the road, I saw my brother and father in an embrace, both weeping. Greg looked up and said simply, "Dad's mother died."

After trying to comfort one another, it was decided that Dad and Greg would take one car and leave immediately on the five-hour drive to Dad's house. I'd follow in the station wagon with the gear and five boys. As they pulled away, I turned to find all five looking at me with questioning eyes. I didn't know how to begin explaining death to those boys. We finished packing in silence and drove away. After a few miles, I said, "Boys, Grandpa is very sad because his mother died. That means she fell asleep and woke up in Heaven, and we won't see her again until we are in Heaven."

The youngest of them started to cry, and some of the others joined in. They were crying for their grandpa, because he was so sad. At that moment, the Lord brought the verses from I Thessalonians 4:13-18 to mind. I remembered how Dad's mom had quoted them to me almost twenty-five years before on the morning after her husband died. So as best I could, I quoted the message that death is sleep, and we will be one day united with the Lord Jesus.

A camping experience was over and a deeper reality about life had set in—for both me and the young ones. Our shared togetherness in the wilderness gave us strength to face a great loss. As we took one last look around at the beautiful God-created wilderness where we had grown so close, we knew that we would find comfort—in one another and in the gentle embrace of our Heavenly Father above.

Lord, thank You for the gift of belief that helps us to see death as a door to the next room—a room where someday we will be reunited with those we love. —Eric Fellman

Thursday **12** *Fireside Friend*

God loveth a cheerful giver. —II Corinthians 9:7

In Ireland, we have an abundance of native saints. The most famous of these is St. Patrick, the slave boy who brought Christianity to Ireland, defied the pagan king and finally converted him. Then there is St. Brigid, a feisty maid who gave away her family's butter to the poor and refused to marry the man her father had chosen for her. By all accounts, these Irish saints were quite a dynamic bunch.

But we Irish also frequently refer to living people as saints. "That woman's a saint," someone will say of a particularly kind, patient person. Or "Sure, you'd need the patience of a saint," when referring to a difficult situation. Saintliness, when we refer to living people, does not mean splashy heroism or bravery, but rather quiet forbearance, patience and generosity.

My friend Pat, for example, is a saint. She attends law school, takes care of two small children (one of whom is handicapped), volunteers for everything and yet always has time to listen to my problems. So is Dr. Gross, who faithfully returned my annoying telephone calls during the long bout of hypochondria I developed after my cancer operation. And where would I be without dear Lynne, a devoted mother of three, who always answers the question "Can you do me a favor?" with a resounding "Yes!" *before* she knows what the favor will be.

I bet there are a few saints in your life—those quiet people who give abundantly of themselves, who seldom grumble and never seem to expect anything in return. Why not call one or two of your saints today and tell them they make your life heavenly right here on earth!

Gentle Lamb of God, bestow on me qualities of kindness, patience and meekness, that I may walk among Your earthly saints as an emissary of Your love. Amen. —Stephanie Oda

Friday

13

Beloved, if God so loved us, we also ought to love one another. —I John 4:11 (RSV)

Years ago, on a trip out West, our nine-year-old, eager to be on his best behavior in a restaurant, sprang to his feet after the waitress introduced herself. "Glad to meet you, Janet. My name is Mallory." He then went around the table presenting the family: "This is my mother, this is my dad. This is Mark, this is Mickie, and this is Melanie." The girl laughed, obviously as surprised as we were.

"Honey, you didn't have to do that," we told him, when the waitress had taken our orders and hurried off. But mistaken courtesy or not, the service was prompt and attentive. And when we got ready to leave, the young lady gave all the children cowboy souvenirs, and even came to the window as we piled into the car to wave us a merry good-bye. As we drove off, we all decided that, whatever the customs, we couldn't go too far wrong just by being friendly.

How often today I think of that well-meaning little boy. Whether it's a plush hotel or a hamburger stop by the highway, if a waiter or waitress greets me like that, I want to respond as he did, "Glad to meet you. I'm Marjorie." I want to introduce my family, if they're there, and ask about his own. I don't, of course—there isn't time, for one thing. But there is time to smile, to encourage, to show appreciation and respect. And when we leave, to tip as generously as we can.

Sons and daughters, working their way through college, mothers helping support their children, older men and women cheerfully bending under heavy trays. Sometimes we do exchange bits of information about ourselves. For a little while our lives touch, we are family, we are friends.

Etiquette books don't deal with this—they don't need to. The Bible tells us we are all God's children, here on Earth to serve and to love one another. Only then can we truly serve and love Him.

Thank You, God, for all the wonderful people who help us throughout the journey of life. My son was right: It's not only correct to be friendly, it's Christian. —Marjorie Holmes

Saturday

14

Fireside Friend

...A time to be silent.... —Ecclesiastes 3:7 (NIV)

The Thunderdome. Minneapolis' Metrodome, where I work, acquired this nickname during the 1987 World Series, when crowd noise consistently topped the 120-decibel level, equivalent to a jet plane taking off. As I lead tours at the dome, I'm often asked to describe this. I recall my five-week-long earache, the bobbled balls dropped by outfielders who couldn't hear each other calling for the ball, Kent Firbek's sixth-game grand slam that broke the noise level meter.

But the most thunderous experience I can recall at the dome was not the World Series, but the day the Names Project spread the gigantic AIDS quilt over the entire baseball field. Each small square was made by friends or family of someone who had died of AIDS. As thousands of mourners walked among the thousands of names, there was unbroken silence. I found a square for Baby Jessica, an infant from a neighboring church, who had received the virus from a transfusion. Her panel had teddy bears sewn on it, and was made by people who had never met her. Farther over, a purple panel with a white cross bore the name of Reverend Randall Kingsbury, a friend I had not seen for years. I laid a white carnation by his name.

I was struck by the silence, because grief was the most thunderous sound I'd ever heard. But in this silence there was also healing, as tears were shed, hugs exchanged, wordless prayers said. The dome had finally earned its nickname, I felt—not at high decibels, but at none at all.

God of thunder and might, reach through the silence to touch all who grieve today. —Tammy Rider

WINDOWS INTO WONDER
One in a Crowd

John answered... There standeth one among you, whom ye know not.... This is the Son of God.
—John 1:26, 34

I wonder what I'd have done if I'd been in the crowd by the River Jordan that day as John was baptizing and telling about One Who was coming to baptize with fire and the Spirit. I wonder if I'd have looked around at the crowd and sized up the people. Would there have been some I'd want to know better, others who would repel me? What about that man next to me whose sandaled feet were dirty, his long hair windblown, his beard gritty-looking from the desert sand? Chances are I'd have moved away a bit. Imagine how I'd have felt if John suddenly stretched out his hand to *that man* and said, "Behold the Lamb of God, which taketh away the sin of the world" (John 1:29), and the heavens opened, a dove descended and a voice proclaimed, "This is my beloved Son" (Matthew 3:17).

What a vision! But I wasn't there, of course. I've never stood next to Jesus in a crowd. Or have I? It was He Who said that whatever we do "to one of the least of these" (Matthew 25:45), we are doing to Him. During the past week, I've asked God to let the vision of the dove be a reminder to me to treat others as I would Jesus. It's amazing how often that picture of the descending dove has flashed into my mind. I was shopping for new eyeglasses, and it seemed to me that the girl who waited on me was a bit rude. Just as I was ready to make a sharp retort, I blinked my eyes... and saw a dove in my mind's eye. Would I make that remark to Jesus? On another day, a woman whose child was in trouble called in the late afternoon, interrupting a special birthday dinner preparation I wanted to finish before five. As I sat there, drumming my fingers on my desk, the thought of the dove flashed into my mind. Would I listen if Jesus called me?

Where will you see Jesus this month? Perhaps you'll ask God to send a dove into your mind to remind you that He's in "the least of these."

Lord, help me to recognize Your face in the crowd.

—Marilyn Morgan Helleberg

July Prayer List Reminder

Return to your Monthly Prayer List on the calendar opening page and review your requests. Give thanks for prayers answered, renew old prayers and add new concerns today. Then pray once again our *Family Prayer for July.*

Monday

16

And I say also unto thee, That thou art Peter, and upon this rock I will build my church....

—Matthew 16:18

On my first trip to Rome, we visited St. Peter's Basilica. Its great dome was a manifestation of Michelangelo's engineering genius, and the sculpture inside was a tribute to his unmatched talent as an artist, but the church overwhelmed me and seemed cold. This largest of all Christian churches had too many statues and tombs, it seemed to me, and too little focus on God.

I returned five months later with my wife Sally. Just as before, a rush-hour mob crowded around shouting and pushing. "Want a guide, only twenty-five thousand lire [about twenty dollars]?" called a plump woman who seemed too old to be walking these marble corridors each day. "Let's do it, otherwise we are just going to wander around and not know what we see," Sally suggested.

And so this time we saw St. Peter's through the eyes of our guide. The Latin inscriptions around the ceiling became the personal words of Christ to the Rock upon whom He was building His future church. Statues came alive as her stories breathed into them a fresh vitality. And she talked in loving tones about her priest, the world's Pope. In reverent excitement she described the worship planned for the next month. Her church, she assured us, was the biggest, most beautiful church in the world.

My church isn't. It has concrete block walls and the artwork was done by our high-school art teacher. But you'll misunderstand my church, too, if you don't get to meet Ralph, or Frank, or Emily... people who belong to it and love it and are proud of it.

Not in a tent or a temple but in our hearts, Lord; that is where we may meet with You.

Dear Lord, I praise You that You choose to meet us wherever we call on You, in so great a building...or so small. —Scott Harrison

Tuesday

17

If any man offend not...the same is a perfect man....
—James 3:2

The car wouldn't start this morning and I was furious. I kicked a tire and muttered nasty thoughts about machines. Later I was overcome with remorse when I realized that this was the first time our three-year-old car had failed to start. That's once out of nearly eleven thousand starts, I figure. Besides, I was the one who left the dome light on all night, running down the battery!

Sometimes I make the same unfair judgments of people. I'm annoyed when the paperboy misses the porch now and then, or when the postman gives us the neighbor's mail by mistake. I grumble when my wife Sharon forgets to wash my favorite shirt, and sigh when (only once) the kids leave the TV on all night.

From now on, I plan to pay a little more attention to what people do *right*. I'm going to praise my students who have good attendance and compliment those who ask me hard questions in class. I'm going to ask God to make me more patient with those now-and-then failures we all have.

And I'm going to apologize to my car.

Perfect Father, remind me that You alone have the ability not to make mistakes. —Daniel Schantz

Wednesday

18

Though our outer nature is wasting away, our inner nature is being renewed every day.
—II Corinthians 4:16 (RSV)

My forty-third birthday dawned a brilliant blue-sky day, but I was feeling lots like the descriptions on my birthday cards: over-the-hill; sluggish; with more wrinkles than an elephant.

Oh, yeah? I decided after moping around the house all morning. I hopped on my bicycle and took off down our big hill. Instead of my usual cautious speed, I hunched low over the handlebars like a little kid, going faster and faster. Suddenly, my front tire wobbled, then my back tire, and I was zigzagging crazily. What was happening? The ground came closer and I twisted the handlebars. Miraculously, I didn't fall and pulled in a driveway where I climbed off, shaking uncontrollably. I checked the tires. No problem, so I climbed back on and continued down the road. Slowly.

Later, at my birthday dinner, I casually mentioned my close call. "High-speed wobble," twelve-year-old Kendall pronounced without even looking up from her plate of *fajitas*. "You always go out of control like that on a bicycle when you overreact to something... like a birthday."

I stopped chewing and stared at her. *Smart kid,* I thought, vowing right then that I wouldn't even wince when it came time for the inevitable jokes about the candles on the birthday cake burning the place down. After all, there's this consolation: No matter how many wrinkles or changes appear on the outside, I'm ageless on the inside... and that's where it counts.

Lord, You made us with ageless, eternal souls. Thank You.

—Carol Kuykendall

Thursday

19

For the mountains shall depart, and the hills be removed; but my kindness shall not depart from thee....

—Isaiah 54:10

The summer after my senior year was a fun time. I was out of school, I had my friends and I didn't have a care in the world. I didn't know what I wanted to do, but I knew I didn't want to go to college. Neither of my parents pressured me at first, but as summer started drawing to an end, they suggested that I start getting ready for school.

Finally, the weekend before fall semester arrived. On Saturday, Mom came into my room, tears in her eyes. "I love you," she said, "and it tears me apart inside to make you do something you hate so much, but sometimes change is necessary. This afternoon we're taking you up to enroll in college."

I'd like to be able to say I saw her point of view, but I don't think I said three words the entire two-hour trip to the university. They helped me enroll, unpacked my belongings in my dorm room and left me.

As it turned out, college was a wonderful, positive experience. It gave my life direction and helped me grow. And I never would have had it if my parents had let me have things my way. I'll never forget the courageous love my parents showed me by their firmness. It makes me wonder if God does the same. If God doesn't give me what I want, isn't it possible He's giving me what I need?

Lord, love me with a parent's brave love. And help me to recognize the gift of firmness better than I did when I was young! —John Coen

Friday

20

Fireside Friend

Come ye, and let us go up to the mountain of the Lord, to the house of the God of Jacob.... —Isaiah 2:3

When I was seven years old we lived for a time on the outskirts of Indio, California. I remember blue skies and miles of desert unfolding to the distant mountains. My dad, born in 1898 of a Chumash Indian mother, used to take my sister Pat and me for hikes into this vast land. He would point out medicine plants like *Yerba Santa* (sacred herb) used to cure stomach troubles, or *Kanotillo,* a low green bush we called "stick tea." He taught us to sharpen our senses to everything around us, like lizards or the direction of the faintest breeze.

An important part of the hikes was to teach us how to take our bearings, noting the sun's direction and particular landmarks that would point the way home. When he took us over sand dunes and down into washes, following animal tracks or investigating rock formations, we never lost our way. At some point Dad would say, "Find home," and Pat and I always did.

I wanted my kids to have that sense of holiness and awe of God's nature that Dad taught me. And even though we raised them in the city, we'd often take them out to wild natural places. Recently, my grown-up daughter Cynthia and I went to the Morongo Reservation in Banning, California. Like my dad and I, we gathered sage and *Kanotillo,* and went into the San Jacinto Mountains for a picnic. I was unwrapping the food when, to my surprise, Cindy said, "Mom, wait. Can we pray?" And then she began, "Thank You, God. Thank You for our time together. Thank You for the mountains, for the lakes, for gathering sage...."

As I saw my daughter's head bent over the food, sunlight glinting on her dark hair and the mountains behind her, I smiled. My Father was still pointing my family in the right direction...toward Home.

Father, through all the generations, lead us Home.

—Georgiana Sanchez

Saturday

21

The Lord's unfailing love surrounds the man who trusts in him. —Psalm 32:10 (NIV)

It was my first summer at camp. And while all the other kids splashed playfully in the pool, I sat on the sidelines—wrapped in my beach towel, hugging my knees. I was a non-swimmer, and my clumsy efforts in class that morning had earned me the nickname "Rock." So I was understandably terrified a few days later when everyone in my cabin went canoeing. "Don't worry," my counselor said as she strapped on my fat orange life jacket. "This is your very own PFD—personal flotation device. It will keep you afloat no matter what!" I climbed aboard, gripping the sides of the canoe. Later in the day, we came to a shallow place in the river where everyone went wading. I decided to try out my PFD. To my amazement, it worked! I bobbed in the water like a huge orange balloon.

I seldom go canoeing these days. (My nickname's still "Rock.") But I've discovered another kind of "personal flotation device" I carry with me always. God's love. It's there when I lose my temper with the kids, when my grand plans don't work out, when I feel awkward or alone. It surrounds me and keeps me afloat. Even when the waters get very deep.

Thank You, Father, for Your love. Today I'll rest in its sure buoyancy.

—Mary Lou Carney

Sunday

22

Whither have ye made a road today?

—I Samuel 27:10

My favorite work of painter Bob Judah was a collection of roads he'd known and loved since his boyhood days. Bob's friendship with the roads dated back over seventy years: paved, dirt, rocky, slick, obscure, open—they led me through an adventure of seasons and locations. I marveled my way through fresh fallen snow, then instantly wandered amidst piles of bronze and golden leaves. Deep within some cool woods a subtle but glorious hint of spring blossomed, and I also followed a dirt road through lush green trees and startling summer sunlight. No figures on the roads, not even animals. Yet, Bob had somehow painted life, emotion and something almost spiritual into the pictures.

"Bob," I said to him once, "all the roads have a curve in them! They beckon me—make me wish I could go around them. Seems like there's something waiting for me around the curve, something good."

Bob looked pleased. "That's right. When you get discouraged about the future, start believing that God really has something for you—just around the next curve—and keep moving toward it."

Now when I'm traveling, I find myself looking for "Bob Judah Curves." And when I get disheartened, I try to create a road in my mind, reminding myself that just around the next curve is something good... something from God.

Father, help me make mental roads of faith and expect You around each curve. —Marion Bond West

Monday

23

Those who are loving and kind show that they are the children of God.... —I John 4:7 (TLB)

When is it my turn? I asked God. *When do I get to be the bride instead of the bridesmaid? Will I end up living my life alone?*

I had just been a bridesmaid for the fifth time. First, it had been for my sister Melanie, then my sister Valerie, then my friends Cindy and Vicki, and now Missy. I was beginning to feel very sorry for myself. Everyone else was falling in love and finding a mate.

Then, throughout the workday, little things started to chip away at my bitterness. I got a few phone calls from friends wanting to plan get-togethers for the week. My nephew Ryan sent me one of his finger paintings, and my coworkers asked interested questions about my new life in the city. Small events, to be sure, but each one was saying, "I care."

I felt warmed and my spirits lifted. God was showing me that I wasn't alone and that I was loved. Maybe I don't have a spouse, but

I do have loving relationships with family and friends and co-workers... and God.

Are you feeling today that you have no one to love and no one who loves you? Take another look around you. You might change your mind!

God, open my eyes to the many gifts of loving and caring You have placed around me. Let me express gratitude and thanksgiving for them all. Amen.

—Stephanie Samoy

Tuesday

24

But now they desire a better country, that is, a heavenly....

—Hebrews 11:16

It was the summer of 1965. I was only nineteen and had been called to Vietnam. Like other young men of the time, I was eager to serve my country. I had trained as crew chief and door gunner with a helicopter unit in the States for a year before we were shipped overseas.

By the end of our first day in combat, we had expended a couple of loads of rockets and M-60 machine-gun ammunition into the jungle. Back at camp we heard that one of our helicopters had been hit by enemy fire. I made a dash to investigate. The two bullet holes in the side of the chopper reminded me of the holes I'd made in tin cans with a twenty-two back home in Oklahoma—smooth going in, but jagged going out. I was almost jealous of that other crew chief, wanting a battle-scarred helicopter of my own. How young and naive I was then!

Nearly a year after being sent to Vietnam, I was boarding the plane that would take me on the first leg of my journey back to the States. I had seen too many bullet holes, too many fearful nights, too many frightful battles. As I sat in my seat, one of the soldiers up the aisle started weeping and blurted out, "I can't believe I made it." A few other guys started sniffling, and all of us began fighting back the tears. We weren't excited young soldiers ready for battle. We were old men who knew that there is nothing glamorous about war, that it is a terrible scourge for all humankind, and that we who survived could only thank God with all our hearts that we were still alive and were going home.

Lord, help us all to remember how precious life here on earth is, but most of all, we thank You for the victory of an eternity in Heaven with You. —Brian Miller

Wednesday

25

Not my will, but thine, be done. —Luke 22:42

I was at work in the garage and had the radio on while Frank Sinatra was singing "My Way." What a thrilling song! I sang with him (an octave lower), and finished with a great flourish: "I did it m-y-y wa-a-a-y-y!"

But then I stopped and said out loud, "What am I singing? That's not the way I do things!" I learned a long time ago that I could get into a lot of trouble when I did it "my way." There was the class project in college where I attempted an experiment without consulting the textbook. I knew better. The experiment was a flop because I had overlooked some important steps. Months of wasted time, energy, materials and calculations because I stubbornly insisted on "my way." All through my early adult life, it seems, I had to guard against that same collegiate-minded self-will.

Today, in small and large ways, I bring God into my choices and decisions. Someone cuts me off in traffic; my way is to respond with anger. *God's way is to live in peace with everyone* (Romans 12:18). Someone deliberately wrongs me; my way is typified by the bumper sticker that says, "Don't get mad; get even." *God's way is the path of forgiveness and love* (Genesis 50:17). It seems that everyone else is looking out for number one, get all you can and never mind who gets hurt in the process. *But God's way is not* get *but* give (Acts 20:35).

Now which way should I live? I sometimes fail in my purpose, and I do not always react as I should, but I am determined that when I am faced with a "fork in the road"—my way or His—I'll choose to walk God's path.

Dear Lord, I pray that every day, in all my thoughts, words and deeds, that my way becomes more and more Your way.

—Lee Webber

Thursday

26

Fireside Friend 

We are Christ's ambassadors. God is using us to speak to you.... —II Corinthians 5:20 (TLB)

"God told me to change churches!" "God told me to change jobs!" The young woman spoke with such assurance that I wondered why God doesn't "speak" so clearly and decisively to me.

The past few years have held a litany of traumas for our family: unemployment, foreclosure, major moves, health problems for my husband Dennis and me, and all the traumas that come with parenting teens and young adults. So many times I have longed for God to speak to me, preferably with a loudspeaker and blazing neon lights.

Then I thought of the different ways God has spoken to me through the difficult times:

- through the church body that provided us with food during Dennis' time of unemployment.
- through a concerned realtor who provided interim housing for us.
- through friends who packed boxes, loaded furniture and held my hand when we moved.
- through the prayers of friends and strangers and the wisdom and skill of doctors as health was restored.

Thank You, Lord, for speaking to me through the lives and love of Your earthly voices. —Bonnie Wheeler

Friday

27

And he took them up in his arms, put his hands upon them, and blessed them. —Mark 10:16

My dream had come true. Like everyone else, I stood as applause thundered against the walls of the auditorium. A slight woman, her white sari vivid against her dark face, stepped upon a black box so that she could see over the podium. A rosary dangled from her clasped hands and she nodded humbly. Mother Teresa of Calcutta stood before us.

After the crowd quieted, she told stories about the "poorest of the poor" in India. She told of a man lying in an open sewer in Calcutta; he was covered with sores and maggots. She had offered the dying man her opened arms. Her words saddened me. *How could I help others the way she helped them?*

Then, as if hearing my thoughts, Mother Teresa said, "People come to me and say, 'Mother, what can I do? How can I help?'" She pointed her finger at us and said, "I tell them to go home and to love their family."

Hope flowed through me. For the great lady of love had commissioned me to a task I could accomplish. She had not asked me to go to some distant port—only to my corner of the world. There, too, open arms are needed—for spouses and children and sisters and brothers and neighbors and friends. Yes, I, too, can reflect God's love. Maybe not in Calcutta, but where I live—and where you live, too: Main Street, Park Avenue, Oak Drive, Barton Way or Rural Route 1.

Dear Heavenly Father, in Your name, let me open my arms to those around me. —Terry Helwig

Saturday

28

"This day shall be for you a memorial day...."
—Exodus 12:14 (RSV)

From the time I was a girl of twelve, I enjoyed summer fishing trips with my father in his fourteen-foot aluminum boat *The Charu.* Dad always sat in the stern handling the motor controls, but whenever I had a trout on my line, he jumped up beside me ready with the net. He'd help unhook the slippery fish and then pass me bait for the next cast. When Dad died, my son Phil was just two and not yet under the spell of hook and line. It wasn't long, however, before he was out trolling with his dad in that same dependable boat.

By last summer Phil had grown to a boy of twelve...and one evening he took me fishing. Suddenly I felt that old familiar tug, and hollered as I always used to, "I've got one!" Phil was right there to grab the line and swing a fat *kokanee* into the boat. "That's a beauty,

Mom," he whistled. And, just like Dad, Phil unhooked the wriggling fish and passed me more bait.

We cruised awhile longer without catching anything—or so it appeared. But for me, the evening had been an unexpected cast backward in time, and the childhood memory I had hooked was a beauty. As we headed for shore, I looked at Phil manning the controls, squinting into the setting sun, and I prayed, "Help me, Lord, to fill his net with a good catch. Among his memories let there be some real beauties."

Dear Lord, guide me by Your understanding to stock my days with tomorrow's prize-winning memories. —Carol Knapp

You have taught the little children to praise you perfectly. —Psalm 8:2 (TLB)

It was "Kids' Day" in our church, the one Sunday a month when the children are brought into the sanctuary to take part in the adult worship service. At a signal from the children's choir director, rows of kids filed forward. The *thud* of sneakers echoed down the center aisle, while tiny heads turned up in awe of vaulted ceilings and stained glass. As the kids filed onto the risers, several indulged in grins and waves of recognition to people in the congregation. Some still had sunburned noses from their last trip to the beach. Several chewed bubble gum. The director raised her hand, and every eye was on her. They sang "I'm in the Lord's Army," their voices filling the sanctuary with unself-conscious enthusiasm.

After the children left, the service was different for me, somehow. I read the responsive Scripture, not with mumbling indifference, but with firm voice. I listened—really listened—to the offertory. The words of the soloist seemed sung for me. And the pastor's message was just what I needed.

What made the difference? Perhaps it was the invisible energy the children brought with them. Maybe it was their spontaneity. Or the sincerity with which they sang. Now, whenever my worship seems dry or rote, I remember the color and clamor and unaffected praise of those children. I rouse myself to really take part in the service. After all, I'm in the Lord's army, too!

O God, strip off the shroud of formality and familiarity I too often wear to church. Teach me to worship You naturally as little children do.
—Mary Lou Carney

Monday

30

Blessed are the peacemakers: for they shall be called the children of God.
—Matthew 5:9

Every day the noisy bluejay flew to its perch on the eaves of the porch, right above the sunny spot where Mom and Dad's little Yorkshire terrier Sassie likes to sit. Then the squawking began, that high-pitched, aggravated squeal. Sassie barked back loudly, but the bird kept it up. The dog jumped up and ran around the yard barking, but the bird would tease her and fly away.

This continued for weeks; the little dog became more and more frustrated by the bird's teasing and her own helplessness. Then one day, it stopped. Not the teasing, but Sassie's reaction. The bird began its tirade, Sassie shot it a glance, then coolly walked away. She finally accepted that she couldn't change that bird, and so turned her helplessness into a powerful defense. Unable to get a rise out of Sassie, the bird gave up and flew away. It still returns to the yard, but it doesn't taunt Sassie anymore.

I thought about Sassie's lesson soon after, when I started a new job. A coworker had been testing me, as the "new kid on the block," with little jabs and intimidation tactics. Our relationship was a nonstop argument. But once I accepted her behavior instead of trying to fight her, things were easier. And eventually, my choosing not to fight took the fun out of it for her, just like Sassie's bluejay, and she became my friend.

Is there a situation or someone in your life today that is bothering you? Maybe the best reaction is not to react at all, but to back away and call a truce.

Dear Lord, help me to accept the things I cannot change, a first step toward peace.
—Gina Bridgeman

Day Brightener

Have courage for the great sorrows of life and patience for the small ones; and when you have laboriously accomplished your daily task, go to sleep in peace. God is awake.

—Victor Hugo

Tuesday

31

Fireside Friend

Be careful for nothing.... —Philippians 4:6

Remember the story of the ant and the grasshopper? The ant spent the summer storing up food while the foolish grasshopper frolicked in the meadow. When winter came, only the provident ant survived. But was the grasshopper really so foolish?

By nature, I've always been an ant. I work hard, save for a rainy day and never waste my time. Then, one day, I turned into a grasshopper. Let me explain: A friend invited me to join some neighbors at her home for lunch. I enjoyed this get-together very much, but when lunch went on for two hours, I began to think of all the work I had left undone at home and got a bit "antsy." I wondered how I could make a graceful exit, when Felicity, a sprightly grandmother, spoke.

She confessed she had been a hopeless spendthrift all her life, squandering time and money as if there was no tomorrow. One summer she and her husband impulsively emptied their savings account and took their two young sons on a glorious three-month vacation to England, realizing a longtime dream. When they returned, Felicity's husband—barely in his forties—died of a heart attack.

After the shock of silence abated, someone suggested that we meet once a month and call ourselves the Grasshoppers. Before our monthly meeting, we each had to do at least one frivolous thing, like letting the housework go or buying something totally impractical.

If you tend, as I do, to be too much of an ant, try out the spring of a grasshopper. Go play in the meadow once in a while. Discover some new terrain (nurture a new talent, visit a foreign city, make a new friend). Find the joy and beauty of a new experience that was meant just for you—now, today, this moment.

Beloved Friend, be a guest in my heart, as You were at Bethany, and chide me gently, as You did Martha, when I am troubled by too many things. Amen. —Stephanie Oda

Thank-You Notes to God

1 ____________________

2 ____________________

3 ____________________

4 ____________________

5 ____________________

6 ____________________

7 ____________________

8 ____________________

9 ____________________

10 ____________________

11 ____________________

12 ____________________

13 ____________________

14 ____________________

15 ____________________

16

17

18

19

20

21

22

23

24

25

26

27

28

29

30

31

AUGUST

S	M	T	W	T	F	S
			1	2	3	4
5	6	7	8	9	10	11
12	13	14	15	16	17	18
19	20	21	22	23	24	25
26	27	28	29	30	31	

SPIRITUAL TREASURE

Take the Hard and Narrow Way

"Enter by the narrow gate; for the gate is wide and the way is easy, that leads to destruction, and.... the gate is narrow and the way is hard, that leads to life...."
—Matthew 7:13-14 (RSV)

Hammock time. August is that lazy, hazy month that seems designed for leaning back and taking it easy. Leisure is important, but lolling away in a spiritual hammock can be destructive. This is just the month to aim at a difficult spiritual challenge, one of those "hard and narrow way" kinds of tasks that you need to accomplish. Come on, get up, get going! Take a few steps toward your goal each day. It might be hard, but it's the way that leads to new life!

My Monthly Prayer List

Family Prayer for August

Jesus, this month I pray for peace in the world—and where I live. Help me to surrender to You the part of me that is not peaceful. And help me become a peacemaker.

Wednesday

1

THROUGH AN OPEN WINDOW
Obey

If you will walk in my statutes and obey my ordinances and keep all my commandments...then I will establish my word with you.... —I Kings 6:12 (RSV)

From my window this morning, a bright summer day beckons me out of doors. I suddenly recall an adventure I had one wonderful summer. I'd gone to Costa Rica as part of a turtle-tagging team. Since our work with the turtles was done at night, our days were free for swimming, fishing, photographing or exploring the surrounding rain forests.

One afternoon, Terry and Jack, two team members who were experts on crocodiles, announced that they were going out in a boat to trap a "croc" for study purposes—not to kill it, of course. I begged to go along. Terry looked apprehensive. "Well, I don't think...."

Again, I pleaded. They relented. "You must do exactly as we tell you," Jack said. "It will be your job to steady the boat." I nodded.

The boat turned out to be little more than a dugout canoe, and with the weight of the three of us, it sat fairly low in the water. When we reached the riverbank where the crocs were sunning, Terry stretched out in the bow, his rope noose ready. Jack knelt behind him, holding the net. "Put your hands on each side of the boat and don't move," he ordered me.

Splash! A croc slithered into the water and swam in our direction. "Get ready!" Terry yelled. A moment later he aimed the noose at the croc's jaws; Jack leaned over the side. Suddenly, I decided that part of the net might become entangled in the bottom of the boat, so I let go of the sides and bent down to fix it. Just then Terry's noose made contact with the croc. The boat rocked wildly. The noose missed its mark. The reptile dove underwater. Terry had to grab Jack's leg to keep him from falling overboard.

"Why did you let go?" Terry roared.

"I thought I should...."

"You should have obeyed us!" Jack interrupted. "We could have all been endangered!"

"I'm terribly sorry," I answered.

I guess I looked it because they soon forgave me. "We'll try again," Terry said gently.

We did. This time I did exactly as I'd been told. I kept both hands firmly on the sides of the boat. We trapped the croc, and after taking some measurements, we let it go.

But that day, for the first time, I saw clearly the value of obedience. Terry and Jack knew far better than I how to manage the boat. Surely, God knows far better than I how I should conduct my life. That's why His plan contains rules for us. That's why you and I should obey them.

Dear Father, every day during this month, I'm going to think of You as a loving Parent Who wants the very best for me. Help me to obey You.

—Eleanor Sass

Thursday

2

[Love] beareth all things, believeth all things, hopeth all things, endureth all things. —I Corinthians 13:4, 7

Without any enthusiasm, I grocery shopped. It seemed discouragement rode in my cart. Although I had made trips home, I hadn't been able to persuade any of my grown children back in Georgia to come out and visit since I'd remarried and moved to Oklahoma. Conflicting schedules, finances, other reasons made it impossible just now. Then a loud, happy voice caught my attention. A young man over on the other aisle was speaking to a young woman. *"Hi, I've seen you around. You work here?"*

"Yes." (No warmth in her reply.)

"Me, too. What about having lunch with me tomorrow?"

"No. No, thank you." (She didn't hesitate.)

How disappointed he must be. I guess he felt as I did this morning.

"Why not?" he persisted in a hopeful voice. I couldn't see them, so I leaned a bit closer to a shelf of green beans and listened, pretending to read the label.

"I go home for lunch. I live nearby."

"Could you make an exception just one day?"

"Actually, I don't eat lunch. I just drink something."

"Would you drink something with me tomorrow and maybe eat a small salad?"

"I don't think so." (She didn't sound too convincing.)

"Tell you what. I'll meet you right here at this very spot tomorrow, and we'll eat a salad right across the street. You'll like it."

Silence. *Say yes!* I thought excitedly.

"You might forget," she blurted out.

"Me! Never. I'll even be here early waiting for you."

"Promise?" (Shy voice, but I knew somehow she was smiling.)

"Promise. Tomorrow at noon."

"Okay!"

I almost cheered. As they parted, I heard him singing at the top of his voice, *"Tomorrow, tomorrow...."* The young man's hope and belief had penetrated right through shelves of canned goods and reached my doubtful heart. Discouragement fled. Hope now grocery shopped with me. And when I went home, there was a letter from my twenty-year-old son Jeremy saying that after some reworking of his schedule, he'd be coming to visit after all!

Thank You, Father, for strangers who show us how to keep on keeping on.

—Marion Bond West

Friday

3

Live in harmony with one another....

—Romans 12:16 (RSV)

On our wedding anniversary last year my husband presented me with a small package wrapped in beautiful silver paper. It was about the right size for a bracelet.

I tossed Sandy a smile and opened the box. Inside was a metal chain, composed of three links. Not three links of delicate gold chain, mind you, but the kind of heavy chain you use to fasten the gate on a fence.

I could think of nothing to say. Somehow, "Thank you for this portion of chain link fence" didn't seem appropriate. Sandy reached over and lifted the three links from the box. "Do you notice how the two links on each end are joined by the center link?" he said. "They are separate and complete in themselves, yet they share a common space together. I think it is a picture of marriage at its best—two people, complete and independent in themselves, but joined in a common bond of intimacy."

As I took the chain in my hands, I felt a slight stinging in my eyes. Even the bracelet I received from him later did not affect me so deeply as that strong and tender symbol of what a relationship can be. Whether husband and wife, parent and child, or simply close friends, the link needs the balance of autonomy and intimacy in order to remain strong.

Father, link me to others in ways that are loving, balanced and healthy.
—Sue Monk Kidd

Saturday

4

For God maketh my heart soft.... —Job 23:16

One of the fascinating things about life is to observe how God moves in a mysterious way, as the poet William Cowper said, to perform His wonders. Sometimes in great natural events like hurricanes or volcanoes, sometimes in tiny episodes that leave people changed.

For example, I have a friend who lives in a big city; an impatient, somewhat intolerant man who has a seven-year-old son. Someone gave the lad a kite for his birthday. The only place to fly it was a small park near their apartment. But the park had been allowed to deteriorate into a meeting place for derelicts and panhandlers and other social misfits. My friend always gave it a wide berth to "keep away from the riff-raff," as he put it.

But the child begged so hard that at last the father consented to take him. "And you know," he said to me later, "it was amazing. When those people saw a child with a kite, something in them was changed. Some of them spoke to us and smiled. They watched the kite soar up over the grimy city, and the same look was on many faces—a look of far-off happiness, of remembered joy. It made me realize how different they might have been if things had been easier for them. I don't think I'll ever be quite so harsh and scornful of them again."

You see, he went to help his child fly a kite and was handed this little surprise package containing a deeper insight, a changed attitude. Remarkable, isn't it?

Lord, teach me to watch for Your mysterious ways and be grateful for them.
—Arthur Gordon

Sunday

5

How good and how pleasant it is for brethren to dwell together in unity!
—Psalm 133:1

Despite many invitations, I have never persuaded a good friend of mine to go to church with me. We share a common interest in many things, especially sports, but he has a million reasons for avoiding church; e.g., the services are too early, too long, too boring.

I recently read the story of a sports fanatic (or fan as in the Latin word *fanaticus,* which meant excessive religious enthusiasm) who has kissed off all athletic events, sworn off all sports, quit attending all games—cold turkey. These are some of his reasons: The seats are too hard; the people I sit with are not very friendly; some of the games went into overtime and upset my schedule; events are scheduled at inconvenient times; I've read the rule book and know it better than the referee; as a youngster I was taken to too many games by my parents, a mistake I'm not going to repeat with my children.

A philosopher once observed that in life we always find time for the things that are really important. Christ put it another way: "For where your treasure is, there will your heart be also" (Luke 12:34). He didn't make churchgoing a requisite for finding the kingdom of Heaven; He only promised that He would be present wherever two or three are gathered in His name (Matthew 18:20). That, it seems to me, is good enough reason for His fans to huddle up regularly at the meeting house.

Whenever worship becomes a bother,
Heal my blindness, O heavenly Father.

—Fred Bauer

Monday

6

Fireside Friend 

If thou seekest her as silver, and searchest for her as for hid treasures.... —Proverbs 2:4

A friend was visiting San Francisco from England, and all she could talk about was her dream of walking across the Golden Gate Bridge. She told me she had dreamed of this for years. On a glorious, sunny day, we headed for the bridge and walked across it, marveling at the blue sky, the picturesque buildings on the nearby hills and the colorful boats below. "This must be old hat for you," she said apologetically, then asked, "How many times have you taken this walk?" Shamefacedly, I mumbled that although I'd lived in San Francisco for five years, I hadn't walked across the bridge even once. I suppose it was too available, too easy to get to, so it was easy to put it off.

A similar thing happened when a friend of mine commented after coming to my house for dinner, "We really enjoyed ourselves. The meal was excellent, and you know, your husband has a wonderful sense of humor." I thought how true that was—and I also realized with guilty surprise that I had begun to take that sense of humor for granted (which I much admired when I first met Paul). Like the Golden Gate Bridge, I guess it was just there, so I didn't give it enough value. That night, I made sure to tell Paul, "I really enjoy the way you make me laugh."

What treasures are there in your hometown—or in your home—that you haven't paid attention to lately? Why not thank God for them—and enjoy them—*today*?

God, keep me alert to the treasures all around me this day and thankful for the special people, places and things in my life. Don't let me take them for granted. —Linda Neukrug

Tuesday

7

You died with him [Christ], so to speak, when he died; and now you share his new life....

—Romans 6:5 (TLB)

I left my husband's field glasses out in the rain one night at Lake Erie. "Honey, I'm so sorry," I told him when he found them the next morning. "I'll have to buy you another pair. I'm afraid these are ruined."

But these were his favorite, and he hated to part with them. Patiently he took them apart, dried them, cleaned them thoroughly and reassembled them; and now, to my surprise, we see through them more clearly than ever. Ships on the distant horizon, friends out fishing, kids swimming, birds we can now identify in the trees, geese and seagulls soaring or riding the waves.

"Thank goodness," I marveled, "we didn't throw these old glasses away!"

And putting them back in their case, I thought of the many problems that beset all families, including our own. How often disaster seemed imminent—and sometimes was. Yet lives, too, can be cleaned and reassembled after disappointments and estrangements, or even tragedy and sin. Human relationships can be mended—between parents and children, husbands and wives, friends.

If you're thinking of throwing something valuable away, wait. Pick up the pieces. Ask God to help you. If it's worth saving, He will show you how to put it back together, sometimes better than new!

Lord, help us to recognize the value in what we have. Give us the faith and patience to reclaim it. —Marjorie Holmes

Wednesday

8

By my God have I leaped over a wall.

—II Samuel 22:30

Our son Willy, at the age of twenty months, is willing to try any new word. He points at what he wants to know and says, "This is...? This is...?" I answer, "Pickup truck...flag pole...garbage can...mail box." He dutifully repeats what I've said—leaving out a consonant or two—and then goes on to the next item that has captured his fancy. I start to wonder if this game is worthwhile when I have to name things like "incinerator," "storm drain" and "fire hydrant." Undaunted, Willy tries them out (something like "erter," "stumdane" and "irdrent"). It doesn't quite matter that he doesn't know exactly what they are. The point is, he's not afraid to try something new—even if it's beyond his grasp.

It's this fearless attitude I think of when I'm faced with a new challenge, such as a new assignment at work, an unfamiliar solo in choir or serving as the new head of the parents' group in our apartment complex. Part of me wants to retreat, going back to what's comfortable. "The challenge is beyond me," I say to myself. "I sing better with the group," I rationalize, or "I'm a better Indian than chief." But then I think of Willy picking up a new word, a new phrase.

"Act boldly," I tell myself. "Just try it. Don't be afraid of making mistakes. You'll learn. Be like Willy." I take a deep breath, ask for God's help, then leap.

Lord, bring all Your mighty forces to aid when I take a leap of faith.

—Rick Hamlin

Thursday

9

"You have been trustworthy in a very small matter...."

—Luke 19:17 (NIV)

Several months ago I saw a sign on the cash register of my local supermarket: ROUND OFF FOR THE NEEDY. "What's that?" I asked the checkout girl, pointing at the sign. She said, "If people want to donate the odd change from their grocery bill, we funnel it to organizations to help feed needy people." Odd change? "Here," I smiled, dumping my thirty-six cents back into her hand.

While doing my grocery shopping this week, I was amazed to see a huge banner: OVER $10,000 RAISED FOR THE NEEDY. THANKS! Ten thousand dollars? From small change? Incredible!

Later, as I put away groceries, I thought of my life. Was I discrediting the "small change" opportunities that came my way? I didn't have time to direct the children's pageant at church, but I could spend a few evenings painting sets. I couldn't chaperone the week-long teen ski trip, but I could make a giant batch of chocolate chip cookies for them to take along. My offering when the missionary visited was small, yet daily I remembered her in prayer. Little things. Christ knew how important they were—and I'm learning.

Father, still the part of me that yearns for only grand displays. Keep me faithful in little things. —Mary Lou Carney

Friday

10

[Love] is not rude, it is not self-seeking, it is not easily angered, it keeps no record of wrongs.

—I Corinthians 13:5 (NIV)

My dad has spent his whole life in baseball, first as a player, then as a broadcaster. I like to kid him because no matter what situation comes up, he translates it into a baseball analogy. "That's like the guy who convinces himself he can't hit a certain pitcher," he'll say, or "It's like when the bases are loaded, two outs, and two strikes on the hitter...."

One of his favorite analogies compares a good umpire with a good spouse. "A good umpire," he says, "has one eye and one ear. He doesn't see everything the players do, and he doesn't hear everything they say. If an umpire saw every gesture, or heard everything the players hollered at him from the dugout or after getting called out on strikes, he'd be throwing everybody out of the game. A good umpire doesn't notice a lot of little things that he knows would make him mad."

I thought of my dad's advice today when I snapped at my husband over a little inconvenience. Like a good umpire, Paul quietly ignored my behavior until my anger passed. I later wondered how many annoying little things he overlooks in loving me, as I hope I do with him. For it seems that in looking with just one eye, and listening with just one ear, you catch only the good things.

Loving Father, give me patience and wisdom to be a "good umpire," so I might see and hear the best in people. —Gina Bridgeman

Saturday

11

It was not with perishable things such as silver or gold that you were redeemed...but with the precious blood of Christ. —I Peter 1:18–19 (NIV)

"How are you doing?" a friend asked me cheerily not long after I'd had a heart attack.

"My number-one job is just to stay alive," I answered.

"No," he told me, "your number-one job is the same as everyone else's—to feel good about yourself."

His answer made me realize that I'd been feeling low and useless and that I wasn't of value to God anymore. And then I remembered a story I'd heard a long time ago.

A boy made a toy boat carefully, with much love and attention. But when he took it out to the lake to sail it, a gust of wind caught it and blew it out beyond his reach. He watched it drift and thought it was gone forever. But months later, he saw his boat again—in a shop window. "Even though it's yours," his father explained, "you'll have to buy it back now." As the boy walked out of the store with his boat, after paying the price asked, he said, "Little boat, now you're twice mine. You're mine because I made you, and you're mine because I bought you back."

I had been forgetting that I did have value to God. He not only made me, but He "bought" me. He loved me enough to give His Son for me. To know that I am precious to God restored my dignity and sense of value, and helps me continue to feel good about myself, even when my parts slow down or my spirits sag.

Dear Lord, when I lose sight of the joy of living, the knowledge of Your love restores my sense of self-worth and makes me thankful to be alive. —Lee Webber

Sunday

12

Be strong and of a good courage.... —Joshua 1:18

I keep markers bearing inspirational Bible verses in my Bible and in the devotional books I read each morning. One marker, however, is a cartoon, laminated to withstand endless readings. I found it years ago in a magazine I'd taken to lunch with me, planning to read while I waited for a friend.

It had been a downbeat morning. I awoke depressed. My husband Carl had already left for work so I poured coffee, flipped on the newscast and opened the morning paper. Both depressed me further. A sudden rainstorm made driving to town hazardous. Truckers splashed muddy water onto my windshield, and a driver pulled out from behind me, sped around and slammed on his brakes. I was ready to give my friend an earful of the morning's near disasters. Then I opened the magazine.

The cartoon before me depicted a motherly looking woman gazing down affectionately at her dog, a springer spaniel. "Thank you," she was saying, "for not talking about recession, inflation, the weather or your health." I got the message and chuckled. We had a pleasant lunch.

I'm sure you already have book markers bearing Bible verses. But could you perhaps find a place for this gentle reminder to spread sunshine instead of gloom? Perhaps you could write it under a snapshot of *your* favorite animal. I'm sure God would approve.

Dear Heavenly Father, You give us so many wonderful gifts each day. Help us to keep our thoughts and our conversations on them.

—Aletha Jane Lindstrom

Monday

13

And the peace of God, which passeth all understanding, shall keep your hearts and minds through Christ Jesus. —Philippians 4:7

My wife Cherry and I sat amid a sea of boxes, feeling both thankful and apprehensive. For the past four years we had lived in a mobile home on the farm, but then when our partner retired, we fell heir to his spacious farm home. This move meant that now we would be the sole owners of the 460-acre dairy farm. With more work, more financial stress and all the uncertainty that goes with a new adventure, we were excited but a little scared, too.

We had spent many hours of prayerful reflection the past few months, and as we sat there in the middle of clutter, we decided to bow our heads once again. *Oh, Lord, please stay with us through all the changes we'll be going through*, I prayed.

Refreshed, we started unpacking again, when Cherry exclaimed, "Oh, look, John!" She pulled out of a large box the Scripture we had framed when we were married six years ago: "The peace of God, which passeth all understanding, shall keep your hearts and minds through Christ Jesus" (Philippians 4:7).

I immediately hung the Scripture in a prominent place in our new family room. We were moving to a new house and starting a new phase of our lives. But I understood that there was no need to fear. There would be challenges and maybe even frightening changes in our lives, but in loving Him, and concentrating on the peace He gives us, we can always be "at home."

God, help me with the challenges You have set before me this day. I know that in You I can always find the strength and security that make up a home.

—John Coen

Tuesday

14

Be...slow to wrath. —James 1:19

A magazine article asked, "How would you respond to this? You ask one of your children to go get a rake, and he dents the car with it as he's bringing it around."

I hate to think how I'd respond!

The article advocated viewing such incidents "from God's eternal perspective," such as asking, "How much is that dent going to bother me a year from now?" The author said, "In God's economy, it doesn't amount to a hill of beans."

It wasn't long before a test situation arose. I went to take some cheese from the refrigerator and found part of the outside dried out. What a waste of good money! I had purposely bought a larger piece than usual because it was on sale. "Who forgot to put the cheese back in a plastic bag?" I started to bellow accusingly.

I took a second look at the orange wedge on the butcher block. How important would this be in a year?

I trimmed off the dry part and tossed it on the back porch for two grateful cats. Then I sliced some, wrapped the rest and placed it back in the refrigerator. A reminder was in order for the family. But not a tantrum.

Not in God's economy, anyway.

Father, please give me Your perspective. —B. J. Connor

Wednesday 15

WINDOWS INTO WONDER
A Look Beyond

And his face did shine as the sun, and his raiment was white as the light. —Matthew 17:2

Some Bible scholars believe the transfiguration of our Lord was a dream, because Luke says, "Now Peter and those who were with him were heavy with sleep" (Luke 9:32, RSV). Others maintain that a physical change took place in Jesus' body. But consider this: Could it be that there was actually no change in Jesus Himself, but that the change was in the *seeing ability* of the disciples? Could it be that Jesus wore His Heavenly body all the time that He walked the earth, even though it was clothed in flesh, but that people couldn't see it because their eyes were not capable of perceiving spiritual reality? And could it be that, during those life-changing moments on the mountain, Peter and James and John actually saw, not with the eyes of the body but with the eyes of the spirit?

When I was a child, my Aunt Alta played with me, prayed with me and introduced me to her friend Jesus. But little girls grow up and aunts grow old, and one gray December day, I stood by Aunt Alta's hospital bedside, holding her frail white hand. Just before she died, Aunt Alta opened her eyes very wide and said, "There He is! Oh, He is so beautiful!" That memory hovers in my heart like a bird, not only because I loved my aunt, but also because, at the time of her death, Aunt Alta was totally blind. How could I *not* believe that the spirit has its own eyes and that every moment of our lives we are truly surrounded by the divine?

For us, as for Peter and James and John, there can be moments during this lifetime when we experience, for an instant at least, an awareness of that divine reality. The point of entry may be a symphony, or a sunset, or a line of Scripture. It may be a welling-up of praise from within, or a cry of the heart that knows its own insufficiency. And suddenly there is the knowing—the deep, sure inner verification of spiritual truth. Maybe you'll take a minute or two now, to think of one of your own mountaintop moments. Hold it. Trust it. During the month ahead, keep that moment handy in your mind, calling it back whenever you need affirmation. It can be your sure footing through all the climbings and descents of your days.

I'll trust my mountaintop moments, Lord Christ, for they are evidence of Your shining truth. —Marilyn Morgan Helleberg

August Prayer List Reminder

Return to your Monthly Prayer List on the calendar opening page and review your requests. Give thanks for prayers answered, renew old prayers and add new concerns today. Then pray once again our *Family Prayer for August.*

Thursday

16

He is a new being; the old is gone....
—II Corinthians 5:17 (GNB)

It was time for the Kentucky State Fair. I ate hot dogs, melted mouthfuls of pink cotton candy on my tongue and quenched my thirst with fresh lemonade. The sun blazed overhead. Eventually, I sought relief in an air-conditioned exhibit hall. I joined the crowd gathered around an incubator.

Inside, fluffy chicks closed their eyelids and dozed beneath the warm lights. Several eggs remained intact amid broken eggshells. One egg sported a hole the size of a dime. A small yellow beak appeared from inside. The beak pecked against the eggshell, flaking it like paint. Another chip, and still another. The progress was slow, and the chick rested from time to time. But it never gave up. Every time it started pecking, I found myself inwardly cheering for it. About thirty minutes later, the chick, streaked with wet black feathers, tumbled out of the egg, and a small cheer rose from the crowd.

Watching that chick gave me new determination. Now, whenever I encounter an obstacle and the odds seem insurmountable, I remember that tiny beak pecking away, millimeter by millimeter, until all that remained was an empty shell... and a new life!

Lord, help me to remember that becoming a new creature may take a lot of work and persistence. —Terry Helwig

Day Brightener

LADDER OF ACHIEVEMENT

100%—I did.
90%—I will.
80%—I can.
70%—I think I can.
60%—I might.
50%—I think I might.
40%—What is it?
30%—I wish I could.
20%—I don't know how.
10%—I can't.
0%—I won't.

Friday

17

Doth a fountain send forth at the same place sweet water and bitter? —James 3:11

Misery was etched on the face of the man who sat near us in the fast-food restaurant. For a while he ate in silence; then he held a little box against his throat and spoke to his friend with a strange, buzzing sound. I realized his voice box had been removed and he was speaking with the aid of a machine.

I was about to say to my wife Sharon, "How wonderful that science can correct such problems," when suddenly I got the drift of what he was saying with such difficulty. His remarks were a caustic commentary on the world conditions and every other word was a swear word!

"Goodness, you'd think he'd be grateful to have his voice back," I whispered to Sharon.

She grinned. "Oh, I don't know. He doesn't sound much different from you when you get in a blue mood, except that you don't swear."

I laughed uneasily, suddenly remembering all the times I grumbled at and about my students. Too often my conversation is only a long growl about the weather or the cafeteria food or the long wait in traffic. If we were allowed voices only if we deserved them, I'd probably not qualify too well!

I left the restaurant determined to be more positive. Sure, there is much that is wrong with the world, but complaining does little to change it. Instead, I will look for what I can praise and show appreciation for both my life and my voice.

Dear Lord, You have given us the miracle of speech. Teach us to use it with respect and reverence. —Daniel Schantz

Saturday

18

But we have this treasure in jars of clay to show that this all-surpassing power is from God and not from us. —II Corinthians 4:7 (NIV)

Several years ago I spent two weeks in the tiny mountain village of Danli, Honduras. When it came time to go, I wanted a special memento of my visit. "Buy this, señorita," the vendor said, shoving a brightly painted jar into my hands. I shook my head. "I want that one," I said, pointing to a plain jug on the shelf behind him. "No, no!" he fussed. "It is ugly! How about one with gold trim?" I shook my head. "That one," I insisted. Finally he sold me the piece, a plain, unfired pot made from the clay of Danli. "You'll never get it home," the missionary said. "It's too fragile." But I was determined. So I wrapped it in my beach towel, tucked it in my carry-on tote, and hugged it to me all the way home.

Now that clay pot sits in my family room, a fond reminder of my days in Honduras. But it reminds me of something else, too. God's "treasure," the Spirit of His Son, is housed in me, a plain, vulnerable vessel. A vessel dependent on God's care: on His granting me sleep at the end of a hard day; sending me a cheery phone call from a friend when I feel blue; helping me merge into the crowded freeway traffic; guiding me through His Word.

I've never thought of my clay pot as ugly. And its frailty has made me cherish it even more. Perhaps that's the way God feels, too.

Hug me to You, Father. Let Your light shine through the fragile fiber of my being. —Mary Lou Carney

Sunday

19

He maketh the storm a calm.... —Psalm 107:29

A storm howled outside the concert hall, as inner turmoil raged within me. Money problems, an argument with my wife and a friend's acid comments about my competitive nature bombarded me like the rain and winds whipping the trees. My attention then returned to the soloist, whose lovely voice filled the hall. Her ease of manner was attractive and her face glowed as she sang. For the moment I forgot about the storm.

After her performance, I made my way through the guests to congratulate the soloist. When I reached her, I was amazed to see that she was supported by two metal crutches grasping her forearms! But her handicap didn't dampen her or her enthusiasm for music or for life. "I was a music teacher before my hip problem," she told me, "but now I sing all the time." She had risen above her illness to enrich others' lives.

The storm outside continued, but I went away feeling her inner peace. The soloist reminded me that I could use God's gift—be it a financial problem, a handicap, or even a crisis—to quell any storms

I might face. Today or any day, no matter what may impede me, I have a Buffer to help me through any inclement condition. And so, too, do you.

Heavenly Father, knowing Your gifts are within my reach, I can face head-on any storm that may be brewing. —Oscar Greene

Monday

20

He heals the brokenhearted, and binds up their wounds. —Psalm 147:3 (RSV)

When I first started teaching college in New York City, I admired a veteran professor named Jim. He was a happy-go-lucky person, until he lost a valued promotion. Then I watched him slide into depression. I wanted to make Jim feel better, but I didn't know what to say. Though I sympathized with his pain, I had never gone through what he had. So I did nothing. Finally, out of cowardice, I wrote Jim a note. I avoided the issue of his promotion and focused on his fine teaching. Then I slipped the note in his mailbox, hoping I hadn't done the wrong thing.

The next day, as I was tiptoeing past Jim's office, his door opened. I looked up to find Jim's face beaming at me. "Thanks," he said. "That note was just the comfort I needed. You did exactly the right thing."

It's so hard to know what is the "right thing" to do when friends are depressed or grieving. Yet looking back, here's what I learned from my experience with Jim.

1. *Don't* give in to your own indecision.
2. *Do* something as soon as possible.
3. *Don't* give advice unless asked.
4. *Do* listen with patience and sympathy.
5. *Don't* tell your friend that you know exactly how he or she feels. You don't, exactly.
6. *Do* something practical and tangible. Treat him or her to a meal, give a small gift, write an upbeat note.

Lord, where there is hurt, let me be brave enough to try to heal.

—Linda Ching Sledge

Tuesday
21

And be ye kind one to another.... —Ephesians 4:32

I'll never forget one summer day when I was eight and my mother sent me out for milk. She wanted it in a hurry, so I rode my bike to the grocery store down the road. Carrying the glass quart bottle in my hand as I steered home, I hit a bump, and I, and the milk, went sprawling. The bottle shattered and milk spilled everywhere.

My knee was scraped up and I hurt all over, but I was even more afraid of being yelled at when I got home. My family didn't exactly have extra money to waste, and it was just before dinner. But when I wheeled my bike into our yard, my father rushed toward me. "Are you all right?" he asked, seeing my forlorn face. "Did you get cut?" Only after carefully checking me over did we go to clean up the glass.

When my son Tim was eight years old, he wanted to help by feeding the horses when his dad was sick. As he carried a big armful of hay through the gate, he forgot to close it behind him, and all the horses escaped. When he told me, I wanted to scream! "Tim, how c—" I began. But a picture rose to my mind of my father's face. He'd had to make a split-second choice: to yell at me for my mistake or to react toward me with love and concern. I had to go out and get the horses back, but I had something else I had to do first. I took a deep breath and reached my hand out to touch Tim's tearstained cheek. "Are you all right, son?" I asked.

Lord, when the people I care about make mistakes, let me react with love and forgiveness—just as You do with me.

—Aletha Jane Lindstrom

Wednesday
22

Fireside Friend 

What wilt thou have me to do? —Acts 9:6

As the wide-bodied DC-10 prepared for takeoff, the attendant announced over the intercom that this was the farewell flight of the captain, a man who had been a pilot with that airline for thirty-two years.

A spontaneous round of applause from the passengers followed the announcement. Then the captain got on the intercom and announced his intention "to really grease it in" when we reached our destination.

Grease it in... I knew that must have something to do with landing the plane, something to do with one's ability, skill and thirty-two years of practice putting three hundred thousand pounds of plane on the ground.

The flight went smoothly—clear sailing and a landing where the ground seemed to come up and meet the plane halfway. On the captain's last flight, he did indeed "grease it in."

I know we will all have a "final flight," a last conversation with "the Tower." I need to remind myself of that and remember Who's really at the controls. Let's all do a few practice takeoffs and landings today—while we're at it, why don't we stay on our knees long enough to make sure we have a clear signal from the Tower. I don't know about you, but when it's all said and done, it sure would be a great feeling for me to have developed enough faith "to really grease it in."

God, remind me daily to check in with You about my flight plans.

—Debbi Smoot

Thursday

23

Fireside Friend

If ye have faith as a grain of mustard seed... nothing shall be impossible unto you. —Matthew 17:20

Do you worry? Or can you turn everything over to the Lord, always confident that He will take care of things? I can't. By nature I'm a worrier. I used to feel badly about this, because when you think about it, worry and anxiety are a symptom of flawed faith. If I really believed in the Lord's wisdom, goodness and mercy, why couldn't I just turn my problems over to Him?

The answer to my question came through one of the great faith stories in the New Testament. In Mark 9:14-29, a man approaches Jesus and asks Him to heal his son of convulsions. But the boy's father admits his faith is far from perfect, saying, "Lord, I believe; help thou mine unbelief" (Mark 9:24). The Lord heals the boy, and the message is clear: The Lord doesn't expect perfection in our faith.

I have now adopted these words as my own personal faith prayer. Recently, my husband left on a trip to Japan only days after a tragic plane crash had shocked the world and other terrorist threats of more plane bombings had been looming. As the monitor in the airport lounge flashed "Departed" next to his flight number, my stomach began to tighten. It would be fourteen hours before he would be on the ground again, and I was in for a real worry marathon.

Then my prayer came to me: "Lord, I believe; help thou mine unbelief." I kept repeating these words to myself, until the din of fearful "what-ifs" was replaced by feelings of calmness and confidence in the Lord. My husband returned safely, of course, but more than that, my faith was steady once again. That's not to say that faith protects us from life's sorrows or tragedies. But always, we can believe in Him Who carries us through anything. And that kind of faith is guaranteed to make our travels through life secure.

Lord, Your love and patience are boundless. Shield me from my fears; rescue me from the barren wastelands of my unbelief.

—Stephanie Oda

Friday

24

I have played the fool, and have erred exceedingly.

—I Samuel 26:21

The scraggy, snaggy red cedar, a gift from the previous owner, stood sentinel at the northwest corner of our yard for years. It crowded the walkway that led into the back, but because I like trees I resisted the urge to remove it for several years. Then, it got to bothering me. The tree certainly was not pretty, it was obtrusive and it didn't even provide much shade. So one day, I took a bow saw from the garage and proceeded to lay the twenty-five-footer low. But as it fell, something scurried from its branches, and even before I saw what it was I knew from the whirring sound of wings that in addition to a tree I had uprooted a turtle dove.

My heart sank as I investigated and found a nest. Fortunately, it was in late summer so it contained no fledglings. I had discovered too late that the cedar had had a value unperceived by me. It was not the first time I have made an error of this sort. More seriously I have done it with people. Perhaps you have, too.

Even though we know we can't judge a book by its cover (or, as they say where I hail from, the depth of a well by the length of its pump handle), we do it every day. And our misjudgments are humbling reminders that we have daily need of the Lord's reproof and correction. Our only hope is that in time through prayer and God's grace we will receive second sight, the kind that sees beyond superficials and reveals the Christ in others, the kind that helps us distinguish between lasting and passing, wise and foolish, worthwhile and worthless.

Give us wisdom, Lord, and understanding, too,
Forgivings that are many, judgments that are few.

—Fred Bauer

Saturday

25

Lo, children are a heritage of the Lord: and the fruit of the womb is his reward. —Psalm 127:3

Our whole family sat together in a circle on a blanket, munching fried chicken at the end-of-the-season Teen Tennis picnic one August evening. Correction! Four and a half members of our family sat together. Lindsay, fourteen, was only half there, which is the way she had seemed most of the time lately. She perched on the edge of the blanket, her back to us, laughing with her friends. I missed her constant chatter and little-girl grin in our family circle. I started feeling sorry for myself and my sad turned to mad. *Insensitive, inconsiderate, uncaring* were some of the "mad" words buzzing through my head as the tennis coaches began announcing the annual awards.

First was Most Improved; then Most Valuable; next was Sportsmanship. "This award goes to the person who knows the importance of being a team player. She's always a good sport, no matter how many changes we make. She's consistently the most *sensitive, considerate, caring* member of our team. Lindsay Kuykendall!"

Lindsay turned around, flashed us her little-girl grin and marched up to claim her trophy. I sat in stunned silence for a moment, and then started clapping loudly. Not only for her, but for the lesson I'd just learned about the importance of being a team player and a good sport on our family team—especially as our circle gently changes shape.

Lord, a family is the first team You created. May we all learn to be good sports and considerate team players. —Carol Kuykendall

Sunday

26

Fireside Friend

Be filled with the Spirit. —Ephesians 5:18

"Mom, come quick! Boppo's dead!"

I ran to the sound of the frantic screams and found my five-year-old son Timmy kneeling beside his quickly sinking friend. Orange hair, a big smile, bright clown suit and sand-weighted bottom. Boppo the Clown. Timmy's favorite toy.

No matter how hard or frequently Timmy punched, old Boppo faithfully bopped back up. But Boppo developed a slow leak and came up a little slower each time. We ignored the leak, but the day of reckoning had arrived. One last punch; Boppo lost his infilling of air and just couldn't get back up.

In the past, as I coped with the demands of three small children and multiple miscarriages, I had often identified with that toy: No matter how many blows came my way I just kept bopping back. I consoled my son beside the "body" of his companion and wondered if one day I too would receive one blow too many and not be able to get up.

As I pondered over the "Boppo Syndrome" I realized that there are two keys to keep me from becoming like that discarded toy: I must seek daily the infilling of the Holy Spirit through prayer and Bible study, and be diligent in spotting those "slow leaks," like lack of devotional time and overlooked bad habits. I realized how quickly those slow leaks could rob me of that infilling power.

When I make those two steps part of my daily life then I can remain upright... or at least keep boppin' back.

Lord, thanks for using the simplicity of a child's toy to remind me of Your indwelling presence. —Bonnie Wheeler

Monday

27

Do not judge by appearances, but judge with right judgment. —John 7:24 (RSV)

A few summers ago, I auditioned for a community theater production of *Fiddler on the Roof* and won the role of Chava, Tevye's youngest daughter.

"Maybe you'll meet an interesting guy," my best friend suggested. *Interesting* was too mild a word. Actors were a little too weird for me. The theater students in high school and college always dressed the wildest, stood on tables and sang the loudest at parties, and talked to themselves, memorizing dialogue while walking to class. I was too normal for that crowd.

Later I found out that the actor who played opposite me in *Fiddler* felt the same way about theater people. He doubted he'd ever meet someone and fall in love doing a show. Yet that's exactly what happened to us. Paul and I have been married for three years now, and we often laugh at how God brought us together when we least expected it.

Next time you catch yourself trying to shut people out by slapping neat labels on them based on their jobs, where they live or the color of their skin, consider for a moment why God might want them in your life. After falling in love with a "theater person," I learned that God doesn't care too much for labels. He'd much rather surprise us. And what wonderful surprises come in God's packages!

Open my heart to Your surprises, Lord, and to each exciting new person You bring into my life. —Gina Bridgeman

Tuesday

28

Behold, your king is coming to you, humble, and mounted on an ass.... —Matthew 21:5 (RSV)

Our old green station wagon is definitely a candidate for the endangered species list. Once the gear shift fell off in my hand, and another time a minor explosion caused black smoke to billow out from under it. But somehow my husband has coaxed it from extinction on innumerable occasions.

By far the most humiliating incident for the whole family occurred the day we had a flat tire driving into another town. We suffered a second flat leaving town and had no spare to replace it. There was nothing to do but rattle and shake two miles back to the nearest gas station with our tire flopping uselessly around its rim. As other cars passed us (we were going only fifteen miles per hour), our children slouched way down in their seats out of embarrassment.

I understand perfectly the children's reaction because my own has often mirrored it. I like to "look good" in the eyes of others. If I'm driving and get lost, I often hesitate to seek help. Sometimes I'll refuse to try a new project for fear I'll bungle it. Or, in conversation, I might nod my head pretending to comprehend what another person's saying, even though I'm confused or don't agree.

I wonder how the Lord would feel about climbing in my old rusted-out car? Or riding beside me when I'm hopelessly lost? Or knowing of my inner confusion? Maybe He would note my discomfiture and graciously tell me, "Let go of the pride that so easily clings to appearances. I'm using this moment to teach you humility."

Could it be that humility is on the "endangered values list" these days? If so, what is God using in your life to save this rare attribute from extinction?

Lord, remind me:

If I live by pride I will surely slide,
But a heart that's humble will not stumble.

—Carol Knapp

Wednesday

29

Fireside Friend 

I have calmed and quieted my soul, like a weaned child...like a weaned child is my soul within me.

—Psalm 131:2 (MLB)

We had been staying in Lupton, Arizona, a small town on the edge of the Navajo Reservation. We were visiting my nephew Tony, who works at a trading post with Navajo silversmiths, when we decided to take a drive to nearby New Mexico.

As we crossed the state line, there was an elderly Navajo woman tending sheep. She wore a gray sweater over her forest-green velvet blouse and her faded green cotton skirt hung to her ankles. Her face was wrinkled and weathered, but what I have never forgotten was her complete stillness and serenity as she stood there looking down at the sheep. She was still standing there, in almost the same spot, on our return trip three hours later.

My own life is so hectic that it is sometimes very difficult to slow down to the point of stillness. And yet, it is those times when I recollect my scattered forces, when I am still enough to wait upon the Lord in quiet prayer, that I am filled with a deep peace and joy.

Whenever I get the feeling that I have to be in several places at once, I remember the elderly Navajo woman tending her sheep. I see again the acceptance and patience and serenity on her face, and I stop and make time for a few quiet moments to sit in the presence of God.

Father, help me to slow down long enough to hear that still, small voice within me, Your voice, filling my soul with peace.

—Georgiana Sanchez

Thursday

30

Thou shalt rise up before the hoary head, and honor the face of the old man.... —Leviticus 19:32

I can count on the fingers of one hand the number of times the kids have used the pool this summer. Only a few years ago we practically lived out there. Our industrial-strength swing set in the woods hasn't heard a child's laughter in years, and the Flexible Flyers hang on the garage wall gathering dust, while the ancient toy chest squats beside my youngest child's bed, sulking.

They're all tangible reminders of yesterday, all useless now. No, not useless—*unused*. There's a big difference between those two words. Once I give these things to the grandchildren for whom they're being saved, they will again be used and useful.

The same principle applies to people, of course. The retired man down the street may be unused by any business, but he is not useless. An ignored relative is an untapped source of strength and acceptance—unused, not useless. Someday soon, I'll be old, too, with no children to care for, no family meals to prepare. I hope I have the grace to stand tall and proud like our unused swing set. I hope I'll remember the distinction between unused and useless then. I pray my children will, too.

Father, don't ever let me allow those I love to feel useless. Remind me to make that telephone call on Sunday and write that note this week.

—Toni Sortor

Friday

31

Follow the truth at all times...and so become more and more in every way like Christ....

—Ephesians 4:15, 16 (TLB)

When my son Patrick was ten, he chose gardening as his 4-H Club project. The summer was unusually dry, and invading grasshoppers ate more beans and lettuce than we did. By County Fair time, the small vegetables were gone and the vine crops weren't yet ripe.

Pat had to exhibit to complete the project, so he chose a huge, beautifully shaped pumpkin. He cut the stem to the precise one and one-half inch length specified in the rules book, then polished the olive green shell until it gleamed.

A pumpkin that wasn't orange caused quite a stir among fair-goers. Grown-ups stared. Little kids asked, "What is it?" A fellow 4-H member even asked, "Why did you bother bringing that weird green thing?"

To everyone's amazement, the pumpkin received a purple ribbon: Grand Champion. "It's still immature," the judge explained, "but it has good qualities and great potential."

I try to remember Pat's pumpkin when I'm tempted to judge from appearances or actions. Instead of criticizing that teenage boy who wore ragged jeans to church, I'll compliment the way he read the Scripture lesson, making a difficult passage come alive. It's up to me to discover the hidden potential in people, to point out their good qualities and to encourage them as they grow.

Dear Jesus, help me remember that beneath many a weird green exterior, there is a person with the potential for godly perfection.

—Penney Schwab

Thank-You Notes to God

1 ______________________________

2 ______________________________

3 ______________________________

4 ______________________________

5 ______________________________

6 ______________________________

7 ______________________________

8 ______________________________

9 ______________________________

10 ______________________________

11 ______________________________

12 ______________________________

13 ______________________________

14 ______________________________

15 ______________________________

16 ____________________

17 ____________________

18 ____________________

19 ____________________

20 ____________________

21 ____________________

22 ____________________

23 ____________________

24 ____________________

25 ____________________

26 ____________________

27 ____________________

28 ____________________

29 ____________________

30 ____________________

31 ____________________

SEPTEMBER

S	*M*	*T*	*W*	*T*	*F*	*S*
						1
2	3	4	5	6	7	8
9	10	11	12	13	14	15
16	17	18	19	20	21	22
23	24	25	26	27	28	29
30						

SPIRITUAL TREASURE

Be Tolerant

Judge not, that ye be not judged. —Matthew 7:1

Plump fruit, ripe grain, harvest moon. In September we celebrate the abundance of the fields and orchards, which has come after a long season of growing and tending.

Human beings develop through long seasons of growing and tending, too. This month resolve not to judge and criticize, but recognize that the people around you are in the slow process of becoming. God isn't finished with any of them. So be patient. You'll find your own tolerant spirit being extended back to you.

My Monthly Prayer List

Family Prayer for September

Father, help our children to learn in school, not from books alone, but also about friendship and play. Help teachers, also, to bring forth the potential hidden in each child.

Saturday

1

THROUGH AN OPEN WINDOW
Be a Peacemaker

Let us therefore follow after the things which make for peace.... —Romans 14:19

From my window this morning I can see a flag fluttering on a building not far away. It brings back memories of September 2, 1945. V-J Day. The Japanese had formally surrendered to the Allies and World War II was over.

I was eleven years old that day when the news was announced over the radio in my little hometown on Long Island. I recall the shouting, the smiles, how joyful everyone was. Mike Spina, a young soldier who happened to be home on furlough, rounded up all the kids in the neighborhood to form a parade. Everyone who had an American flag carried it. My cousin Daniel ran to get his trombone; a friend Freddy Demarest beat his drum. Up and down the streets of our town we marched. It seemed as if everybody's parents and grandparents had come to stand on their sidewalks, laughing, crying, applauding. As we marched past Mrs. Lagenfeld's house, she rushed up to Mike, her apron flapping in the breeze, and gave him a big hug. "Now my Johnny will be coming home!" she shouted.

I have never forgotten that association of peace with coming home. Isn't that where all of us hope to find "the peace of God, which passeth all understanding" (Philippians 4:7)...at our ultimate homecoming someday?

Meanwhile, shouldn't we be trying to make the dream of world peace a reality? This month, let's pray—really pray—daily for peace in the entire world. Don't let negative thoughts interfere, such as "I'm only one. How can I possibly bring about world peace?" Suppose, for instance, that every reader of *Daily Guideposts,* wherever they are, prayed at noon every day for peace. That would be a powerful lot of praying.

And remember what God said: "If my people, which are called by my name, shall humble themselves, and pray, and seek my face, and turn from their wicked way; then will I hear from heaven, and will forgive their sin, and will heal their land" (II Chronicles 7:14).

Lord, as I pray for peace throughout the world, I also ask You to remove any strife or animosity that is within me. —Eleanor Sass

Sunday

2

Yet will I not forget thee. Behold, I have graven thee upon the palms of my hands.... —Isaiah 49:15–16

I put my papers away, zipped my bag closed, picked up my pen and started out of the room where I'd just given a talk about "Letting Go of Our Children" to a group of young mothers. One lady hesitantly motioned to me as I neared the door. "Could I speak with you?" she stammered, her eyes suddenly brimming with tears.

"Of course," I said, dropping my bag and taking her hand.

"I'm Susan from Louisiana and my friend Andrea...a young mother in our church...just lost her baby... my godchild... a terrible accident... a bureau fell...." Then she sobbed.

"Let me pray for you," I said, aching for their loss. But even as I spoke, I knew my words sounded hollow. Two strangers meet, one reveals a deep need or hurt. "I'll pray for you," the other vows, but does she remember? And here I stood, empty-handed except for my pen. *Aha!*

"Andrea," I wrote on the palm of my hand, as I used to in grade school when I wanted to remember a phone number or homework assignment. "Susan," I added below "Andrea." We talked a few moments and she left.

I prayed for Andrea and Susan until their names began to fade. Then I opened my hand to God, asking Him to keep them in the palm of His hands, healing their hurt and covering their needs. Since that day, "palm prayers" have become a regular habit.

Lord, what a privilege to carry the names of others in the palm of my hand, reminding me to pray for them, and then to lift them up to You as they fade from me. —Carol Kuykendall

Monday
3

For we are laborers together with God....
—I Corinthians 3:9

Today, as we take a break from our working lives and celebrate Labor Day, let's think about why it is we're working and whether we're working too much or not enough and whether we're doing our job well.

My neighbor drops her first-grader off at my house every morning at 6:40 to wait for his school bus so that she has time to drop her preschooler off at the babysitter's and then drive the twenty miles to her job that begins at 7:30. Her husband has a good-paying job from 8 A.M. to 5 P.M., but he goes to bed early so that he can go to his moonlighting job from 2 A.M. till 7 A.M.

I wonder if these friends aren't laboring too hard. Where is the time for a long walk? Some relaxed talk? A leisurely bedtime story with the children? A family picnic? "Alone" time?

When I became a single parent, I decided that even though I could use the extra money that a full-time job would bring, my most important job was raising my four children. I decided to tighten the budget and continue to work part-time, and I've never regretted it.

Is it time for you to take inventory of how hard you work and why? Maybe a change in your work habits will make all the hosts of Heaven and earth proclaim, "Here lived a great worker who did her job well and still had time to enjoy life."

Father, help me not to labor so hard that I have no time to enjoy this wonderful world and the people I treasure most. —Patricia Lorenz

Tuesday
4

Fireside Friend

In everything, do to others what you would have them do to you.... —Matthew 7:12 (NIV)

For years our children were those unsung heroes, news carriers. Each of our four sons took his stint at delivering papers, and their two sisters helped.

They soon learned all the excuses customers give for not paying the monthly bill on time, all the houses where vicious dogs resided, all the bushes to avoid when throwing papers. They learned to cope with snowstorms, blistering heat, undependable substitutes and circulation department errors for which they were invariably blamed.

Yet it was good training for the future. Through the years, the children have worked in discount stores, restaurants, hospitals, banks, swimming pools and schoolrooms. Each of them meets the public well.

My children's experiences prepared me for the future, too. I've learned to be more tolerant, not only with our news carrier, but the TV repairman, plumber and electrician as well. I try to be courteous to sales clerks, receptionists, telephone solicitors (although that's a struggle!) and door-to-door salespeople, knowing that he or she is trying to earn a living.

Come to think of it, that's one way of putting the Golden Rule into practice in my daily life.

Today, Newspaper Carrier Day, I'm thankful for all the folks in jobs of service who make others' lives easier. And, Lord, help me express my love for You by showing tolerance and kindness to them.

—Shirley Pope Waite

Wednesday

5

Love does no harm to its neighbor. Therefore love is the fulfillment of the law. —Romans 13:10 (NIV)

Sometimes I think you can learn more from an episode where you are in the wrong than from one where you are in the right.

During World War II, our Army Air Force authorities took over several hotels in the town of Cannes on the French Riviera. It was a pleasant place to go if you had a few days leave. The French, a proud and sensitive people, had had a hard time under the German occupation, but we American soldiers were comfortable and well-fed.

Cigarettes had considerable value then, and it was considered amusing sometimes to toss a couple to the ragged street urchins and watch them scramble and fight over them.

One day, as a variation on this, we placed four fresh cigarettes on the curb of the street in front of our hotel and settled back on a bench in the hotel garden to see what would happen. Nothing did for a while. Then along came a very pretty French girl. She had no stockings and she was wearing *sabots,* those uncomfortable wooden shoes that many of the French wore because they had nothing else. When she saw the cigarettes, she stopped. Then, slowly and deliberately, with her wooden shoe, she stepped on the first one and mashed it flat. One after another, she ground them all into the pavement. She raised her head, and gave us a stare as savage and superb as the gaze of a lioness. Then she went on down the street while three American soldiers looked at one another and said nothing, because there was nothing to say.

But to this day, whenever I'm tempted to do something thoughtless that may be hurtful or offensive to someone else, I remember the hollow sound of those *sabots* retreating down a sunlit street. And I try not to do it.

Father, help us to feel the hurts of others... before they happen.

—Arthur Gordon

Thursday

6

He kneeled upon his knees three times a day, and prayed, and gave thanks before his God....

—Daniel 6:10

During the second year of our marriage, Carol and I established the half-hour rule: That is, we must talk together half an hour a day. As a busy couple with various commitments, we'd discovered that we always managed to discuss the essential things, like checking the phone bill or balancing the checkbook, but it was easy to forget more important things, such as how I felt about work or maybe how Carol felt about an unresolved argument she'd had with her mother. Moreover, these matters didn't come out until we sat together by ourselves. We had to put aside distractions and think about each other. A quick "How are you?" call from the office was not enough.

I bring this up because I think it's for similar reasons that so many books (including the Bible) suggest a person pray at a set time for a certain length of time every day. Before I close my eyes in the morning to pray, I can blithely convince myself, "Not much bothering me. Not much to pray about today." But when stillness settles over me, festering problems have a way of asking for attention. As in my conversations with Carol, I discover important matters that need to be addressed. For instance, I become aware of my envy for a colleague and I ask God to rid me of it. My anger with a friend comes out and I know I need to forgive him. Or I think of all my wonderful blessings (like conversing with my wife), and I thank God.

Lord, You see what is in our hearts even before we know what's there. Help us respond to those needs in prayer. —Rick Hamlin

Friday

7

When I begin, I will also make an end. —I Samuel 3:12

I didn't look forward to picking the kids up from school. It would be the first afternoon in six weeks that Daniel wasn't in the car waiting for them.

Daniel. The snuggly infant we fostered while steps were taken to place him with the right family. Nikki, nine, and Sean, five, adored his squinty blue eyes and loved to rub his knobby little bald head, calling him "Peachhead." But this morning Daniel left with his adoptive parents. Although we were happy for them, we felt our hearts ripped apart.

The kids trudged to the car, weighed down with more than backpacks and lunch boxes. Instead of going home as usual, we detoured to an ice cream parlor. We all chose "Superman" ice cream, a food dye critic's nightmare of brilliant turquoise, red and yellow. "Three hot fudge sundaes made with Superman, please," I ordered. We sat at a booth and prayed—a combination of thanks for the treat and Godspeed for Daniel.

And as I prayed, it became clear to me: Yes, our time with Daniel was ended, but for Daniel's new parents, it was just beginning. One day Nikki and Sean would leave me, too, to start their adult lives. But the end of their childhoods would give me a chance to become new again also, to discover parts of myself and face different challenges.

"Now we need to toast Daniel," I said, raising a spoonful of Superman sundae. Nikki hoisted her dripping spoon, and Sean followed suit. "To Daniel."

In that moment, the tendrils of our hearts began to heal. And with the clinking of three spoons, we anticipated a new day.

Dear Lord, remind me that with You, endings always lead to new beginnings. —B. J. Connor

Saturday

8

As ye abound in every thing, in faith, and utterance, and knowledge, and in all diligence, and in your love to us, see that ye abound in this grace also.

—II Corinthians 8:7

It's bulk trash pickup on our street tomorrow, and all week beside the road the piles of castoffs have been growing. Discarded storm windows, an old TV, a broken trike. Driving past these heaps of discards, I've been seeing another street—the road past our house in Uganda—and a man literally leaping for joy as he walked....

The house we'd rented was in a neighborhood of mud-walled homes strung along a red-earth track. There was no trash pickup there; nobody threw things out. Our house, in fact, had the only trash can along that road: a small lidless barrel, which we would take at infrequent intervals to a nearby dump.

One morning I answered a knock to find a neighbor standing at the door. In his hands was an orange-soda bottle I had put in the barrel the evening before.

"Pardon for this disturbance," he began in the formal school-learned English of Uganda, "but as I passed your house my eyes beheld this." He held up the empty bottle. "I have asked of myself..." he stammered on, "is it that you have no further plan for it? I am not a thief," he added hastily. "It is only that finding it here in this barrel...."

I was the one now to stammer for words. "Of course... take it," I said. "I'm just sorry I didn't—I should have offered it in a more...."

But at the words "take it," he had headed off up the road. The last I saw of him he was running, leaping, all but dancing along that dirt track in the exhilaration of sudden wealth.

I've been thinking about that man as the trash piles grow along our street. Ours has been called the throw-away society—stripping the forests, polluting the seas, despoiling the earth. If we made do with less, I've been asking myself, might we too dance with the joy of gratitude?

Father, we would not be rich in things, poor in soul.

—Elizabeth Sherrill

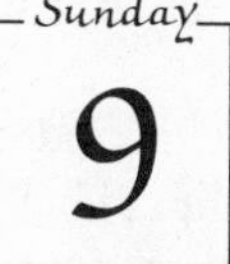

You are no longer strangers...but you are fellow... members of the household of God....

—Ephesians 2:19 (RSV)

In Sunday school one morning we launched into a discussion of how much darkness there was in the world. War, hunger, hate, homelessness. "When will it end?" a woman asked.

Her question reminded me of the rabbi who asked his students a question. "When does night end and day begin?"

One student asked, "Is it the moment you're able to perceive the difference between an olive tree and a fig tree?"

"No," said the rabbi. "That's not it."

"Is it the moment you can tell the difference between a sheep and a dog?" asked another.

The rabbi shook his head. "No, that's not it either. Rather it is the moment you look at the face of a stranger and recognize that it is really the face of your brother."

Perhaps that *is* when night ends in our world and day begins. Today, if I practice seeing the strangers who come my way as brothers and sisters, I suspect I might find a new attitude dawning in my life. And who knows, maybe there will be even a bit more light in the world.

God, give me the vision of love. —Sue Monk Kidd

Monday

10

So exercise yourself spiritually and practice being a better Christian.... —I Timothy 4:8 (TLB)

Recently my friend Kathy visited her long-lost relatives in Switzerland. Their first moments together were a bit awkward. But Kathy says real unity came when, before dinner, her cousin announced, "In this house we are practicing Christians. Let us pray."

Downstairs I hear my sixteen-year-old daughter Amy Jo at the piano, working on those tricky fingerings in the *Warsaw Concerto.* Outside my window I see thirteen-year-old Brett kicking the soccer ball, trying to get his dribble just right. Both are practicing. Why? Because they know that practice makes... well, *better.* They know their hard work will pay off in improved performance.

So today I'm going to work hard, too. I'll try to be a little kinder when my hardworking husband tracks in mud. More patient as I help Brett with long division. And a little calmer when Amy Jo wants to use the phone—again. I'll listen to my grandmotherly neighbor Katie tell me—for the fourth time this week—about her bursitis. I'll flip off the TV and read my Bible instead. Today I'm going to *practice* being a Christian. Won't you join me?

I'm not all I should be—or could be, Father. But I'm working on it! You will help me, won't You? Thanks! —Mary Lou Carney

Tuesday

11

And what is the immeasurable greatness of his power in us who believe.... —Ephesians 1:19 (RSV)

In a recent news article, I learned that a man from Alaska expects to collect a thousand tons of ice every week for shipment to Japan. The ice is broken down from icebergs and measured into sacks weighing a few pounds, then sold for around seven dollars. Glacial ice, it seems, produces a refreshing crackle while floating in a beverage and lasts twice as long as ordinary ice cubes.

These mammoth glaciers began when a few snowflakes clustered together, trapping tiny air bubbles inside. The weight of additional snow and ice eventually forced out the trapped air, turning the grains of ice a startling blue. Year after year they continued packing, forming a thick sheet that began to slide over the land. Permanent traces of their presence are still seen in misplaced boulders, smooth rounded rocks and isolated ponds.

A snowflake, by itself an insignificant crystal of ice, can in great numbers become a gigantic moving force capable of rearranging mountains. Yet, I know what it is to feel like a "singular snowflake." My husband had gone ahead of us to Alaska, and I was left to pack, to organize a garage sale, to sell a car, to rent our home and to watch four children. As snowflakes go, I would quickly have melted if not for all the people who clustered around and helped me. Together we created our own moving force, and I was transformed from weakness into strength by the presence of these caring friends.

Snowflakes cluster and become mighty forces; God's people joined together also become mighty channels for His wonder-working power! Today, can you think of a single snowflake you can cluster with? Maybe, together, you can move mountains.

Lord, use the unparalleled message of the glacier to advance Your kingdom in our lives this very day. —Carol Knapp

Wednesday

12

Give us this day our daily bread. —Matthew 6:11

Do you ever think about the bread you eat? Flaky buttermilk biscuits... crunchy bran muffins... feathery crescent dinner rolls?

I do, because we grow wheat on our farm. Each September we drill the tiny seeds into fertile brown soil. The green blades push through the ground, but lie dormant through the winter. They begin rapid growth in the first warm days of spring, and combines harvest the golden grain in midsummer.

This year we planted *Vona,* but we've also grown *Tam* and *Satanta*. There are many varieties of wheat grown on the plains, but the one I think of the most is *Turkey Red.* Turkey Red was brought to the United States in 1874 by Mennonite immigrants from the steppes of Russia. They arrived with little more than their faith in God and their faith that this wheat would thrive in their adopted land—and it did. In fact, all of the various kinds of hard red winter wheat grown on the plains have a common ancestor: Turkey Red.

So when I look at bread, I see more than a fragrant loaf. I see those Mennonites traveling across continents with their tiny seeds, trusting to God that they would grow. And when I see rustling, waving fields of wheat I see more than a crop—I see a powerful testimony to a people who had faith that God could make their dreams come true. It's the kind of faith I pray to have more of—every day.

Dear Lord, help me take the tiny seeds of my dreams and trust that with Your help and my faith and hard work, they can grow to something magnificent—as magnificent as bread. —Penney Schwab

Thursday

13

Fireside Friend

For the same Lord over all is rich unto all that call upon him. —Romans 10:12

It was my sixteenth birthday and I had just returned from spending the summer with my cousin, only to discover my best friend and my boyfriend had fallen hopelessly in love.

Sensing my devastation, Dad's imagination swung into action. "Imagine your body's an empty vessel, Mary Jane. The top of your head a golden lid. And God, high above, silver chalice tilted...."

"I can't play games right now, Daddy," I interrupted him.

"Sure you can, honey. Besides, this is no game. God *is* there, waiting to fill your emptiness with the love of forgiveness and understanding. *All you have to do is open yourself to Him.*"

Everett and Jewelle have long since married and raised a family, and I have long since discovered the true magic of Dad's imagination—and when I become distressed, disappointed or just plain frustrated with life and the people in it, I draw on it. Because Dad was right. God *is* always there, waiting to drain the anger, envy or just plain weariness away and fill me with the balm of His healing love.

Do you seem to be losing the battle with painful hurts today? Why not give Daddy's imagination and God a chance?

Father, this moment I open myself to You. Fill me.

—Mary Jane Meyer

Friday

14

If any of you lack wisdom, let him ask of God....

—James 1:5

On the wall of a local auto parts store, a sign reads:

—PRICE SCHEDULE—

Due to the volume of questions directed at counter personnel and the amount of time taken to answer them, we are forced to institute the following policy:

Answers $1.00
Answers that make sense $2.00
Right answers $5.00
Dumb looks are still free!

There is a truth buried within that wry humor: Wisdom is a precious commodity. The author of Proverbs declared over and over that wisdom is "more precious than gold."

Lately I've needed wisdom more than ever as my kids are nearing adolescence. Like so many others, my sons tend to leave a mess wherever they go. When my wife Joy took a part-time job last winter, the house began to look like a disaster area.

One day it got to be too much for overworked Joy. What could we do? I'd tried reasoning with the kids, and it wasn't working. With a sigh and a "flash prayer" asking for wisdom, I headed upstairs. When I faced the three culprits, I blurted out, "All right, no more living like slobs. From now on, no one will pick up anything for you. Things left out after bedtime will disappear. That's final!"

That first night three dollars and two favorite toys disappeared off bedroom floors. More disappeared the next day. But after five days, my sons had the neatest bedrooms in town—and a dad who'd learned a little more about parenting from his Heavenly Father.

Do you, like me, face problems you need answers to right now? Stop and pray, asking for God's wisdom, and then step into confronting them. As James says in the Bible, wisdom is something "He gives generously to all" (James 1:5, RSV). All we have to do is ask!

Dear Lord, help me live in trust that no matter how confusing the challenges I face today are, You will give me whatever wisdom I need to confront them. —Eric Fellman

Saturday

15

WINDOWS INTO WONDER
When the World Closes In

Behold, I see the heavens opened.... —Acts 7:56

Men full of fear and irrational hatred had been tracking young Stephen like a pack of hungry wolves. Now they were moving in for the kill. False witnesses testified that this faithful apostle of the crucified Christ was saying blasphemous things about the Temple and the Law of Moses. Stephen bravely accused his attackers of being "betrayers and murderers of the Just One" (Acts 7:52). The mob became enraged and gnashed their teeth at him, a signal threatening death. Imagine the terror that must have gripped Stephen as he saw those raging men start to gather rocks with which to stone him to death! He could have tried to run, or pleaded for his life, or collapsed in panic. Instead he stood firm and steady, raising his eyes to the heavens. In that moment when the world was closing in on Stephen, the heavens opened up for him, and he saw a vision of the glory of God, and Jesus standing on the right hand of God. It was all the reassurance he needed. Jesus lived. Knowing that, he could face the pain, and he went to his death with a prayer that echoes Jesus' last words, "Lord Jesus, receive my spirit" (Acts 7:59).

You and I will probably never have to face a threat as dire as Stephen's, but there are times in every life when the world seems to be closing in. Friends betray us, or we lose our job, or a beloved family member becomes gravely ill, and we feel as though we're falling into a deep abyss from which there is no escape. I felt this way during a recent family crisis. I kept praying about the problem, asking God to change the situation, but all that focusing on what was wrong made me feel even more hopeless. One gray fall day, my emotional pain seemed almost unbearable. I had to do something, so I went for a walk. About three blocks from home, the clouds broke, and it seemed to me that the sky split open. Golden rays of sun streamed down on me. Suddenly, I had a deep inner assurance that Jesus lives, and that, *no matter what happened,* I could go on, and that I would never be alone.

There is a truth in this that is practical, even in those little daily crises that can so easily destroy our peace of mind. This month, whenever the world seems to be closing in on us, let's try to focus on God instead of on our problem. We might even want to go outside and look up at the sky, as a reminder of Stephen's vision and the courage it gave him. Then we can pray the most important prayer of all: *Lord Jesus, receive my spirit.* —Marilyn Morgan Helleberg

September Prayer List Reminder

Return to your Monthly Prayer List on the calendar opening page and review your requests. Give thanks for prayers answered, renew old prayers and add new concerns today. Then pray once again our *Family Prayer for September.*

Sunday

16

But lay up for yourselves treasures in heaven... where thieves do not break in and steal.

—Matthew 6:20 (RSV)

After an absence of twenty years, my friends Eliska and Ludvik—Elsa and Lou—planned a summer visit to their native Czechoslovakia and Europe. Everything went smoothly until they got to Italy. Someone broke into their car and stole several hundred dollars. After that, Elsa and Lou hid all their valuables in hard-to-reach places throughout the car. Elsa's Bible, a one-hundred-year-old family treasure, and several pieces of heirloom jewelry were buried in a suitcase and packed safely in the trunk.

Then, on the last day in Italy, another unfortunate accident: A driver rammed their auto and the gas tank exploded, instantly engulfing the car in flames. Lou and Elsa fled the car with no time to grab their valuables. All but one treasure was lost. Sifting through the charred wreckage, they found Elsa's family Bible, smudged with ashes and smelling of smoke, but not a single page singed.

When she showed me the Bible, I handled it reverently. It seemed I was holding eternity in my hands...the treasured Word of God, withstanding all manner of opposition through the ages. Still it proclaimed the one message that cannot be destroyed, the one I clasp tightly every day: There is a Savior, Christ the Lord, Who has promised never to fail or forsake me. He is the Treasure in Elsa's Bible.

Gracious Father, when I'm feeling impoverished, don't let me overlook the priceless treasure inside the pages of Your Holy Book.

—Carol Knapp

Day Brightener

Tell him about the heartache,
And tell him the longings, too.
Tell him the baffled purpose
When we scarce know what to do.
Then leaving all our weakness
With the One divinely strong,
Forget that we bore a burden
And carry away a song.

—Phillips Brooks

Monday

17

Children are a gift from God.... —Psalm 127:3 (TLB)

Several years ago I flew to Kansas to interview Glenn Cunningham, one of America's premier runners in the thirties. He had set the world record for the mile and won a silver medal in the Berlin Olympics. What made Cunningham's feat pure Horatio Alger was a childhood accident that he overcame. He was burned so badly at age twelve in a one-room school explosion that doctors feared he would never walk again. But he not only regained the use of his legs and walked, he ran—for a while faster than any mile-runner alive.

But I didn't go to Kansas to hear about his miraculous recovery or his headline-making athletic accomplishments. Rather, I wanted to learn about his life work that began after the glory days. Glenn and his wife Ruth were remarkable Christians whose deep love for children led them to start a ranch for troubled and orphaned youngsters. They didn't have much money, but they invested all they had in this work, and over the years they cared for nine thousand abused and delinquent boys and girls, many of whom have gone on to productive lives.

Today, I read in the newspaper that Glenn Cunningham has died at age seventy-eight. His obituary naturally highlights his athletic victories, but for me they are only footnotes to his real greatness. What I remember is a single sentence that capsules his all-consuming passion. It should be written on the heart of this nation and embraced by everyone who shapes the lives of young people—parents, grandparents, coaches, youth workers, teachers. "Nothing," he said simply, "is as important as a child."

Don't let us forget, Lord...
When our race is over and life is summed up,
The winner's the giver with an empty cup.

—Fred Bauer

Tuesday

18

I have planted, Apollos watered; but God gave the increase. —I Corinthians 3:6

I worked with a woman whose office temperament skyrocketed or plummeted depending on her romantic situation of the moment. If she and her former husband had an argument, she was hostile and sullen. If she and her new boyfriend had a good dinner date, she was jovial and productive.

I felt sorry for her unsettling quest for Prince Charming and Happily Ever After. When she announced she was moving, I wanted to talk with her about anchoring her life in Jesus. We had lunch together on her last day, but I didn't have the nerve to bring up God's Word.

When we got back to our desks, I mentally kicked myself. There was only one more opportunity. I rolled a piece of scratch paper into my typewriter and whipped off a rough note referring to Psalm 118:8–9: "It is better to trust in the Lord than to put confidence in man. *It is better to trust in the Lord than to put confidence in princes."* I told her I cared about her and that every man would disappoint her sometime, except Jesus. Embarrassed, I pressed it into her hand as she headed for the door.

A few years later, I got a letter from her from out of the blue saying that she had found the Lord. She explained that my note was part of a chain of influences leading to that transformation. She no longer depended on her human relationships for happiness; she trusted her circumstances to God.

Seeing how God "gave the increase" despite my clumsiness has encouraged me to keep "planting" and "watering" ever since.

I hope it will encourage you, too.

I praise You, Lord of the harvest. Give me boldness to speak of You to someone You bring across my path today. —B.J. Connor

Wednesday

19

He found nothing but leaves; for the time of figs was not yet. —Mark 11:13

I was raking leaves one late September day when a small brown-backed bird with a spotted chest flitted out of the woods and just as swiftly darted back. A wood thrush. Not much to look at with his drab coloring: His glory is his song. On spring evenings he's a liquid voice from the forest edge, a flute song at twilight.

Not a sound did this one utter, of course—wrong time of year. Still I gazed longingly into the trees where he had vanished, hoping in vain for some reprise of his rhapsody of four months ago, some thrush-style September song.

What melody that small bird was endowed with, I thought—and how parsimonious he was with his great gift, spending it on his narrow concerns of territory and mating, locked into his cycle of seasonal behavior.

Do we humans, too, have neglected gifts, I wondered, *channeled by habit into narrow repetitive paths, clutched selfishly to our own small uses?* Is God even now looking longingly at His most gifted creation, telling us: "You could sing, if you would!"

Father, I want to spend myself for Your kingdom, in season, out of season. —Elizabeth Sherrill

Thursday

20

Now Israel loved Joseph... and he made him a coat of many colors. —Genesis 37:3

My mother was nervous when she started her new job at a needlecraft shop the year after my father had passed away.

One day, a big car pulled up to the shop, and the driver helped an elderly gentleman to the door. He looked very forbidding and was rather gruff. Although he was a regular customer, everyone in the shop dreaded waiting on him, but my mother was intrigued by this man wanting yarn in somber blacks, whites and beiges. She made a point of being friendly and helpful to him every time he came in. It turned out that he had been a prominent physician, now retired, and that he had lost his wife six months ago. He was lonely, but to keep active, he made alphabet blocks out of yarn and donated them to a nursery school.

Then one day the doctor came in with a bounce and announced, "Today, I want all new colors!" My mother helped him pick out warm reds, sunny yellows, cheery greens and blues for his nursery school blocks.

Puzzled by his change in colors—and disposition—my mother said, "Why, you're so different today. Like a new man—cheerful and happy."

"Yes, my dear," he said, clasping my mother's hands. "Your warm smile helped me realize that the dark times would pass." After that, he always asked for the brightest colors.

Every so often, I have days when everything seems black and white; my moods feel dark and somber. I think of my mother helping the old gentleman through his hard time. Perhaps I could do some giving myself—like the doctor, I could keep active by doing something creative (I've tried growing azalea and rhododendron in our backyard), or like my mother be friendly or helpful (I made lunch for my new neighbors who were moving into the house next door). Small, doable acts, but they helped lift my waning spirits.

Do you find yourself in a dark mood today? Find something to do—for yourself or another. The change may not happen overnight, but sooner than you think, you may hear yourself saying, "Today, I want all new colors!"

Lord, when my life gets gloomy, remind me that helping out—whether myself or another—is the quickest way to brighten up my world.

—Anne Moiseev

Friday

21

Therefore when thou doest thine alms, do not sound a trumpet.... —Matthew 6:2

I found a wallet at the post office recently. It was hefty with credit cards, personal photos and money. The owner's address indicated that it was within walking distance, so I headed to the place, thinking how happy the woman would be to get her precious possessions back.

I knocked. The woman cracked open the door. I explained what happened. She reached out, snatched the wallet and closed the door.

I was stunned. That was it? No thank you? No pat on the back? No nothing? As I walked slowly away, thoughts raced through my head: *Wasn't this unfair? Why should I give my best if what I do isn't overtly appreciated?*

I stopped in my tracks. That was a human reaction, but it wasn't God's way. Of course I'd continue to help. As God works through people—in the child who welcomes the new kid in the neighborhood, in the volunteer who gives her time to a hot line, in the low-income family that contributes canned goods to a food drive—so I, too, can offer up myself to do His will... quietly. Just knowing I'm doing it is reward enough.

Lord, let me be a nameless offerer of help, expecting nothing in return each day of my life. —Oscar Greene

Saturday

22

Even as the Son of man came... to give his life a ransom for many. —Matthew 20:28

As I care for my eighty Holsteins, I often remember my first calf. We didn't have a dairy, but even as a nine-year-old, I wanted to be a dairyman one day. So my dad and I headed over to our neighbor Jack's dairy farm. Jack took us into the calf barn where, back in the corner, were three Holstein heifers, each around three days old.

Jack said, "Now, Johnny, you can pick a calf and raise it as your own. But you have to give me back the first heifer calf she has." I had fallen in love with one calf in particular, and before we even had her loaded in the truck, I named her Patsy.

I bottle-fed Patsy, kept her stall clean and taught her to lead. I kept track of her feed records and veterinary expenses for my 4-H record book. I couldn't have been prouder when I took Patsy to the county fair and showed her to all my friends.

As Patsy grew, I grew—both physically and in learning responsibility. Before I knew it, Patsy birthed a newborn baby heifer. I kept telling myself I wasn't going to become attached to her calf, but when I saw that new baby standing there, it was just as when I first laid eyes on Patsy. When the calf was four days old, we took it back to Jack's. I had a lump in my throat, but I had given Jack my word and now it was payment day. I think Jack knew how I was feeling, but he didn't commiserate or sympathize. He just shook my hand as if I were a man and said, "Johnny, I'm proud of you."

I had a good feeling inside as Dad and I got back in the truck and headed home. I had learned about keeping my word, even when it's hard. As I've grown, I've thanked God many times for this early lesson. Giving up that calf wasn't easy, but it was right. And the sweet memory of Jack's handshake stays with me as a reminder. I always want to have the good feeling of having tried to do right—so God can think, "Johnny, I'm proud of you!"

Dear Lord, You, Who gave up Your life for us, know the tender sadness of sacrifice. When I need to give something up, remind me of the sweet pleasure of pleasing You. —John Coen

Sunday

23

Have compassion, making a difference. —Jude 22

Dorothy Miller had been a nun. She gave it up to become a mother. Never married, she adopted ten severely retarded, brain-damaged, emotionally disturbed children. Doctors insisted one underweight girl would only be a vegetable. Dorothy proved them wrong. There were spina bifida children, Down's syndrome and other diagnoses I didn't even begin to understand.

Dorothy ran a tight ship. There was firm discipline, along with unrestrained love. No pity was allowed. Dorothy taught the children to help one another. It was amazing to watch their feeding, tooth-brushing and getting-into-leg-braces routine.

One Sunday, after I was newly widowed, my teenage sons and I were having a heated argument while eating in a restaurant. I ended up crying, leaving my food untouched. Just then Dorothy and her brood came in—smiling, laughing, limping, some pushing wheelchairs. She saw me and waved, and they got seated. One of her boys kept watching me. Finally, he came over, patted my shoulder, looked me directly in the eyes and said with a slight speech impediment and a perfect smile, "I tan see ooh having hard time. It will det better."

"Thank you," I responded, greatly encouraged, half laughing, half crying. He was right. It did get better. I still marvel over the compassion Dorothy Miller instills in each of her remarkable children. It's something I can learn—and be reminded of—from them.

Lord, teach me to make a difference in someone's life—by caring.

—Marion Bond West

Monday

24

Continue ye in my love. —John 15:9

Barbara was the homely twin. Although I tried not to compare the ten-year-old sisters, I couldn't help being astounded by the contrast between them. Barbara was chubby, Betty was slim; Barbara was painfully shy, Betty was assertive and outgoing. Barbara had straight brown hair. Betty's golden curls were the envy of the neighborhood girls. Whenever company came, Betty would smile and start a conversation. Barbara would stare stonily ahead. Neighbors thought Barbara rude.

Driving home from the train station one day, my husband noticed Barbara walking up the hill ahead of us. "Don't bother waving," I told him. "She'll just ignore you."

My husband rolled down his window and grinned. "Hi, Barbara!" he yelled and waved at her. As I predicted, she gave no response.

"See? I told you," I said.

"Look back," replied my husband, watching the child in the rear-view mirror.

I turned and saw Barbara shyly wiggling two fingers at us.

"That little girl needs someone to wave at her," my husband said, "because she doesn't think anyone wants to."

Teach us to see other people's deepest needs, Father, and where there is hurt, sow love. —Linda Ching Sledge

Tuesday

25

Pray without ceasing. —I Thessalonians 5:17

Until recently I always felt that I didn't pray enough, as if there was some specific quota of words or minutes to fill each day.

This may sound irreverent, but one morning I was angry over something that had happened to me and I blamed God. As I drove to school, I muttered like a pouting child, "God, I'm not speaking to You today. I'm upset with You." I didn't realize I was speaking to Him at that very moment.

As the day unfolded, I caught myself starting to pray on more than one occasion.

"Lord, what a beautiful sunrise... *oops.*"

"Father, help me teach this class... *uh, cancel that.*"

"Thank You for friends like... *well, never mind.*"

By the end of the day I had accepted my part in a hurt that had been bothering me that morning, but more important I realized just how tightly my life is woven with prayer. Perhaps you, too, speak to Him more often than you know. I have a growing feeling that God has no "rule of thumb" for the frequency or quantity of prayer. Maybe He meant for prayer to be as normal and sporadic as conversation with a friend, and not some stiff and formal chore done with a grimace and a growl.

Whatever your mood today—fair or foul—it's natural to share your thoughts with your Friend above. Try it now.

Father, help me learn to pray as naturally as I breathe.

—Daniel Schantz

Wednesday

26

For where your treasure is, there will your heart be also. —Matthew 6:21

One evening while my parents were home, two cat burglars broke into their house (police evidence determined there were two). They stole several pieces of jewelry with great sentimental value, including their wedding rings and the ring my dad earned for playing in the 1946 World Series. Although my parents weren't hurt, the goods were never recovered. The timing couldn't have been worse. For months, Mom and Dad had been planning a big party for the following night.

"Why don't you call everyone, explain what's happened, and cancel the party," I told Mom. "Our friends will understand." But Mom and Dad were determined to go ahead with their plans, even though we all felt angry and depressed, and far from a partying mood.

A few hours later, laughter and love filled my parents' home. "I'm here if you need me," said one friend, with a warm hug.

"At least nothing they took had a heartbeat!" said another.

Looking around, I realized that my real treasures are "burglar-proof"—the people I love and our memories together. Too often I'm tempted to cherish things, forgetting the people who give them their meaning. Even my dearest mementos are only reminders. If they're stolen, the memories are still mine; riches that I'll keep forever and leave behind as my legacy.

Dear God, help me treasure people, not things, remembering that all good gifts come from You. —Gina Bridgeman

Thursday

27

What is man, that thou art mindful of him?...For thou hast made him a little lower than the angels.... —Psalm 8:4–5

Groucho Marx is quoted as saying, "I wouldn't belong to any club that would have me as a member." Groucho was just joking, but having a low opinion of oneself is a problem that touches all of us now and then.

When I was a new mother I made so many mistakes I began to feel that I didn't deserve the title. "Sometimes I hate myself for being such a poor mother," I muttered one day to an elderly woman who kept the church nursery.

She placed her hands on my shoulders and I thought for a moment she was going to give me a well-deserved shake. "My child, you shouldn't be so hard on yourself. If God chooses to love and accept you just as you are, isn't that permission enough for you to do the same?"

Her question dissolved my self-rejection then and there.

When your opinion of yourself dips and you're having trouble accepting yourself, try asking yourself that question and see if it doesn't put a new twist on things.

Help me relate compassionately to myself, Lord. —Sue Monk Kidd

Friday

28

He died for our sins and rose again to make us right with God, filling us with God's goodness.

—Romans 4:25 (TLB)

It had been a hectic morning. And now the washer had broken down—in mid-cycle. Amy Jo came in from the backyard, where half the neighborhood had gathered for a soccer game.

"Can we have some Kool-Aid?" she asked.

I was busy wringing out wet clothes. "If you want to make it yourself," I said without looking up.

Even before I heard the squeal I knew I'd made a mistake. I hurried into the kitchen. Kool-Aid ran everywhere, its red rivulets leaving stains on counters and sink and even throw rugs.

"It's his fault!" Amy Jo said, pointing to her younger brother. "He came in and bumped me just as I started outside."

"You're just clumsy!" Brett yelled.

I evicted them to the backyard and began working on the mess. As I scrubbed, I thought about other "spills" in my life. Unkept promises to clean rooms, the additional committee work I'd had to take on, the flowers I didn't get on my anniversary. As I sopped up the last puddle, I realized that whatever we're filled with is what spills over when we're bumped. I knew that too often lately I had splashed out anger, resentment—even sarcasm.

One of my dish towels still has a tiny red stain. But I don't mind. It reminds me that I need to be filled with God—so filled that everyday jostlings will provide splashings of His love.

Father of love, fill me with You. Transform my "bumps" into blessings. —Mary Lou Carney

Saturday

29

Fireside Friend

Pride goeth before... a fall. —Proverbs 16:18

When my father was a little boy, he became the proud owner of a battered red bicycle. *Proud* is the right word to use, for more than one reason. He was the only boy in the family at that time, and he was too proud to ask his big sisters to teach him how to ride. He mounted the bike from the doorstep, and could keep it fairly steady as he steered down the driveway. But there was a problem: He didn't know how to stop!

He could easily have asked for help, but his pride kept him from that. Instead, when he wanted to stop the bike, he would steer down behind the farmhouse where he'd "bump" into the woodpile to bring his bicycle to a stop. His plan worked fine for a while, but one day he was gone for so long that people started looking for him. They found him down by the woodpile, in a heap with his bike, just beginning to regain consciousness! His was the kind of pride that "goeth before a fall."

Some of Dad's self-reliance has undoubtedly been handed down to my generation. A few months ago I became the proud owner of a computer. How I hated to ask for help in learning how to use it! Typically, I ran into a few woodpiles before I admitted my need. In fact, my pride was responsible for several lost documents, before I finally called on my younger brother for advice.

What woodpiles have you been crashing into lately? Isn't it time to admit you need help? God's just waiting for you to ask.

I admit it, Lord. I need You to help me with _________________. Please show me what to do next.

—Vicki Schad

Sunday

30

He who is slow to anger has great understanding....

—Proverbs 14:29 (RSV)

Participating in a carpool is like dividing up the check at a restaurant—it never comes out fair! And I should know! I've been carpooling most of my seventeen-year parenting career. This morning, for instance, I had my day all planned when the phone rang. "Just wanted to be sure you're doing the soccer carpool today," another mother said cheerfully.

"But it's not my day," I protested.

"According to my calendar it is," she claimed, "and everyone has notes to get off the bus at your house." Assuming I had made a mistake, I meekly agreed, hung up the phone and then grabbed my calendar, counting back and adding up and subtracting for days missed.

Aha! It was not *my day. It's not fair,* I pouted, feeling a growing sense of injustice. I thought about my choices: I could call all the mothers back and set the record straight; I could call the school to change all those bus notes; I could grumble to the kids about the unfairness of it all so they could go home and set their parents straight; I could hold a grudge and feel sorry for myself and get more fanatic about keeping score... or I could merely accept the mistake this time.

I think I know what to do—pack my pride in the trunk of my car and place my hands on the steering wheel... a yellow school bus should be arriving soon.

God, You know when it's fair and when it's not. Let me let You be the Scorekeeper and I'll try to be the gentle responder.

—Carol Kuykendall

Thank-You Notes to God

1 ____

2 ____

3 ____

4 ____

5 ____

6 ____

7 ____

8 ____

9 ____

10 ____

11 ____

12 ____

13 ____

14 ____

15 ____

16 ______________________________

17 ______________________________

18 ______________________________

19 ______________________________

20 ______________________________

21 ______________________________

22 ______________________________

23 ______________________________

24 ______________________________

25 ______________________________

26 ______________________________

27 ______________________________

28 ______________________________

29 ______________________________

30 ______________________________

OCTOBER

S	M	T	W	T	F	S
	1	2	3	4	5	6
7	8	9	10	11	12	13
14	15	16	17	18	19	20
21	22	23	24	25	26	27
28	29	30	31			

SPIRITUAL TREASURE

Turn Loose Your Worries

Do not worry about your life...See how the lilies of the field grow. They do not labor or spin. —Matthew 6:25, 28 (NIV)

Now comes October when trees turn loose their leaves to swirl on fall breezes.

Instead of clinging to your worries, this month learn from nature and practice the healing art of letting go. Choose a worry you've been "laboring and spinning" over and release it to swirl up into the arms of God. Then keep on shedding a worry a day until they're gone.

Like the trees of autumn you'll stand open-armed and free.

My Monthly Prayer List

Family Prayer for October

Lord, unite Your people, and begin with me. Help me to step beyond the borders of my denomination, to see all believers as my sisters, my brothers.

Monday
1

THROUGH AN OPEN WINDOW
Be Patient with God's Timetable

Ye have need of patience, that, after ye have done the will of God, ye might receive the promise.
—Hebrews 10:36

On my bedroom wall, between the two windows, is a watercolor painting, a gift from my Aunt Eleanor. Aunt Eleanor taught me to appreciate art. She also taught me to appreciate the virtue of patience.

I was a teenager when I suddenly announced to her one day that I wanted to knit a pair of argyle socks. Several of my girlfriends were busy knitting argyles to give to their boyfriends for Christmas. It was fascinating to watch the little spools of brightly colored yarn dangling from knitting needles. The fact that I barely knew the basic knitting skills didn't seem to bother me. I knew my aunt was an expert knitter and I thought she'd approve of my project.

But when she heard about it, Aunt Eleanor sighed and pointed out that argyle socks would be a bit too complicated for me. Instead, she suggested I try a simple one-color scarf. I protested. I wanted to make argyles—*now*! But, finally, after a long discussion, I settled down with some dark green wool and a beginner's pair of Number One needles. Weeks later, after I'd mastered knit one, purl two, Aunt Eleanor taught me some other more complicated stitches; then we went to two colors. And one day I did, indeed, proudly present my boyfriend-of-the-moment with a pair of argyle socks.

Today, alas, patience still isn't one of my virtues. I still find myself wanting things to happen right now, this minute. It's often the same with prayer. I make a request to God, then expect Him to answer immediately. I've found that He doesn't necessarily operate that way. Often, His plan is for me to learn what I need to know, step by patient step. Lovingly, He stands by as I struggle, at first, to master each of life's difficulties with a Number One needle.

Lord, this month whenever I need patience, help me to remember that You have a timetable for my life. Urge me to consult it.

—Eleanor Sass

Tuesday

2

Therefore, as we have opportunity, let us do good to all people.... —Galatians 6:10 (NIV)

A few months ago I found myself with too much to do and not enough time to do it. For days I raced from one task to another. Then one afternoon while sitting in the dentist's waiting room, I read about a study that had been done years ago at an Ivy League university.

Fifteen students were divided into three groups. Each group was told they had to go to a building across campus to take a test, and that being late would cause a lower grade.

The first group was told to report to the building immediately. They were dubbed the "high hurry" group. The second group was told to arrive at the building within fifteen minutes. They were labeled the "moderate hurry" group. The third group, known as the "no hurry" group, was simply told to report to the building any time that afternoon.

Unknown to the students, individuals pretending to be in need were planted along the way. Some were crying, some were sick. Some had flat tires or other problems requiring assistance.

Not one of the students in the "high hurry" or the "moderate hurry" group stopped to offer help. But every single member of the "no hurry" group did. The study concluded that as our hurry increases, our caring decreases. We ignore needs to which we would ordinarily respond.

As I left the dentist's office, I walked a little slower and looked around. If I was too busy to love, I was just plain too busy.

Father, do not let me get in such a hurry that I overlook what is really important. —Sue Monk Kidd

Wednesday

3

And he bearing his cross went forth into a place called the place of a skull.... —John 19:17

Sometimes I think that when one sees a certain object or a certain symbol all the time, it's easy to begin to take it for granted. Even the cross, the very hallmark of Christianity.

Ever since I was a child, the cross has been meaningful to me. My brother and I used to spend summers with our grandmother Laura Peale, who lived near Cincinnati. Grandma Peale was a glorious cook, a beautiful character and a very religious woman. She had religious pictures all around the house. In the dining room was one of a stormy sea, scudding black clouds and rising up out of the ocean an enormous cross with a woman clinging to it. She was dressed in a white gown. Her long hair was streaming out across the water and under the picture were these words: *Simply to Thy Cross I Cling.*

Decades have passed, but that picture is as fresh in my mind as if it were yesterday, and the message is the same: *In all of life's strain and trouble, the one thing we may cling to with constant assurance of support and healing is the cross of Jesus.*

And what does the cross actually mean? Simply, it means love. It's God's way of telling us that He loves us. "For God so loved the world, that he gave his only begotten Son..." (John 3:16). *So loved!* Would you love anyone enough to have your son crucified for them? Would I? Would you sacrifice one of your children to bless the world? Would I? God did. What He's saying is "I love you... that much."

So remember, if you're having trouble, if times are hard, you are not forsaken. You are not alone. He loves you, and because He loves you, there is hope, there is joy, there is the blessed assurance that sooner or later all will be well.

Remind yourself every time you see the cross—on an altar, on a chain around someone's neck, on the top of a soaring steeple—and be thankful.

For Your sacrificial love, we bow in gratitude and humility, dear Lord.
—Norman Vincent Peale

Thursday

4

We walk by faith, not by sight. —II Corinthians 5:7

One of the great itinerant evangelists of our time was Vance Havner.

Once he told about a man who went on a safari in Africa. Naturally, he hired a guide, and for a while he followed the native without question. But when the guide tried to lead the stranger into the vine-thick jungle he balked. "There is no path, no road, no way," the man protested. The guide replied, "There is no road. I am the way!"

As long as we can see our path ahead clearly, faith, for many, is a spare tire. While it's nice to know it's there, we don't really think much about it. But when we come to a place in our lives where we can't see our way—and make no mistake about it, all of us sooner or later will reach such a crossroad of confusion—we will need a trustworthy guide. For Christians, Jesus Christ is not only the Way-shower, but the Way—the Way, the Truth and the Life.

Whatever your need today, you have a trustworthy Guide Who has promised to go before you and make the "crooked ways straight" (Luke 3:5).

While life's dark maze I tread,
And griefs around me spread, Be Thou my Guide;
Bid darkness turn to day, Wipe sorrow's tears away,
Nor let me ever stray from Thee aside. (Ray Palmer)

—Fred Bauer

Friday

5

Two are better than one.... For if they fall, the one will lift up his fellow.... —Ecclesiastes 4:9, 10 (RSV)

I used to like the saying, "When life gives you lemons, make lemonade!" But after an experience our daughter had one year, I've changed the words slightly.

Nikki was five then and looking forward to the pet show her kindergarten teacher had announced. She couldn't wait to show off Purry, our black kitten, and admire her classmates' pets as well. Then life dumped a whole crateful of lemons on Nikki in the form of chicken pox. Grotesquely spotted and itchy, she felt too miserable to enjoy staying home. Even the little "get well" toys we gave her didn't sweeten her forced vacation much.

When she returned to school, I hoped she wouldn't be too dejected after hearing about the fun she had missed. Instead, she came home bursting with pride and handed me the reason why. It was a shiny gold foil medallion with two blue construction paper ribbons dangling beneath. The inscription on the foil said, "First Prize for Most Invisible Cat."

Do you know someone too discouraged today to see a bright side? I suggest that "When life gives your friends lemons, help them make lemonade!" Nikki's teacher provided the "sugar" with a few scraps of paper.

How can I?

How can you?

Lord, give us sensitivity and creativity to uplift others.

—B.J. Connor

Saturday

6

For the good man... there is a happy ending.

—Psalm 37:37 (TLB)

It was a two-handkerchief book. The heroine faced perilous plot twists: Evil men tried to cause her downfall; friends betrayed her; happiness seemed to elude her on every page. But still she pursued her dreams—strong-willed, resolute, honorable. And in the end, the very end when I was almost overcome with pity for her, she succeeded. True love prevailed; evil was swallowed by its own sinister schemes. A happy ending!

Sometimes my life seems like that book. Things don't go the way I want. My car battery dies—on the exit ramp of the freeway. My son Brett brings home a note from school saying the teacher wants to discuss his conduct in class—again. My "perfect" dinner turns out charred. The dog slips his collar and disappears. My sinus infection lingers. A coworker gets the job I wanted. I pray for things that never come.

That's when I remind myself that the hassles of day-to-day living are only one part of my story. There's a closing chapter I haven't seen yet, one in which good triumphs. Finally and forever. My destiny is Heaven—a "happy ending" planned by the Author especially for me!

Oh, God, thank You for the certainty of happiness in the end; thank You for Your peace during every chapter of my life.

—Mary Lou Carney

Sunday

7

So we, though many, are one body in Christ, and individually members one of another.

—Romans 12:5 (RSV)

I had a whole year to anticipate a summer trip to Norway with my mother, whose grandparents had left the family farm and journeyed to America one hundred years before. It was like a dream when we arrived in the tiny hamlet of Budal, guests in the sturdy, sod-roofed house my great-grandfather had helped his father build. What a fascinating mystery to meet men, women and children from another side of the world who spoke an unfamiliar tongue, and know that we were inseparably bound together in a common heritage.

This sense of connection was particularly strong on a rainy Sunday afternoon in the home of a plump, rosy-cheeked Norwegian friend. During our conversation, my mother remarked she had no picture of her grandmother, who had lived with the family in Mom's early years. When this was translated, our hostess walked quickly to a buffet drawer and drew out an old photograph showing a buxom woman surrounded by four young children. There was not only my mother's grandmother, but the boyhood image of her own father!

I felt almost giddy at the sight of these faces. My people hidden in a keepsake drawer in a hand-hewn farmhouse set in the Scandinavian mountains. Yet to our hostess, a foreigner to us, these were her people, too. Time seemed to blur. For indelible moments we were one, no longer separated by country or custom or language, but one body around the table, belonging to each other then and now... and always.

Today, World Communion Sunday, we Christians of many nations will gather at the Lord's table to remember Him. Let's pause in our worship to reflect upon the beauty of being one body, joined inseparably in Jesus Christ. For in the kinship of Christ, we are all related, no boundaries to separate us.

Lord, You bid all who believe to partake at Your table, saying, "Kommen, velkommen...*come, welcome.*" —Carol Knapp

Day Brightener

ON ENTERING CHURCH

Pause ere thou enter, traveller, and bethink thee
How holy, yet how homelike, is this place;
Time that thou spendest humbly here shall link thee
With men unknown who once were of thy race.

—Plaque in an English Church

I have called daily upon thee.... —Psalm 88:9

I recently read a fitness article listing several ways we can "sneak" more exercise into our daily lives. Some of the suggestions: Do housework to fast music; park farther away from the store; carry one bag of groceries at a time from the car into the house; take the stairs; stretch during TV commercials.

These ideas made me wonder if I could just as easily "sneak" some extra time with God into my day. So I began to look for such hidden opportunities. Now some of my most comforting moments with God come in what might seem the most unlikely situations:

1. Brushing my teeth and preparing for bed (either reviewing the day just past or the one I'll wake up to in the next few hours).

2. The few minutes before a film or play starts (I pray about a specific problem I need to have more patience with, like a friend's gradual hearing loss that frustrates me and causes me to be short with her).
3. In the waiting room of my obstetrician (I'm going to have my first child soon, so I have a lot to talk to God about there).

Now I really look forward to these times, like a visit with a beloved Friend. Once while driving home from work, I was fretting about a tight deadline for a theater newsletter I had to write. I prayed to God, "What am I going to do?" He helped me focus on one thing at a time, so as not to feel overwhelmed. The job got done—calmly and on time.

And the best part of these "sneak" chats with God? They can be any time, any place.

Loving Father, thank You for being there whenever we need You, with Your love, Your guidance, and mostly just to listen.

—Gina Bridgeman

Tuesday

9

Fireside Friend

Be strong and of good courage....

—Deuteronomy 31:6 (RSV)

When my boss told me I had to give a speech before our managers, I broke out in a cold sweat. I was tempted to say, "I can't do it," but my boss's "I have confidence in you" kept me silent. When the big day arrived, I managed to get through my talk, even though my voice sounded creaky, I forgot a line, I was sure my one joke fell flat and when one man asked a question, I stammered through the answer.

Finally, the managers left and my boss made the surprise announcement that he had videotaped my presentation! I actually looked and sounded a lot more composed than I felt. "I taped it so that you could see how you felt inside didn't show on the outside. Now aren't you glad you didn't let your fear stop you?"

I'm sure God doesn't want fear to stop me from doing what He knows I can do. Maybe He uses it as a spur to get me to work as hard as I can. When I was learning to ski, I hung on the instructor's every word; I didn't break a leg as I had feared. And at work, when I had to handle the switchboard and pager for the vacationing receptionist, I managed admirably without embarrassing myself.

This month, I'm going to have a dinner party for ten people—something I've always wanted to do, but felt intimidated by. I'll assemble my recipes, do far too many trial runs and with God's help, I'll get through the big day.

God, let any fear I feel motivate me to work harder—don't let me use it as an excuse to run away from a challenge. —Linda Neukrug

Wednesday

10

O Lord, open his eyes so he may see.
—II Kings 6:17 (NIV)

Yesterday morning my husband George summoned me into our bedroom to see a strange vision. "Look, look. What do you see?" he said, pointing to the light streaming through a high window. "No, move a little more to the left, toward that picture."

We'd had the painting for years, a scene of the ocean at sunrise. But now, incredibly, poised just above the water, a shadowy yet clear figure had appeared. A robed figure with a nimbus around his head!

"Why, it's Jesus," I gasped. "Jesus walking on the water! But where has it come from?"

"Now step over here and look up at that other window." He guided me and tilted my chin. "See how the light is coming through it too, picking up something on your dressing table." Yes, now I could see another soft banner of light drifting toward the seascape, passing through a little crystal knob on a lampshade. Just a tiny, inconsequential fixture, transformed by the miracle of sunshine into the silhouette of Christ.

"Maybe God's trying to tell us something," I said. "Maybe it's a sign."

George nodded. "Let's hope so." I knew he'd been very worried about one of his patients. He knew how troubled I was about the book

I was writing—I'd wrestled with it half the night. Yet now, this morning, this incredible "accident" of light. A simple lamptop turned into Jesus walking on the water!

We've all heard of such phenomena. I read of one in the Midwest where our crucified Lord appeared vividly on the side of a grain elevator and drew excited crowds—until the farmer across the road moved the large machine that was creating the shadow. But whether explained in human terms or not, such visions do help, encourage and even heal.

I know I went back to my desk that day with a new feeling of peace and promise. And wrote simply but well for hours. And when George came home from his office he was smiling. "I feel better about Mrs. Gran. I found her problem and I think she's going to recover."

If you've never witnessed such a little miracle, look around you. You may be surprised!

Dear Father, give us the eyes to watch for the wonders all around us every day. Only then are we able to witness other miracles that may be waiting. —Marjorie Holmes

Thursday

11

Come unto me, all ye that labour.... —Matthew 11:28

I have a problem. I've overcommitted myself. During the next few months, I must undertake a community project, prepare three talks, have Thanksgiving dinner at my house, visit my daughter in Topeka and get ready for Christmas. I don't know how I can do it all, yet I know I must! Last night, I asked God to show me a way.

Early this morning, I dreamed of a beautiful spider web. The spider moved from the center of the web to the end of one of its spokes, then back to the center and out onto another spoke, continuing this way till it had traveled to the end of every spoke. My son John told me that a spider walks on only one spoke at a time, always going back to the center before moving out on another spoke. It's because the spokes are smooth, but the circular threads are sticky, to catch the prey.

It fits! I've been going around in circles and getting stuck. The message is clear: Work on only one thing at a time; then always go back and center myself in God before moving to the next task. It's the answer to my problem, the only way I can meet my commitments. Let's see, this week I'll begin finalizing my new home-improvement project. Then I'll spend Sunday getting centered in God. Next week, I'll prepare the nursing home talk; then I'll center again and....

If you also have too much to do and too little time, maybe the lesson I learned from my spider dream may help you, too.

I can do what's needed, Lord, because You are my center and the One Who smooths my path. —Marilyn Morgan Helleberg

Friday

12

By faith Abraham...went out....For he looked forward to the city which has foundations....

—Hebrews 11:8,10 (RSV)

All times have had their visionaries and Christopher Columbus was certainly a leading one in his day. His problem, common to all people who dream, was getting others to share it. He was only thirty-one when he first proposed his expedition in search of the East Indies, but his plan lay dormant for ten years until another young dreamer, Spain's Queen Isabella, caught Columbus' enthusiasm. It is said that she was so excited about his voyage that she would have pawned the crown jewels had it been necessary.

But the discovery of America still would not have happened had Columbus not persevered to the end. No doubt the crew of his three ships, a total of ninety sailors, began the trip full of high-spirited anticipation, but it faded by the time they had been to sea for three weeks, longer than anyone before had sailed in one direction out of sight of land. On October 10, 1492—after more than four weeks at sea—the crew petitioned the captain to turn back, but Columbus, believing his dream was at hand, bargained for just three more days. "Sail on!" someone cried and they continued. Two days later, by the light of a two A.M. moon, another cry was heard: "Land ho!"

Today, an ocean voyage may seem little more than a walk in the park, but the requirements for Columbus' adventure and space explorations of today are much the same. The common elements are curiosity, imagination, planning, preparation, courage and one of God's greatest gifts—vision, the belief in possibilities. Every day each of us has a choice to make in our lives. We can stick to safe, familiar harbors or we can sail forth to challenges beyond the horizon. When we pray, "O God, the sea is so great and my ship is so small," He answers, "Fear not, little flock; for it is your Father's good pleasure to give you the kingdom" (Luke 12:32). Sail on!

Lord, stretch our souls with visions glorious
Until we rest in You—victorious.

—Fred Bauer

Saturday

13

Fireside Friend 

Be content with such things as ye have....

—Hebrews 13:5

Do you ever wish you could have lived in another era? For some, the Old South holds special intrigue; others are fascinated by the feudal age of castles and knights. For me, however, the early days of the American colonies were always "the good old days."

Our little home in the woods was built in the 1700s; our area of Maine is rich in the history of the colonial period. As town clerk in our community, I have access to all the old records, dating back to 1754. I have romanticized everything from old quilts and colonial dress to the slower life-style that marked the first European settlers in New England.

Then one day, while researching a request for the history of a family in our town, I found a record that changed my mind. The death record read, "Josiah Mabry, aged three." Then, on the next page, only a few weeks later, "Thankful Mabry, aged eighteen months." Then, "James Mabry, aged four." I thought of their young mother, struggling to keep her family alive in that time of primitive medicine and inadequate hygiene. How lonely she must have felt, with her own parents far away in Europe, as one child after the other lost the battle for life.

I found myself thanking God for twentieth-century America.

Even with its fast-paced life-style and its political and economic problems, it's a good place to live. The "good old days" for future generations are the days I am enjoying right now!

Help me, Lord, to be content with where and who I am, knowing that Your will for me is best. —Vicki Schad

Sunday

14

It is good to sing praises unto our God....

—Psalm 147:1

I can't sing and this embarrasses me. At church, I retire to the back and just struggle along during hymns. But recently, an acquaintance said to me, "Of course you can sing. Why not 'sing' silently to God? I do this often, after retiring at night."

Only at night? I suddenly thought. *Why not during the day?* Then another thought burst into my mind: *Why not let my life do the singing?*

I began Sunday at church. When appointed ushers were absent, I volunteered to replace them without being asked. Following services, I removed bulletins from pew racks, tidied the hymnals and prayer books and pushed in the kneelers. Then I offered rides to those reluctant to ask or too fearful of imposing. In the days since then, I've discovered there are one hundred small ways I can "sing" silently to God through serving others...on Sunday and other days. (And I do sing songs of praise to God in my mind.)

How can you "sing" for God today?

Heavenly Father, with this renewed strength from You, my life is making a loud and joyful sound. —Oscar Greene

Monday 15

WINDOWS INTO WONDER
One Who Got Unstuck

As he journeyed, he came near Damascus: and suddenly there shined round about him a light from heaven. —Acts 9:3

Saul and his group were out to capture followers of the crucified Christ, whoever they were, wherever they could be found. I can see them stalking down that road to Damascus like a gang of angry hoodlums on the prowl, fists clenched, eyes flashing, spikes of hostility bristling out all over them. Suddenly, from out of nowhere, a blinding light staggers them. Saul's legs buckle, he falls to the ground, and a voice speaks. Instead of "I'll get even with you," Christ says to His persecutor, "I want you on my side" (Acts 9:17), and Saul-the-afflictor becomes Paul-the-Good-News-spreader. A complete about-face. At the moment he had the least reason to expect it, Paul discovered the truth his letters still proclaim: that no matter who you are or what you've done, God wants you. And more: that even if you're stuck in negative behavior, it is possible to change.

I keep reading that personality and character traits are firmly set during the first few years of life, and that no matter what you do, they won't change. If you've ever tried to overcome a basic fault, you know there's some truth in that. I have trouble with the sin of envy. I don't like that in myself and I fight it, but just when I think I've got an edge on it, I catch myself wishing I had my friend's musical talent, or my brother's time and means to travel, or my neighbor's spirituality. It's then that I remind myself of Paul on the Damascus road, and I see that, though *I* can never change myself, Christ can.

If you're trying to overcome a fault, here's a way to meet Christ on the road. Whenever you catch yourself acting out your flaw or thinking about doing so, mentally repeat these five words: *Remember Damascus. I CAN change*. It will help you get unstuck!

I will step out onto the road to change, Lord, trusting You to walk it with me. —Marilyn Morgan Helleberg

October Prayer List Reminder

Return to your Monthly Prayer List on the calendar opening page and review your requests. Give thanks for prayers answered, renew old prayers and add new concerns today. Then pray once again our *Family Prayer for October.*

Tuesday

16

Fireside Friend

Lo, I am with you alway.... —Matthew 28:20

Recently, in New York City, I was running an errand during my lunch break—or trying to. I'd had some difficulty locating a text for the class I was taking, and I wasn't sure the bookstore across town would have it in stock either. "Should I or shouldn't I?" I sighed, already feeling exasperated. *Better at least try,* I thought, looking down at my feet and frowning. Unenthusiastically, I turned to start the long walk west.

Just before an intersection, I saw a small crowd forming. There was a film crew, a camera and lights. My curiosity was piqued. *A celebrity was nearby, I just knew it.* I quickened my steps, hoping to catch a glimpse of someone famous, which for some silly reason always thrills me. My eyes widened with anticipation as I looked in the direction of the bright lights. Sure enough, there was a celebrity—Andy Griffith.

I watched for a few moments, then resumed my walk to the bookstore. But now my mood was lifted. I thought admiringly of Andy Griffith's staying power, of how his television career had taken him from "Mayberry" to the "law courts." I even whispered a quick prayer, "Thanks for letting me see Andy Griffith. Somehow he's given me a boost." But an inner voice seemed to whisper back, "You've had a Celebrity with you all along."

That's right! I thought sheepishly. Jesus had been with me all along, but I'd been too annoyed to be thrilled by His special presence!

"Lord, You are a Celebrity—and much more," I whispered, lifting my face up into the cool autumn air. "Thanks for always being there for me."

And I continued my walk to the bookstore, managing to muster up a little "staying power" of my own!

Lord, You have all the star quality I want to emulate. And at all times, let me not forget You are my constant Companion.

—Robin White Goode

Wednesday

17

Be thou an example of the believers, in word, in conversation, in charity, in spirit, in faith, in purity.

—I Timothy 4:12

I suppose we've all had teachers like Mr. Clopper. Gruff, demanding, rigorous, he would never settle for anything less than our very best. "Clop"—that's what we called him, although never to his face—taught acting and directed plays at our high school. He ran a tight ship. If you were one minute late for a dress rehearsal, you were kicked out of the show, no questions asked. If you hadn't memorized your lines by the appropriate rehearsal, you had to stay late until you knew them. If you mishandled a costume, set or prop, you shuddered in your boots.

Why did we put up with it? Partly because we knew that the finished product would be worth it. The shows we put on were amazingly polished and we basked in the appreciation of family and friends. But also because we knew Mr. Clopper truly believed in us.

On opening nights we assembled backstage for some final words of wisdom. Clop would congratulate us on our hard work. He'd smile slyly, and say, "I'll bet a lot of you never knew you could do it." Then he'd walk out slowly, turning around at the last minute. "God is love, angels," he always said. We weren't exactly angels, but, in loving us, Mr. Clopper was willing to ask for our best because he *knew* it was there.

Let me, Lord, be a fitting example of Your grace, seeing and nurturing what is best in colleagues, family and friends. —Rick Hamlin

Thursday

18

Therefore I tell you, do not be anxious....
—Luke 12:22 (RSV)

"Mom!" Kendall's voice quivered over the phone. "I'm supposed to be at recess, but I've been so worried all morning. Did I turn off the curling iron? I kept looking out the classroom window to see if our house was on fire."

How did I grow such a worrier, I wondered regretfully. "It's okay, honey," I assured her. "I check the bathroom every morning after you leave because I *always worry* that someone might leave it on."

"Oh, thanks, Mom," she said with relief. "See you this afternoon."

As I hung up, my own words hung heavily over my head. I had wondered how I could grow such a worrier and there was my answer: I grew one by example. I sometimes caused my whole family to stare at me in disbelief as I let little "what-if" worries turn a potential problem into a major crisis. *What if I left the back door unlatched and the wind blows it open and the cat gets out and runs away and gets hit by a car?* No wonder I've created a worrier who can't concentrate in class.

Worrying is taking on a responsibility that belongs to God, I once heard. That's true. Surely God wants me to act responsibly, but letting my imagination run wild with "what-if" worries is a sign of not trusting Him. That's bad enough, but passing the trait on to a child is even worse! The curling iron didn't burn down the house that day, but Kendall's phone call burned an impression in my mind about the worry-example I pass on to others.

Lord, let me increase my trust and decrease my worry...and pass on that example.
—Carol Kuykendall

Friday

19

And a little child shall lead them. —Isaiah 11:6

My granddaughter Tracy and I share a "big day" once a week when I pick her up from nursery school and take her to lunch. I teach her new games and songs, hoping to shape her into the kind of person God would want her to be. And she is learning... but this three-year-old is teaching me, too.

I fell and broke my hip recently and had to walk with a cane. After that, Tracy noticed everyone who walked with a cane and formed a kinship with them. Last week, during our "big day," a woman who had suffered a stroke struggled along with her cane. Tracy went up to her and said, "My grandpa used to use a cane. He fell and hurt himself. He was in the hospital, and when he came out, he had to walk with a cane. But, see, he is better now. You will get better, too."

The woman, who had been so intent on her struggle to walk, stopped and smiled. *You will get better, too.* It was a simple thought, yet I would never have gone over to speak to that woman on my own. She would have missed a moment of joy, and I would have missed a moment of sharing.

Tracy showed me that even as an adult, I, too, could learn (or re-learn) to approach someone with whom I share a common mishap and let them know, "You will get better, too."

Is there someone who needs to hear those five words of encouragement from you today?

Dear Lord, let me share compassion and kindness to a friend or stranger who needs to feel my childlike concern. —Lee Webber

Saturday

20

After he had patiently endured, he obtained the promise. —Hebrews 6:15

Back in October 1967, as I wrestled a log two-and-one-half-feet wide into position for splitting, I should have felt invigorated and enthusiastic. But as I gripped the axe handle, I felt defeated. After working for a few months as a supervisor in a home for boys, I was discouraged. I was twenty-one, with what I considered good potential. But instead of advancing my career like the rest of my friends, with my partner Ben I was fighting what seemed like a losing battle trying to keep our program afloat.

I eyed the huge log and knew I'd have to pop it pretty hard to crack it. All six feet two inches and two hundred pounds of me went into that first swing. But when the axe struck the wet log, it rebounded like a sledgehammer bouncing off a tractor tire. I took five more swings and five more times the axe bounced off. I threw the axe down—I was no match for this log. *I was no match for the business I was in either,* I thought. Like the log, work with the boys was just too tough.

"What's the problem?" Ben asked as he walked into the clearing. I explained that the log was too big and wet to split. "Let's see," he said, grabbing the axe. I was almost glad when the blade bounced off with his first three swings—I wanted him to know what it felt like to lose. When he turned to me, I thought he was going to admit defeat, but instead he said, "You just have to keep after this thing. It'll crack, just like the work we're doing with these boys. We'll make a successful program if we're persistent."

Ben kept popping that log until finally, after another dozen blows, the big log split down the middle and the two halves plopped on the ground. Ben handed me the axe and said, "You do the next one." It took me two dozen blows to start that log cracking, but finally it split. And today I'm still helping Ben with the boys.

Lord, give me the wisdom and courage to persist. —Brian Miller

Sunday

21

Ye...outwardly appear righteous unto men, but within ye are full of hypocrisy and iniquity.

—Matthew 23:28

My husband and I were first-time visitors in the Sunday school class. We were dressed appropriately and smiled warmly as we were introduced. We had our Bibles. No one could possibly know that we'd had a misunderstanding en route and that I had unforgiveness in my heart. The teacher was detained and someone asked, "Who will volunteer to teach the lesson?"

God seemed to say to me, *You and Gene are to teach this lesson.*

I argued silently, *I'm angry, Lord. I can't teach today.*

I glanced at Gene. Smiling, he said, "For some reason, I believe

God wants us to teach the lesson." I nodded. No one else volunteered.

Gene explained to the class that since we hadn't studied the material, we'd just share what God was doing in our lives now and in our new marriage. He instructed me to speak first.

Facing the class I heard myself say, "I have unforgiveness in my heart. I need to ask my husband's forgiveness." I glanced at him. He smiled and nodded a quick *"everything's-okay-I-love-you"* nod. I saw several couples smile and reach over and hold hands. I felt differently on the inside, as if God had reached down and removed the junk from my angry heart and put love in its place.

Gene and I taught the Sunday school lesson that day, but I'm sure the lesson I learned was more powerful than the one we shared with the class. God wants our insides and our outsides to match.

Lord, when my insides aren't as appealing as my outward appearance, help me to reach deep within for Your hidden gloss of goodness. Amen. —Marion Bond West

OUR TRAVELS TOGETHER

Crisscrossing this country and globe some 150,000 miles a year for most of their married and professional life, Norman Vincent Peale and his wife Ruth know well the joys and adventure of world travel. They know the strains and pressures, too. In the next three days, Ruth Stafford Peale gives us a peek into some valuable insights she and her husband have learned from the many years—and miles—of traveling together, with their Master Pilot guiding them each leg of their journeys. —The Editors

Monday 22

Day One—Making a Home

Because thou hast made the Lord, which is my refuge, even the Most High, thy habitation. —Psalm 91:9

What with our two busy schedules and far-flung speaking engagements, Norman and I do an enormous amount of traveling. Though it seems that we are away from home a lot, in a way we're not, and that's partly because of a few things we've learned along the way.

Whenever we arrive at our hotel, for instance, the minute we're shown to our room, I begin the same routine. I unpack. I take everything out of our suitcases, seeing to it that clothes are properly placed in closets and bureau drawers, toilet articles neatly arranged in the bathroom and the suitcases stowed out of sight. Then I place our familiar little clock on the nightstand and last, but hardly least, I find a prominent spot to put the picture we always carry with us, a photograph of our family. That done, the room is ready. It is our home for the night.

"But Mother," one of our children said to me once, "you do that even for one night?"

"*Especially* for one night," I told her, "because that's when travelers feel most like transients, a bit uneasy in unfamiliar surroundings."

So when you travel try to make your hotel room a haven of peace and order, a resting place where you can find renewal and strength. And remember, before you retire at night, to put your soul in order, too. That's what Norman and I always try to do. We say our prayers. We deliberately put aside the cares and stresses and problems of the day. We turn them over to our loving Father, and when we do we find that restful sleep comes quickly and easily.

Here's a small prayer that a traveler might want to use just before turning out the light:

Lord, let me not forget that there can be no place like home unless You are dwelling there. —Ruth Stafford Peale

Tuesday

23

Day Two—Into Sure Hands

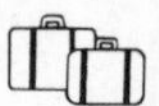

If I take the wings of the morning, and dwell in the uttermost parts of the sea; even there shall thy hand lead me.... —Psalm 139:9–10

I looked through the plane's window. Outside it was rainy and foggy, not a good night for flying. "Flight attendants, prepare for landing," came the order over the intercom. Norman and I rechecked our seat-belts and sat back as the plane started its descent.

Suddenly the plane rose and headed away from the airport beneath us. Norman and I looked at each other questioningly. For fifteen minutes or so the plane circled, then headed down, only to roar up again. The passengers around us began to tense. Once more the plane circled, headed in, and this time, at last, we landed safely, as the cabin filled with a rousing cheer.

We were taxiing into the gate when a voice came over the loud-speaker once more. "This is your captain speaking. Generally at this point in a flight I thank you for flying with us. Now, however, I want to thank you for something else. I have a feeling that you back there were praying for me in what was obviously a difficult landing. I *felt* those prayers. I'm grateful for them. And now, one more thing: Drive safely on the way home."

It was true. I for one, and Norman for another, had been praying for him. He had no way of knowing, however, that it was the second time we'd prayed for him. Indeed, in all our years of travel, we've never taken off in a plane without first praying for the passengers and crew. We ask the Master Pilot to take charge, then we sit back and relax.

And now, before we left our seats, we said a third prayer: that the captain, too, would drive home safely.

Lord, in this risky world, thank You for letting us put our lives into Your sure hands.

—Ruth Stafford Peale

Wednesday

24

Day Three—Happy Landing

He that is soon angry dealeth foolishly....

—Proverbs 14:17

Even though he's more than ninety years old, when we're traveling Norman always tries to pick up our heavy suitcases—that is, until I move in to stop him. Recently we were about to enter a taxi at a New York airport when he started to do it again, and all over again I stepped in, this time with a rather vigorous "Don't pick that up!" Then, in an angry tone I turned to the driver waiting unconcernedly behind the wheel and shouted, "We need some help!" Reluctantly he got out, picked up the bag, and we drove out of the airport with the driver sitting ahead of us in sullen silence.

I didn't like that silence and I didn't like myself either. Whenever I lose my temper, even in what seems like a just cause, I try to remember something that Will Rogers once said: "People who fly into a rage always make a bad landing."

In this case, by the time we came to a tollbooth, I did as the sign posted in the cab said and had the two dollar toll ready. As I leaned forward to hand it to the driver, I said, "My friend, I shouted at you a little while ago. I'm sorry and I hope you'll accept my apology."

The driver stared at me, then mumbled something that I didn't understand. We didn't hear anything else from him until we arrived at our apartment building where he bounded out of the cab, came around to open the door and hauled out the heavy bag. When I handed him the fare (with a generous tip included), he touched his hat. "My friend," he said, "it's been a pleasure."

So you see, even Will Rogers could be wrong. If you can get to the controls soon enough, you *can* have a happy landing.

Lord Jesus, make me kind and forgiving to others, even as God has forgiven me, for Your sake. —Ruth Stafford Peale

Thursday

25

Love one another: for he that loveth another hath fulfilled the law. —Romans 13:8

On a recent TV program, mythology expert Joseph Campbell, the late author of such bestsellers as *Hero with a Thousand Faces* and *The Power of Myth,* had some interesting things to say about reverence for life. In talking about American Indians, for example, he noted with admiration that they addressed all of life—trees, animals, rivers, people—as *thou,* that is touched by the divine. "The ego that sees a *thou* is not the same ego that sees an *it,*" he observed.

Our spiritual orientation certainly has much to do with how we see and treat one another. During wars, for example, part of the psychological strategy for motivating people into battle is to picture the enemy as an *it*—barbaric, strange, unfeeling, ungodly. In other words, to remove all of his *thou* qualities and paint him as subhuman. It's easier for a soldier to fire at an *it* than a *thou*.

But we can bring the application of this principle much closer to home. Today in the grocery store I saw a man and a woman get into a finger-pointing donnybrook over how many items were permissible in the express line. Judging by the anger vented they saw each other as an unredeemable *it*.

For Christians the mark of spiritual maturity is Christlikeness. We witness to His life-changing power when we turn the other cheek, when we don't lose our tempers, when we aren't judgmental, when we are loving and giving and forgiving. In other words, when we treat others as sacred *thous* instead of unworthy *its*.

Consecrate me now to Thy service, Lord,
By the power of grace divine,
Let my soul look up with a steadfast hope,
And my will be lost in Thine. (Fanny Crosby)

—Fred Bauer

Friday

26

Fireside Friend

The spirit of man is the candle of the Lord....

—Proverbs 20:27

It wasn't yet Halloween, but as I drove by a singles apartment complex one Saturday night, there it was—a pumpkin on a porch, carved and lighted, smiling its jack-o'-lantern smile. All the things that singles do on a Saturday night were going on: a couple kissing, three girls laughing as they walked to a car, two boys still trying to pass a football in the dark.

The pumpkin was smiling down on all of them. The football players couldn't see any better because of the pumpkin; its light wasn't bright enough. I don't think the girls walking to the car or the couple wrapped around each other even saw it; it was too small. But no matter how small, it was lighting up a little piece of the world, and

I couldn't help thinking how brightly the place would have been illuminated if every porch in that complex had a lighted pumpkin.

That's God's whole idea, I think; not two or three people with floodlights, but everyone doing his or her best with what little light they have to offer.

By the way, there is a wonderful side effect to such a choice. It makes you happy. How do I know? Oh, that's easy. I could tell just by looking at that pumpkin's face.

God, no matter how bright or dim my candle, help me light it.

—Debbi Smoot

Saturday

27

It is love, then, that you should strive for....

—I Corinthians 14:1 (GNB)

Youth club was just about over at church when I saw my daughter Mandy coming toward me. Big tears slid down her cheeks as she held up her bare wrist. "Mommy, I lost my bracelet."

I knew how much the colorful, braided yarn bracelet meant to her. She had been wearing it to bed ever since her friend Kisha had made it for her. I patted her back and smoothed her hair. "I'll help you look for it," I promised.

We retraced her steps to the classrooms and playground. She even looked under the fallen autumn leaves, but no bracelet. Finally, the search was over. It was time to go.

A fifth-grade boy walked up. "Why's Mandy crying?" he asked.

I hoped he wouldn't make fun of her. "She lost a friendship bracelet," I said.

Instantly, he pushed up the sleeve of his sweater, revealing three such bracelets. He pulled off the prettiest one and handed it to Mandy. "Here, you can have one of mine," he said. Then he smiled and bounded off.

I smiled, too. That boy was in my recreation class. Sometimes his energy and exuberance exceeded my patience. More than once I had wondered what I should do about him. Now I knew. I looked inside my heart, selected my prettiest circle of love and slipped it over his shoulders.

Father, whenever I wonder what I should "do" about people, let the answer always be "love them." —Terry Helwig

Sunday

28

And he said unto them, Take heed, and beware of covetousness: for a man's life consisteth not in the abundance of the things which he possesseth. —Luke 12:15

I feel wealthy today. It has to do with a classmate's Thoreau quotation I came across in my old high school yearbook: "A man is rich in proportion to the number of things which he can afford to let alone."

As I've written before, I like to enter contests, and I guess I'm on somebody's "pigeon" list, because I get deluged with entries. The latest sweepstakes is a thick packet of twenty-two separate papers with numerous glossy pictures of prizes, and extensive directions. "Match the number revealed on your Secret Combination Certificate against the numbers below." "Remove this label and place on the Shipping Address Verification Tag." "Wipe this spot with moist tissue or wet fingertip to discover your Jackpot Symbol."

I get weary trying to figure it all out. Suddenly it's not alluring, just dizzying. Which is more important to me: the slim prospect of this company's giving me something, or the precious time it would take to fill out the forms?

Check our trash can to find out. I feel very rich right now.

Lord, knock some sense into me when my greed makes me undervalue time or people, and overvalue things. —B. J. Connor

Monday

29

So, two good things happen as a result of your gifts—those in need are helped, and they overflow with thanks to God. —II Corinthians 9:12 (TLB)

The 1988 Olympics left a legacy of inspiring moments, but one of them took place after the competition had ended. Teresa Weatherspoon, a member of the gold-medal women's basketball team, was at the Seattle-Tacoma International Airport on her way home. She was carrying her team basketball and a poster signed by all of her teammates.

Army Sgt. Paul Patricio was also at the airport, en route to a military hospital. Earlier in the year he'd saved the lives of seven soldiers after a helicopter crash near Chico, Texas. In the process, he'd suffered third-degree burns over half of his body, lost both hands and a forearm.

When she heard about Sgt. Patricio, Teresa gave him her prized Olympic treasures. "He's a courageous young man to save those people's lives and I just admire him for it," she said.

I admire both of them! Their selflessness prompted me to examine my own actions. I've never saved anyone's life or won a gold medal, but perhaps I could do small acts of kindness for another. I could help feed the victim of Alzheimer's disease who shares my mother's hospital room, write a note of appreciation to a Good Samaritan mentioned in the newspaper and give a treasured trinket to a friend who has long admired it.

The world needs all kinds of heroes...including "everyday" ones such as you and me.

Lord, thank You for Bible heroes, modern stars and the best example of all, Yourself. —Penney Schwab

Tuesday

30

And through us spreads the fragrance of the knowledge of him [Christ] everywhere.
—II Corinthians 2:14 (RSV)

Do you have some favorite scents? I do. When I was a child, I remember my mother giving me whiffs from the vanilla bottle while she was baking, and now, years later, I still enjoy that smell. Another favorite is the smoky odor of a campfire, recalling the evenings of family talks around the firelight. I also savor the scent of wild roses in spring, turkey baking on Thanksgiving, sagebrush after rainfalls, a freshly cut Christmas tree, and the earthy aroma of hay and livestock.

There are other smells I would rather avoid. One time my father-in-law gave us a turtle shell he found along the railroad track. I dropped it in a pot of boiling water to clean it out and the stench was terrible. Then, last week, our daughter plugged in the waffle iron, only to fill the house with the unwanted odor of a forgotten leftover moldy waffle.

What a contrast there is between a pleasant and an unpleasant odor. One invites and the other repels. The Bible describes the knowledge of Christ as a fragrance—a most pleasing scent—and declares that His aroma is spread to others through Christians. Maybe I had better test the air quality in my immediate vicinity. Is there a sour attitude? A bitter spirit? An offensive thought? A spoiled behavior? Or anything emanating from me that would produce an unsavory scent where there should be sweetness?

Lord Jesus, make me a distiller of Your fragrance in this garden called Earth.

—Carol Knapp

Wednesday

31

Fireside Friend

Children, obey your parents in the Lord....And, ye fathers, provoke not your children...but bring them up in the nurture and admonition of the Lord.

—Ephesians 6:1,4

I love Halloween. That first tang of frost in the air, the menacing grins of pumpkins, and the little ghosts and goblins coming to my door fill me with childlike excitement.

Perhaps because trick-or-treating was not part of my own childhood tradition in Ireland, I couldn't wait for my son Jason to be old enough to dress up and join in the Halloween fun. So the year he turned three, I took Jason to the fabric store. Browsing through the pattern book, I found the perfect costume—a charming clown suit with a big, floppy collar and baggy pant legs, each a different color. "Oh, look, honey," I said excitedly, "you can be a clown for Halloween."

Jason, normally a cooperative child, shook his head emphatically. "I want to be Superman!" he declared.

"But sweetheart," I said, "Superman's for big boys. You'll look adorable as a clown."

Jason insisted, loudly now, "Superman, Superman!" And before I knew it, he burst into tears.

An older woman was standing nearby, watching. "He wants to be Superman for Halloween," I explained, embarrassed.

The woman smiled kindly and said, "And why not?"

I couldn't think of any good reason why Jason shouldn't be Superman for Halloween and that small incident taught me a valuable lesson about child-raising. Almost always, children must do as we adults say. This is necessary, of course, for their own protection and nurture. But as Jason demonstrated, children are also individuals. The trick is finding ways to allow that individuality to blossom while at the same time firmly guiding little ones in the way they should go.

Today, are there some ways you can yield to your child's individuality without compromising your authority as a parent? And how about other adults or peers? Can you let those around you freely be who they are, enjoying their uniqueness and celebrating their differences? (By the way, Jason made an impressive Superman!)

Dear Lord, help us to raise our children in Your ways, helping to guide them onto the right path and allowing their uniqueness to flourish. Amen.

—Stephanie Oda

Thank-You Notes to God

1 ______________________________

2 ______________________________

3 ______________________________

4 ______________________________

5 ______________________________

6 ______________________________

7 ______________________________

8 ______________________________

9 ______________________________

10 ______________________________

11 ______________________________

12 ______________________________

13 ______________________________

14 ______________________________

15 ______________________________

16 ______________________________

17 ______________________________

18 ______________________________

19 ______________________________

20 ______________________________

21 ______________________________

22 ______________________________

23 ______________________________

24 ______________________________

25 ______________________________

26 ______________________________

27 ______________________________

28 ______________________________

29 ______________________________

30 ______________________________

31 ______________________________

NOVEMBER

S	M	T	W	T	F	S
				1	2	3
4	5	6	7	8	9	10
11	12	13	14	15	16	17
18	19	20	21	22	23	24
25	26	27	28	29	30	

SPIRITUAL TREASURE

Discover Your Treasure

Lay up for yourselves treasures in heaven.... —Matthew 6:20

Children dressed as pilgrims, families gathered around turkey and pumpkin pie, football on the front lawn, cold crisp air, a fire in the grate. These are the treasures of November.

How long has it been since you've counted the treasure buried in your life? Your challenge is to unearth a unique spiritual treasure each day of this month. Uncover a hidden potential God has placed inside you. Discover a new friend, rediscover an old one. Dig up a forgotten promise in the Bible. Open your eyes to the invisible ways God is loving you. You will find that you are richer than you think.

My Monthly Prayer List

Family Prayer for November

Heavenly Father, bless families and friendships this month. Help us to reconcile differences, overlook little injuries, reach out in stubborn love.

Thursday

1

Fireside Friend

For the trumpet shall sound, and the dead shall be raised incorruptible.... —I Corinthians 15:52

Our pastor held a short service on All Saints' Day to honor those members of our small church who had died during the past year. It was a solemn moment when Eula, our worship chairperson, lighted a candle as each name was called.

The eyes of many filled with quiet tears as memories of fellow members filled our sanctuary. But there was more than tears and memories. The silence held within it a deep peace, a feeling of oneness with those saints who had left us behind as they went to meet their Savior and King.

And hidden in the sanctity of the moment was a clearer understanding of the death of a believer—or, perhaps I should say the life, because that *is* what it is. We, the living, are really the dead, waiting and working toward the new and eternal life with the saints we so honor.

What a startling truth!

What a comforting thought!

Father, help me to prepare each day for the great day when I, with all the saints, will see clearly the mystery of You.

—Mary Jane Meyer

Friday

2

THROUGH AN OPEN WINDOW
Try Something New

In whom we have boldness and access with confidence by the faith of him. —Ephesians 3:12

It snowed last night. A light dusting covers the outside windowsill as I peer through my window this morning.

I remember this time last year when I was planning a skiing vacation in Colorado. At first a friend had expressed an interest in joining me, then had changed her mind. *Should I go alone?* I wondered. Something inside me hedged. I'd never tried cross-country skiing. I might not like it. *Suppose the other guests at the ranch are unfriendly?*

Suppose I break a leg? The more I thought about it the less enthusiastic I felt.

Then I shared my apprehension with another friend. "I hope you do try it," he said. "I know it seems a bit scary to tackle on your own, but the more new things you attempt, the more alive you are. People say, 'When in doubt, don't.' And sometimes they're right. But sometimes it also works the other way. 'When in doubt, do.' Anyway, why don't you pray about it? Then go ahead and make your reservations. If all goes smoothly, it could be God telling you that this is for you."

I did as my friend suggested. And I went on my ski adventure. All did go smoothly and I enjoyed one of the best vacations of my life. Learning a new sport was exhilarating. The other guests were delightful.

As November begins, I'm going to promise myself that I will try one new thing every day. It might be something as simple as a new route while walking to work. Or as complicated as a new needlepoint project. And one Sunday this month I think I'll visit a church other than my own, just for a change. But whatever I do, I'll pray before doing it.

Lord, give me boldness and confidence, and faith in You to try new things.
—Eleanor Sass

Saturday

3

If any one is in Christ, he is a new creation; the old has passed away, behold, the new has come.
—II Corinthians 5:17 (RSV)

On my desk is a handprinted sign that holds special meaning for me. It says, "Warm with hope and start gnawing." You see, many years ago when I was starting a career as a nurse, I was full of doubts about my skills. "I just don't know if I have it in me," I muttered to my new husband.

Then while reading Thoreau's *Walden*, Sandy happened upon a story that he could not resist sharing. It went like this:

There was a table made of applewood, which stood in a farmer's kitchen in New England for sixty years. One day a gnawing sound began to emanate from the table. It kept up for several weeks, until at last a strong and beautiful bug emerged from the table, unfurled its wings and took flight.

An insect egg had been deposited in the trunk of the apple tree before it was made into a table. The egg remained in the wood all those years. Then warmed, perhaps by the heat of a coffee urn placed on the table, it hatched, and the little bug gnawed its way out.

After relating that remarkable story, Sandy said, "Who knows what unhatched potential lies in your life? *Just warm it with hope and start gnawing.*"

And I did.

Lord, when failure and self-doubt strike, remind me that I am an applewood table, seeded with hidden promise. —Sue Monk Kidd

Sunday

4

Fireside Friend

[Jesus] went up into the hills to pray.
—Matthew 14:23 (TLB)

My then four-year-old son Benji quickly picked up the piece of dirty gum from the sidewalk and started to pop it in his mouth. "No, Benji!" I scolded. "We don't chew 'A.B.C.' gum!"

He threw the gum back down. "What kinda gum is that? Never saw that kind."

I explained that "A.B.C." wasn't a brand name. "It means the gum has *a*lready *b*een *c*hewed."

As an adult I recoil in horror at the very thought of second-hand gum, yet how often am I guilty of trying to survive on "A.B.C." religion? In my busy life, it is so easy to let the pastor study *his* Bible to feed me on Sundays; during the week I can let Christian TV and radio worship and praise for me; at mid-week prayer meeting others can do the praying for me.

How often have I waited until someone else has prechewed and predigested religion for me before I pick it up for myself? Just as that piece of gum that little Benji picked up wasn't at its best, so my walk with Jesus needs to be centered with personal private time with Him.

Lord, forgive me for those times when I am content to settle for second best in my relationship with You. —Bonnie Wheeler

Monday
5

For God...hath shined in our hearts....
—II Corinthians 4:6

The letter from my friend had a notation in the lower right corner: "Be a sundial, M." It was rather mysterious. What could it mean? That I should guard my time better? Get out in the sun more often? Surely not that I should cast shadows! Of course I wrote back right away, asking what it meant. "Mark only the hours that shine!" she wrote back.

Oh, what a good thing for me to hear, because it came during a time when I really needed that reminder. Family and financial concerns were occupying me. My friend's message helped me to let go of minuses and focus on the pluses. I thought of the shining hours my son John and I spent recently, talking of many deep things in our hearts. Then there was the spur-of-the-moment birthday gift from a friend—a two-hour car trip to Lincoln, Nebraska, for a cultural excursion. I also wanted to mark those hours that seemed like ten minutes because I was having fun with my grandchildren, or because I got outside of myself by helping someone else.

Wouldn't it be good, at the end of each day, to write down the hours and minutes that have had a special light about them, and let go of all the rest, asking God to blot out the shadows? I think I'll begin tonight.

You are my light, Lord. I'll mark where You shine in my days.
—Marilyn Morgan Helleberg

Tuesday
6

Give diligence to make your calling and election sure....
—II Peter 1:10

Did you know that the lowly louse was once an important part of the mayoral selection process in Hurdenburg, Sweden? During the Middle Ages, all the eligible men gathered around a table for the "election." They lowered their heads and waited. A louse, surrounded by the beards of the candidates, was set down in the center of the table. The owner of the beard into which the louse crawled was declared mayor for the following year.

Sounds silly, doesn't it? But no sillier than allowing neighbors and strangers to elect your officials for you. Years ago Edmund Burke said, "All that is necessary for evil to triumph is for good men [and women!] to do nothing."

So today I'm going to vote—in spite of bad weather and busy schedules and tough choices. If you're a registered voter, I hope you will, too.

Keep me, God, from the comfort of complacency. Stir me to do my duty. —Mary Lou Carney

Wednesday

7

A wise [son] makes a glad father....
—Proverbs 10:1 (RSV)

"Does raising kids ever get any easier?" the weary parents of three teenagers asked my wife Shirley and me the other day. They knew that two of our children have finished college and the other two are partway through.

"Yes," Shirley responded, "it does get easier, and someday your children will even thank you for all you've done." The father answered satirically that he hoped to live that long.

The truth is that parenting is full of sweet rewards. Not that being rewarded is the goal. But every day it seems I find something about my children for which to thank God, little affirmations that remind me of the great blessing kids are. A case in point is the bookmark I ran across in my reading today. It was from Laraine, our eldest child and only daughter who is now a mother herself. She lives two hundred fifty miles away so most of our hugs and kisses are via phone or mail. I don't know when she sent me the bookmark, but when I read it, it raised the gray hair on the back of my neck and gave my heart an instant suntan. Alongside three colorful balloons was one of the best compliments anyone can pay another. It read: *You Make Me Happy.* Ditto, Laraine, ditto.

As a parent, Lord, my thanks for children warm,
Their love my overcoat through any winter storm.

—Fred Bauer

Thursday

8

Love is patient and kind.... —I Corinthians 13:4 (RSV)

Does someone you love occasionally have a rough day at work, hold it all in until he reaches home, and then release it all on you? If so, you can identify with a yellowed, frayed cartoon on our kitchen bulletin board. A middle-aged man settles into his easy chair. As he opens the newspaper, he becomes aware of a little dog waiting patiently by his side. The man glares at him. "You've been walked and fed," he snarls. "Now I suppose you want love and affection!"

As a dog-lover (and owner), I'm sure the little dog refuses to take offense. Secure in knowing he is loved, certain that the tirade isn't meant for him, he continues to wait, gazing steadily at his owner with loving, trusting eyes. And soon he will receive the love and affection he's been anticipating. And in petting the little dog, the man will find the release and relaxation he needs so much.

Why, I wonder, *don't we respond to anger as the little dog does? Why, when we know we are loved, do we withdraw into indignant self-pity when we know the outburst isn't really directed at us?*

Perhaps that's why I keep that cartoon on my bulletin board. I still have a lot to learn from that patient, devoted little dog. Does he perhaps have a message for you today, too?

Dear God, help me to respond with love at all times.

—Aletha Jane Lindstrom

Friday

9

A man that hath friends must show himself friendly.... —Proverbs 18:24

"No man is an island," wrote John Donne. How I wish this were true!

One of the saddest experiences of my life was visiting my friend in a mental institution. I was directed to the third floor and rang the buzzer. An orderly peeped through the tiny window, unlocked the door to let me in, and then locked it again behind me. I felt the sad isolation of being shut off from the world. When I talked to my friend but could not break through the shell that surrounded him, I realized that he was an island.

It was then that I promised myself that I will do my best not to become an island, even if failing health limits my activities with others. I realized that if my circle of friends became smaller and smaller, my life would become more restricted. So I am determined to keep my castle door open, the drawbridge down and the friendship flag flying. And I see opportunities to do this where I never saw them before: friendly chats to encourage a teenager next door who's struggling with his math assignments; exchanged fun jibes between myself and the mail carrier who's new on our route and a little shy; and invite to dinner the friendly couple and child who sit next to us occasionally at our local fast-food restaurant.

Today, try to see how many people you can welcome into your circle. Watch your island transform itself into a continent of growing love.

Dear Lord, don't allow me to isolate myself from others. Help me to be friendly, so that I may share the joy of Your communal Spirit. Amen. —Lee Webber

Saturday

10

Fireside Friend 

Thy word is a lamp unto my feet, and a light unto my path.
—Psalm 119:105

I drive a genuine clunker that we affectionately refer to as "The Golden Barge." This car gives new meaning to the word *stall*. On the way to school in the morning, The Barge stalls before I get out of the parking place. It stalls at the first stoplight. It stalls with sharp turns; it stalls going up hills and down hills. When I described this to my dad, he said, "That definitely sounds like fuel deprivation."

Fuel deprivation is a funny way to talk about a car. It's a term, however, that describes my spiritual life at times. There are weeks when I'm guilty of not maintaining fellowship with other Christians, of not reading the Word or not praying. Often, these are the very weeks when things don't go as smoothly as they're supposed to. A little crisis, such as a misunderstanding with a friend, will catch me off guard, and I handle it badly. A major challenge in my life, like finding my first job just out of college, seems too much to bear. Or I'll take on too many obligations and choke on stress. I'm suffering from fuel deprivation. I haven't fueled up on the spiritual things that keep my life running smoothly and help me handle the sharp turns, the uphills and the downhills.

Have you filled your gas tank this week? Check your gauge, and if you're getting low, make a pit stop—open that Bible, include a quiet time with God—before you're on empty.

Father, thank You for Your Word that gives the spiritual energy I need to meet life's many challenges.
—Teresa Schantz

Sunday

11

Nation shall not lift up sword against nation, neither shall they learn war any more.
—Isaiah 2:4

To be a veteran on Veterans Day, as I am, is to live for a while with memories that never fade. It's to live with troubling thoughts, too.

Can the horror that is war ever be fully disguised by patriotic emotions? I don't know. All I know is that soldiers share a bond unlike any other, not only with their comrades but sometimes even with the enemy, if they are brave and honorable people.

I have never forgotten the description written by Union General Joshua Chamberlain of the final surrender of the battered Confederate forces at Appomattox in 1865. Wounded six times in the war and holder of the Congressional Medal of Honor, Chamberlain was designated to receive the actual surrender. His troops were lined up in battle array. The defeated Confederates would march past and lay down their arms. It was the end of four years of bitter struggle and untold bloodshed. Although he knew he would be criticized (and later was), Chamberlain had given orders to his troops not only to refrain from cheers, but when the defeated enemy came past, to salute "these men, now thin, worn, and famished, but erect with eyes looking into ours, waking memories that bound us together as no other bond."

At the head of the gray column was General John B. Gordon, one of the last of Lee's lieutenants who himself had been wounded five times in one day during the furious battle at Antietam. Now let Chamberlain describe the scene:

> Our bugle sounds the signal and instantly our whole line from right to left gives the soldier's salutation, the marching salute. Gordon at the head of the column, riding with heavy spirit and downcast face, catches the sound of shifting arms, looks up and, taking the meaning, wheels superbly, making with himself and his horse one uplifted figure, with profound salutation as he drops the point of his sword to the boot-toe; then, facing his own command, gives word for his successive brigades to pass us with the same position of the manual—honor answering honor. On our part not a sound of trumpet more, nor roll of drum; not a cheer, nor word, nor whisper of vain-glorying, but an awed stillness rather, as if it were the passing of the dead.
>
> With what strange emotion I look into these faces. It is by miracles that we have lived to see this day, any of us standing here. How could we help falling on our knees, all of us together, and praying God to pity and forgive us all!

Honor, pride, courage and forgiveness—what a legacy for us all on this Veterans Day.

Father, help us move into an era where we shall learn war no more.

—Arthur Gordon

Monday

12

When ye shall have done all those things which are commanded you, say, We are unprofitable servants: we have done that which was our duty to do.

—Luke 17:10

The windows of our plane were opaque as we cruised at four thousand feet through the clouds. The control tower informed me that the plane on the approach ahead of me had turned back and gone to another city where the weather was better. I turned to see if my wife Sandy had sensed cause for alarm, but she didn't appear to have noticed. I was nervous, but not frightened. I had made many instrument approaches with worse conditions during my instrument training. The only problem was that this was real life.

The tower now vectored me to line up with the instrument landing system and I flew by the needles on my instrument panel until we broke out of the clouds. I was right over the approach lights and lined up dead-center with the runway. I was pretty proud of myself. I touched down smoothly and taxied toward the parking area. As we neared the ramp, I turned to Sandy and said triumphantly, "What did you think of that approach?"

She looked at me, slightly bewildered, and answered, "I thought that was what you were supposed to do."

Two weeks later I had to take a commercial airline to Houston. The weather at the airport was soupy and I knew the pilot was making an instrument approach as I had done. After we landed, I had to smile. The captain didn't make a big production out of his landing, because as a pilot it was his responsibility to perform his best under any condition. Just as it had been my responsibility to land my plane safely.

When I feel I should be appreciated more, I try to remember that I do certain things because it's my duty, and not for applause.

Lord, when I begin to feel self-congratulatory, help me back to humility with thoughts of Your great "duty," giving Your life for all of us.

—Brian Miller

Tuesday

13

But when you help...do it in such a way that even your closest friend will not know about it.

—Matthew 6:3 (GNB)

It was a cold, blustery day. I turned into our driveway and saw several sheets of wet, pink paper littering the yard. If I didn't pick them up, I knew my husband Jim would when he came home. He liked a clean, manicured lawn. The temptation to leave the papers was strong. *Besides*, I thought, *if I pick them up, Jim won't even know I've done something nice for him.*

Suddenly Ruth's name came to mind. Some years ago, when Ruth used to baby-sit our daughter, mysterious little things happened at our house. After Ruth went home, the chrome on the stove might look shinier, or the smudges of tiny handprints might have disappeared from the kitchen window. A stack of diapers might look neater or the family room tidier.

Finally, one day I asked Ruth if she ever cleaned things while I was gone. Reluctantly, she admitted she did. She said she tried to do one nice thing *secretly* for someone every single day. I was touched. What a nice way to live. And just think how many secret acts of kindness she carried out in a year!

With that memory still fresh in my mind, I wrapped my scarf tightly around my neck, climbed out of the warm car and picked up the papers.

And when Jim came home from work? Well... I just smiled, kissed him on the cheek and basked in the warmth that comes from doing secret kindnesses.

Dear Lord, help me to leave unsigned notes of love wherever I go.

—Terry Helwig

Day Brightener

YOUR OWN VERSION
You are writing a Gospel,
A chapter each day,
By deeds that you do,
By words that you say.
Men read what you write,
Whether faithless or true,
Say, what is the Gospel
According to you?

—Paul Gilbert

Wednesday

14

He giveth power to the faint; and to them that have no might he increaseth strength. —Isaiah 40:29

One day at my job as copywriter for a radio station in Milwaukee, I had to write an ad for the Freedom From Smoking Center. Some of the copy information included a list of things every smoker gets absolutely free with every pack of cigarettes. Things like "dirty ashtrays, sore throats, smelly fingers, possible heart attacks, chronic headaches, tobacco in your pockets, raspy voice, high blood pressure, chest pains, stained teeth, coughs, holes in your clothing, bad breath, emphysema, burning eyes, fatigue, shortness of breath, gum disease, bronchitis and lung cancer."

Goodness, I thought, *what a devastating list!* Although I'm not a smoker, I remembered smoking friends, acquaintances and co-workers who had to fight all those negative things.

And so a prayer for them, and others, tomorrow on the Great American Smokeout:

Lord, help me to be especially considerate of those people who are trying to give up smoking or other bad habits. They need Your help.

—Patricia Lorenz

Thursday

15

WINDOWS INTO WONDER
An Ever-Present Army

Fear not: for they that be with us are more than they that be with them. —II Kings 6:16

One blizzardy night in the late 1930s, my Aunt Alta tucked me into the big brass bed in my grandparents' house in rural Danbury, Nebraska, kissed me good night, and went back downstairs. As soon as her footsteps hit the last step, the creaky noises in the dark corners started. Then something (was it a mouse or a monster?) skittered across the hardwood floor and under my bed. I screamed, and within seconds Aunt Alta came, wrapped me warmly in her velvety crazy quilt and began to tell me a story about a man named Elisha.

The king of Syria had sent his whole army, with horses and chariots, to capture the prophet. When Elisha's servant saw that they were surrounded, he was very scared. But Elisha told him not to be afraid because "There are more on our side than on theirs." Then Elisha prayed that his servant's eyes would be opened, and the man saw what no one else but Elisha could see—that the mountain on which they stood was covered with horses and chariots of fire, sent by the Lord to keep His prophet safe.

"Whenever you're afraid," said Aunt Alta, "remember that God's invisible army is all around you, keeping you safe." I closed my eyes, and it seemed to me that I could picture those chariots of fire, and I just knew I was protected. The next thing I heard was the rooster crowing, and sun was shining through the lacy curtains.

Many times in the years that followed, during moments of fearfulness, I closed my eyes and pictured those chariots of fire, and my fear went away. Even now, half a century later, I remind myself of God's invisible army when I'm fearful—like the night I was home alone and heard a loud thump in the basement, or the day my son John was traveling through snow to get home for Christmas, or when my doctor said, "We'd better do a biopsy." During the month ahead, any time we're fearful, let's close our eyes and picture those chariots of fire. It will help us remember that we are truly surrounded by divine forces, and that, no matter what our opposition may be, "There are more of us than of them."

Open my eyes, Lord, that I may see. —Marilyn Morgan Helleberg

November Prayer List Reminder

Return to your Monthly Prayer List on the calendar opening page and review your requests. Give thanks for prayers answered, renew old prayers and add new concerns today. Then pray once again our *Family Prayer for November.*

Friday

16

Fireside Friend 

I will forgive their iniquity, and I will remember their sin no more. —Jeremiah 31:34

I heard a short story once about a man who collected rocks. It all started with his decision to pick up a rock every time his boss made him angry. Soon his pockets were bulging with rocks. His collection grew as he included rocks when anyone wronged him. It wasn't long before he filled not only his pockets, but his yard, his car, his house. He took great pride in being able to pick up any rock in his vast array and recall the specific details of its origin.

A geology professor heard about the man's collection and asked to see it. Arriving with his students, the professor surveyed the piles of rocks. "But these are just ordinary rocks. Why did you collect them?" When the man explained his reasons, the professor was amazed that the man had spent so much time collecting something so worthless.

I am not, by nature, a vengeful person. But I, too, have collected rocks of all shapes and sizes. Hurts from misunderstandings with friends. Resentments from not feeling appreciated by family members. Envy at successes of my neighbors. And more. Not big rocks—most of them more like pebbles—but something to hurl if I were ever attacked. I have reviewed, catalogued, remembered...just in case I ever needed them. Think of the senselessness of life's imaginary battle lines: people on either side, spending a lifetime piling up worthless rocks.

Today's a good day to make a new start—let's clean out our pockets and throw away the rocks. They are weapons of self-destruction, not self-defense. Let's give ourselves, and someone else, the sweet miracle of a second chance. Today, let's forgive someone.

Lord, give me the courage and faith to walk away from my pile of rocks—to forgive. —Debbi Smoot

Saturday

17

I press toward the mark.... —Philippians 3:14

I think God must love late-bloomers. That's why He gave the mission of leading the children of Israel to an eighty-year-old Moses, why He sent Noah on his watery quest at the tender age of six hundred. And perhaps that's why he created *Puya*.

The giant *Puya raimondii* plant of Peru is a late-bloomer. Very late. A member of the pineapple family, it usually grows for eighty to one hundred fifty years before blooming. But when the time is right, it shoots up a giant forty-foot stalk from its trunk. Here thousands of flowers blossom, producing millions of seeds.

Often I feel like a frustrated late-bloomer. I'd give anything to create a really fine gourmet meal; I want to learn to swim; I'd love to master cross-stitch. Yet these, and other skills, elude me year after year.

But when I'm tempted to give up and declare myself hopeless, I remember the Puya and all the long, arduous years that produce those colossal blooms. So I'll sign up for another adult swim course (I think my prone kick is getting better!). I'll attempt to bake that delicate soufflé. Perhaps this week I'll dig out my half-finished piece of cross-stitch and try to complete it. Maybe I'll even tackle something new: racquetball or stained glass or yoga. I'll keep trying and trying—and *growing*. Somehow, I know that's what God wants all of us to do.

Thank You, Lord, for Your love that reaches out to even late-bloomers like me, giving me the courage to keep trying.

—Mary Lou Carney

Sunday

18

Seek ye out of the book of the Lord, and read....

—Isaiah 34:16

My thirty-year-old Volkswagen had gone over two hundred thousand miles and really needed help. It had almost no brakes, it would not steer properly and every time it hit a bump, it would shimmy and shake uncontrollably. The whole front end needed to be rebuilt. Since I had never done this before, I had the repair manual open before me, checking each procedure to make sure that I did it "by the book."

In many ways I am like that old car, and often I am in need of a good checkup "by the Book."

I need to check my brakes, that is, my ability to stop working. I have always worked longer and harder than is good for me, so when I read the Good Book, I find out how important rest is. Even God rested (Genesis 2:2)!

I need to check my steering. This means checking to see that I go straight toward the goal, not wandering from side to side. In life, I must be sure that I run between the lines so that I am not disqualified (Philippians 3:12-15).

And *how do I react when I hit a bump in the road?* If I shimmy and shake, some things will have to be tightened or even replaced. In the Book, I read about the peace of God, which can keep my heart and mind (Philippians 4:6-7). I know I cannot avoid all the bumps, but with the help of God, I know I can stay on course without being destroyed.

That old Volkswagen drives like new again because I followed the instructions. I am also working on my life with the same care, and "doing it by the Book."

Dear Lord, on this National Bible Sunday, I'm thankful for Your Book, which ever guides me toward a successful life's journey. Amen.

—Lee Webber

Monday

19

This is the day which the Lord hath made; we will rejoice and be glad in it. —Psalm 118:24

Do you ever have those empty and low-down days following a big event or major holiday? If so, you aren't alone! But I've found a remedy that works for me in E.B. White's words: "Life is always a rich and steady time when we are waiting for something to happen or to hatch."

I'm not waiting for something to hatch—not in January or February. My bluebirds won't be back until late March. But I *can* watch for something to happen!

Around Thanksgiving I cut small notches in five or six Heavenly Blue morning glory seeds. (Just looking at the lovely blossom on the packet boosts my spirits!) Then I soak the seeds overnight in tepid water. The next morning I plant them in a flowerpot and place them in a south or east window. I moisten the soil with slightly warm water when it becomes dry. Shortly after New Year's, sprouts emerge and soon vines are twining up a trellis I fashion from coat hangers. Each morning I eagerly count the number of new buds and watch them unfurl. It's like having a little bit of God's springtime right there in my kitchen.

If you care to try my spirit-lifter, you'll find you have sufficient seeds in a packet for several flowerpots. You might find joy in giving them to others who need a bit of God's joy during the dark days.

Dear God, thank You for the many small ways in which we can give—and experience—Your love. —Aletha Jane Lindstrom

Tuesday

20

Well done, good and faithful servant....

—Matthew 25:23

In the midst of all the Thanksgiving festivities, perhaps we should stop and remember some of the selfless, anonymous people whose services we take for granted in our daily lives.

Yesterday, for example, wanting to look up a certain item in last year's edition of *Daily Guideposts*, I turned to the Reader's Guide Index and found it instantly under the name of the writer. I also could have found it if I had remembered the Scripture passage used, or even the subject of the devotional itself. And suddenly I thought: *What a tremendous service for thousands of readers is being performed by the person who puts together this index. I am part of the team that prepares these books, but I don't even know this person's name. All I know is that I could never have the patience, the calm, unhurried persistence to tackle such an assignment and do it perfectly with no fuss, no fanfare, no credit of any kind.*

When one feels a flash of gratitude to an unknown benefactor, there's little one can do about it as a rule. But this time there may be an exception to that rule. So in this Thanksgiving season, on behalf of all the readers of *Daily Guideposts*, I'd like to thank you, Mary Tomaselli, for your splendid work.

And now, Mary, if you'll look at this year's biography section, you'll find at last a very deserving name (and photo!): your own.

Father, give us grateful hearts, today and every day.

—Arthur Gordon

Wednesday

21

A heart at peace gives life to the body....

—Proverbs 14:30 (NIV)

I recently wrote a check for improvement of my mental health. Was it to a psychologist? No, to a cabinetmaker!

It all started when I read a list of twenty-six ways to lessen stress. Many were familiar—reduce caffeine, stretch, breathe deeply. But one was new to me: "Don't put up with something that doesn't work right. If your alarm clock, wallet, shoelaces, windshield wipers, whatever are a constant aggravation, get them fixed or get new ones."

Now, I tend to take an almost perverse pride in "making do" with objects like our deep kitchen drawer that constantly came off its monorail. The drawer holds frequently used items like dish towels, potholders and trivets, so I pulled it out almost daily, gouging a deeper and deeper groove in the wood underneath. The next time I struggled to hoist it back on track, I had to admit, "This really ticks me off!"

I consulted a nearby cabinetmaker, who quoted a nominal fee to make a quick "kitchen call." He replaced faulty hardware on the drawer and on others I didn't even realize were also being damaged. Months later, as I open that drawer, I am still awed at how smoothly the roller glides.

Do you get agitated over some trivial object that doesn't function well? Yet you put off repairing it or buying a new one because it seems extravagant? The stress experts, and my experience, say if it's significant enough to bother you, it's significant enough to fix.

Lord, thank You for the ability to make changes. —B. J. Connor

Thursday

22

Let them give thanks to the Lord for his unfailing love and his wonderful deeds.... —Psalm 107:8 (NIV)

For what are you most thankful today? Your faith, your family, your home, your sustenance, your church, your friends, your freedom are all no doubt high on the list. But the people most thankful this red-letter day are those who have recently recovered something precious that was lost—say their health, a job, their faith, someone's love. I can make that statement with a good deal of certainty because we all have a tendency to take our blessings for granted. Only when our well runs dry do we learn the real worth of water.

For me, a childhood Thanksgiving Day during World War II serves as a case in point. Like many other service families, ours had been separated. But then came the opportunity to be reunited with my father near an army base in Missouri, and it was with great excitement that my mother, brother, sister and I sped to his side. We arrived in late fall and took up quarters in a miniscule cabin, but being cramped was a small price to pay for togetherness. When we circled our Thanksgiving table that year, there were many reasons to praise God, but my tearful father's prayer revealed that which was foremost on his mind when he began: "Thank You, Lord, for making us one family again...."

If you suffered some loss this year and then had it restored, you have special reason for celebrating this Thanksgiving. Others who have not found resolution to long-standing hurts and difficulties need to be remembered with supporting prayers. Whatever our circumstance, one thing for which all Christians can be thankful today is the gift of God's truth as revealed through His Son. We can sing with composer Philip Bliss,

Come to the Light, 'tis shining for thee;
Sweetly the Light has dawned upon me,
Once I was blind, but now I can see;
The Light of the world is Jesus.

Impress upon us, Lord...
That more than a holiday set apart,
Thanksgiving's the mark of a grateful heart.

—Fred Bauer

Friday **23**

Fireside Friend 

And the bow shall be in the cloud; and I will look upon it, that I may remember the everlasting covenant.... —Genesis 9:16

On one of our infrequent journeys more than a hundred miles from home, my husband decided to take the family on a side trip up Mount Capulin, rising some eight thousand feet above sea level in northeastern New Mexico. Having viewed the huge volcano from its summit, we wound our way down its charred sides. A soft mist draped itself across the sun and a rainbow arched before us.

Without warning, a golden eagle soared through the mist from its nesting place. His wings spanned a good six feet, and his taloned feet dangled beneath him. By the time our son Don got his camera out, the eagle was nothing more than a dot. Yet I can still see the wings tipped upward like long, extended fingers, carrying him higher and higher until he seemed to circle far above the rainbow.

If I'd had my "druthers," we would not have taken that unplanned tour of Capulin—and I would not have seen the majesty of the golden eagle! Most of the side trips in my life have been pretty much like that. Several years ago, the unwanted termination of my job of over twenty years with an oil company led me to the much-needed, more-relaxed atmosphere of part-time work at a nearby church—a path I never would have chosen on my own.

Life still takes me on side trips every now and again, in spite of my protests. And when it does, I look at that small dot in Don's picture and I know that if I place my trust in God's vision for me and remember His covenant, I will be lifted high above life's little side trips.

Father, help me to lift myself ever upward above the mists of my life into the arch of Your protecting love. —Mary Jane Meyer

Saturday

24

I have not stopped giving thanks for you, remembering you in my prayers. —Ephesians 1:16 (NIV)

When my brother and his family went to San Diego for a week's vacation, I took care of their poodle D'artagnian. When they returned, my five-year-old niece Meredith came with her mother to pick up their dog.

Meredith was so happy to see Dart, and he was ecstatic. He danced on his hind legs, wagged his tail and reached for her with his front paws as if to give her a hug.

"Did you miss Dart while you were gone?" I asked.

"Oh, yes," Meredith said. "But as soon as we got to San Diego, I forgot all about him!"

I laughed at her honesty, but as I thought about it later, I asked myself: *Are there people in my life I've forgotten about simply because I don't see them often?* I immediately thought about my good college friends. We shared many great joys and sorrows, yet now that we live in different cities and are busy with our lives, we've lost touch.

Right away I made a list of their names and promised myself to write each a short note, just to say I'm thinking about them. Are there people in your life who need to know you haven't forgotten them? Would hearing from you brighten their day? Why not send them a short "hello" today?

Father, remind us to keep in touch with those we love, especially when we cannot be together. —Gina Bridgeman

That their hearts might be comforted, being knit together in love.... —Colossians 2:2

Pastor Jordan loved to preach on loving. Every chance he got, he expounded on the power and practicality of loving. I once asked him why he so often chose that as a topic for his sermons. Pastor Jordan grinned. "Well, I figure you all have hell all week—and you can use a little Heaven on Sunday."

I remember Pastor Jordan's words whenever I'm inclined to let love take a back seat in my relationships with people, when I'm tempted to pound home their failures and faults. Like the times my daughter Amy Jo borrows the car and brings it home with the gas gauge on E. Or when my son Brett wears his muddy soccer cleats into the kitchen. Then there are those Saturdays when my husband Gary seems blind to the huge "Honey-Do" list I've posted on the refrigerator door. That's when I remind myself that maybe their weeks have been tough enough; maybe what they need from me is a little bit of love, a tiny slice of Heaven. So I'll listen to Brett tell me about making that goal. And let my husband catch a few extra winks on Saturday morning. Amy Jo and I will go out for lunch later—and stop by the gas station.

Is there someone close to you who could use a little "Heaven"? Why not show them some this very day?

Father, how I cherish Your love for me! Today I'll pass that love along to ____________________ *by doing this:*

____.

—Mary Lou Carney

Monday

26

Let us run with patience the race that is set before us, looking unto Jesus... who for the joy that was set before him endured the cross.... —Hebrews 12:1–2

One of my favorite stories is about the boy who decided to learn how to play the flute. He went to the flute teacher and inquired about the price of lessons.

"Ten gold pieces for the first lesson," said the teacher. "And one gold piece for each lesson thereafter."

"Good," said the boy. "I'll start with the second lesson."

I recognize myself in the boy. I often want to bypass what is costly and take the easiest route.

In his book *The Road Less Traveled*, psychiatrist Scott Peck points out that our emotional well-being and personal growth are often determined by our ability to face what is difficult instead of skirting around it.

I imagine we all have some first flute lessons we would like to avoid. I sure do. But today I'm going to remind myself that tackling what is difficult in my life is God's way of helping me learn, grow and become.

Teach me to welcome problems in my life as an opportunity to grow. —Sue Monk Kidd

Tuesday

Fireside Friend 

27

Revive thy work in the midst of the years.... —Habakkuk 3:2

"What do you think?" Jennifer asked hopefully. I looked at the table she was offering me. It was awful. It had been used as a plant stand for years; a piece of linoleum was glued to the top; someone had nailed a strip of metal around the edge; chipped varnish discolored the legs. I cleared my throat. "Well, it looks a little small," I began. But she was already putting it in my car.

"You can have it, Vic," she said enthusiastically. "Take it home and see what you can do with it!"

I started very reluctantly. No matter how hard I tried, I just couldn't figure out what Jen saw in that table. I couldn't see past the "ugly." Then slowly, layer by layer, I got closer to the heart of it. Under all the gunk and glue and varnish was a beautiful grain. I began to enjoy working on the table.

As I worked, I thought of a Woodworker Who sees through all the "ugly" in my life. He was able to look past the impatience, the laziness, my selfish motives and protective masks. He looked directly into my heart and saw what I could become. Then, because I would never change on my own, He went to work. He has used pleasant things and difficult ones; He encourages and He convicts; He sends me people, books and sermons. No technique is too complicated for His persistent, steady work in me.

Slowly but surely, His efforts are bringing results. I'm learning obedience; I'm beginning to see that my stubborn masks are just thinly disguised pride. There's still a lot of change to come, but we're making progress!

A few weeks ago, Jen visited my home. It was my turn to ask, "What do you think?" In front of the living room couch was a small honey-colored table. A lovely, smooth finish revealed the warm grain of the wood. It was exactly what I had wanted for that spot! Jen just grinned and said, "You did a good job."

Lord, keep at me till You're done, till I'm glowing with the beauty for which You created me. —Vicki Schad

Wednesday

28

If it [a person's gift] is encouraging, let him encourage.... —Romans 12:8 (NIV)

I was disturbed several years ago because one of my then seventeen-year-old twin sons and I weren't getting along. Jon meant the world to me, but it seemed all we did was snap at each other.

One morning as he left for school I followed him to the door, nagging about yet another thing. "Just leave me alone," he mumbled. I watched him go down the front steps. He didn't know I was watching. He stopped at our picture window and appeared to be examining the bricks on the window ledge. He hurried to his truck and came back with a towel and placed it on the bricks. *What an odd thing to do*, I thought. I stepped outside and asked sharply, "Jon, what are you doing?"

"Look, Mom," he answered in a voice so soft it startled me. "See, bees can't stand the cold. He's almost dead. He's only a baby... shouldn't have to die." As I watched, Jon gently tucked the towel around the bee.

All morning I checked on the bee. Finally about noon I checked again and the bee was gone. When Jon came in from school we actually had a pleasant conversation about bees.

"You really went out and checked on him?" my son asked, still using his gentle voice.

"Oh, yes," I answered, using an even softer voice.

"A lot of mothers wouldn't have cared about a bee," Jon said.

"Neither would a lot of teenage boys," I said.

We were both smiling.

Oh, Lord, show me ways to encourage, not nag, my children—and others. —Marion Bond West

Thursday

29

Even though I walk through the valley of the shadow of death, I fear no evil.... —Psalm 23:4 (RSV)

Ever since I started exercising four years ago, I've become an avid walker. When I first began my walk-for-fitness regimen, I was excited and enthusiastic. I read every article devoted to the topic and even got into competitive race-walking for a time. But as the months slipped by, my spirits began to flag, and I searched desperately for something to keep me interested.

What occurred to me might seem strange to most people, but if you understand that I am an indexer (someone who creates those alphabetical lists at the back of books—like this one!), it might not seem so unusual. I began to wonder how many quotes from the Bible refer to walking. I consulted an index to the Bible, a concordance, and found lots of references to "walk," "walked," "walketh," "walkest." Here are some of the "walking" references I found:

Thus you may *walk* in the way of good men, and keep to the paths of the just (Proverbs 2:20).

Walk in my presence and be perfect (Genesis 17:1).

Therefore, keep the commandments of the Lord, your God, *walking* in his ways and fearing him (Deuteronomy 8:6).

You may not be a race-walker like me, but if there's some area where your interest is flagging, why don't you find a concordance and look up the appropriate heading. If your job seems flat or stale, look under "work" or "task." If you're bored with housekeeping, try "sweep," "wash" or "feed." If you have a problem with one of your youngsters, look under "children." You'll see that the problems that make up our daily lives are not so different from the problems people had in the ancient days of the Bible. And you might find, as I did, that that new knowledge brings you into a closer walk with the Creator of us all.

Dear Lord, let me find the inspiration to do new things that bring me closer to You. —Mary Tomaselli

Day Brightener

The tides of time flow in,
flow out,
Sun dries each flood,
rain quenches dust;
So if a dark cloud hovers low,
This, too, shall pass. Just wait
and trust.

—Phyllis C. Michael

Friday
30

They shall bear the burden of the people with thee, that thou bear it not thyself alone. —Numbers 11:17

I once heard the mother of a teenage boy who was paralyzed in an accident explain how she kept from having a breakdown herself:

"Our church friends formed a circle around us so tightly, there was no room to fall."

I love her description. Can't you just picture people holding hands, surrounding that devastated huddle of a family like children playing "Farmer in the Dell"? Of course, they didn't literally encompass them. But they surrounded them with love. They sent cards and letters of encouragement, brought meals, built a wheelchair ramp, chipped in money for expenses, helped modify the house, visited with jokes and news and tutoring and prayed, and other unnamed kindnesses, all of which helped pull the family through a difficult time.

What a privilege to be fellow participants in this game called "Bearing One Another's Burdens." Because sometimes we're one of the strong ones forming the circle. And sometimes we're one of the broken ones inside.

Lord, motivate us to keep supportive arms so close, "there is no room to fall." —B.J. Connor

Thank-You Notes to God

1 ______________________________

2 ______________________________

3 ______________________________

4 ______________________________

5 ______________________________

6 ______________________________

7 ______________________________

8 ______________________________

9 ______________________________

10 ______________________________

11 ______________________________

12 ______________________________

13 ______________________________

14 ______________________________

15 ______________________________

16 ____________________

17 ____________________

18 ____________________

19 ____________________

20 ____________________

21 ____________________

22 ____________________

23 ____________________

24 ____________________

25 ____________________

26 ____________________

27 ____________________

28 ____________________

29 ____________________

30 ____________________

DECEMBER

S	*M*	*T*	*W*	*T*	*F*	*S*
						1
2	3	4	5	6	7	8
9	10	11	12	13	14	15
16	17	18	19	20	21	22
23	24	25	26	27	28	29
30	31					

SPIRITUAL TREASURE

Give in Secret

But when you give to the needy, do not let your left hand know what your right hand is doing, so that your giving may be in secret.

—Matthew 6:3–4 (NIV)

If months had second names, surely December's would be *Surprise!* Ever since God sprang the surprise of Bethlehem on the world, the days of December have been filled with unexpectedness, tucked full of wrapped astonishments, big and small.

As you enjoy the secrets and surprises of this month, bestow a few of your own. A poinsettia left at someone's door, a warm coat sent to a needy child, cookies delivered to a lonely friend, caroling outside a nursing home... only be sure you do it in secret. For that's where the real joy of surprises comes from.

Your Father, Who knows every secret, will smile.

My Monthly Prayer List

Family Prayer for December

Father God, I already see colorfully wrapped presents under the tree, but more than that, I want Your presence. Let Christ be born in me, live in me and be Lord of my life.

Lighting the Candles of Advent
JOURNEY TO INNER BETHLEHEM

This Advent, join Terry Helwig and light the candles of Christmas in a "Journey to Inner Bethlehem." As the darkened world waited two thousand years ago for the Light of the World to appear, let's discover this Advent season the Light that brightens our own darkened inner Bethlehem. What hidden potential lies waiting to be illumined within each of us? Advent is a time for waiting, preparing and finally discovering the Light of the Christ Child Who fills our lives with meaning at Christmas and all through the year.

May His blessings in this Holy Season illumine your heart.

—The Editors

Saturday
1

JOURNEY TO INNER BETHLEHEM
Lighting Our Inner Candles

For thou wilt light my candle: the Lord my God will enlighten my darkness. —Psalm 18:28

Tomorrow is Advent. And as I sit in my favorite chair and watch the evening shadows creep into the family room, I think about the Advent candle-lighting service at our church that our family will be part of this season. Yet in my solitude this evening, I wish for a more *personal* celebration of Advent—one between just God and me. I long to discover a more private meaning of Christmas, one that will satisfy an inner desire to draw close to Him this Holy Season.

Suddenly I perk up. *Why not create my own* personal *Advent wreath?* Not too formal; one that wouldn't look out of place amid the clutter of books and papers on the table next to my "quiet" chair in the family room. Excitedly, I begin my search for a handmade Advent wreath. In a kitchen drawer, I discover five birthday candles left over from my daughter Mandy's sixth birthday. In a cabinet, I find a round, metal band of a Mason jar lid from the applesauce I canned last fall. I turn the tarnished band upside down and secure the candles in a circle to the inside rim with melted wax. A sprig of holly from the dining table centerpiece completes my wreath. No, my little crown of leaning candles does not resemble the traditional Advent wreath, but I rather like it. Rustic and homemade—like a manger.

Preparing for tomorrow's lighting, I think back to two thousand years ago, when the world waited, like a darkened candle, for the birth of a Savior.... Candles awaiting light. A world awaiting a Savior. *What else sleeps in my world?*

I wonder, *This Advent, could I possibly discover some spiritual,* inner *candles waiting to be lit?* In the coming weeks, together, let's journey within, to an *inner Bethlehem.* There, let's try to discover and light some of the sleeping candles that await us and awaken the hidden potential that lies dormant within. Perhaps I could light the sleepy candle of understanding that could release me from my pride. Or I might ignite the darkened candle of forgiveness, instead of clinging to a long-held grudge. Could these inner candles, if lit with the Christmas flame, also bring to life within me a deeper love for God and others?

So often after Christmas I pack away the tinsel and wreaths and with them my Christmas love and goodwill. Perhaps, this Advent, by lighting my inner candles, I can keep those feelings burning the other 364 days as well!

Dear Father, touch our hearts this Advent as we light candles, both inward and outward, in honor of Your Son. —Terry Helwig

Sunday

2

JOURNEY TO INNER BETHLEHEM
The Candle of Wisdom

Inasmuch as ye have done it unto one of the least of these my brethren, ye have done it unto me.

—Matthew 25:40

Today is the first day of Advent. Beside my Advent wreath is a copy of *The Story of the Other Wise Man,* written by Henry Van Dyke in the late 1800s. Every year I reread that Christmas story hoping to become more like Artaban, the fourth wise man.

As I stare into the flame of my first candle, I recall how Artaban planned to journey with three wise men to Bethlehem. Artaban's gifts were precious stones: a sapphire, a ruby and a pearl. But on his way to meet the others, Artaban stopped to nurse a dying man.

Being greatly delayed, he missed the caravan. Saddened, Artaban sold his sapphire for camels and provisions to continue on to Bethlehem.

Many days later he arrived. A local woman, holding her son in her arms, told Artaban that the wise men had already gone. And the young child he sought had been taken to Egypt. Artaban hung his head and turned to leave the woman's home. Suddenly, cries filled the village as Herod's soldiers approached with bloodied swords. Quickly Artaban stepped in front of the woman's doorway while she ran to hide her son. As a soldier approached, Artaban held the glistening ruby in his palm. "I am waiting to give this jewel to the prudent captain who will leave me in peace," he said. The captain took the ruby and ordered his men to march on.

For the next thirty-three years, Artaban sought the whereabouts of the King. Stories eventually led him to Jerusalem where he was told the "King of the Jews" was about to be crucified. Artaban touched his pearl as he hurried toward Golgotha. But on the way he saw a young woman being sold into slavery because of her dead father's debts. Filled with compassion, Artaban laid the pearl in her hands saying, "This is thy ransom, daughter—the last of my treasures I kept for the king."

Suddenly the sky darkened, the earth shook and a heavy tile fell upon Artaban's temple. He lay dying, grieving that his gifts never reached the King. Then Christ appeared to him saying: "Inasmuch as ye have done it unto one of the least of these my brethren, ye have done it unto me." A radiance lit Artaban's face. His journey had ended. His gifts were accepted. He had found his King.

Journeying inward on this first Sunday of Advent, I discover within me the sleeping candle of wisdom. The kind of wisdom that says the greatest gifts are not sapphires, rubies or pearls. No, the greatest gifts are deeds of love. If I want to draw nearer to Christ, wisdom tells me the best gifts this holiday are those that cannot be wrapped and laid under a Christmas tree.

Thoughtfully, I make out my list. To Brenda, my younger sister who is separated and raising two girls alone, I will give the gift of my support. I'll make more time to call and write her. To Barb, who worked so hard on a church project with me and experienced my impatience on more than one occasion, I will offer the gift of an apology.

And to my husband Jim, who often takes the brunt of my Don Rickles-like humor, I will give the gift of sensitivity that does not seek a laugh at the expense of his feelings.

Make your own list now... what gifts of the spirit have you to offer the King?

Dear Father, may I be wise enough to understand that the love I give to others always ends up in Your Hands. —Terry Helwig

Monday
3

THROUGH AN OPEN WINDOW
Be a Star

And, lo, the star, which they saw in the east, went before them, till it came and stood over where the young child was. —Matthew 2:9

It's ten P.M. Outside my window the air is crisp and clear. High in the darkened heavens a few stars twinkle. This is the month to celebrate Jesus' birth, the time to think of shepherds who heard the angels and kings who followed a star to Bethlehem.

It reminds me of a little story that I read ten years ago. In this story, a little girl had a part in her Sunday school Nativity play. Her role was to hold high an aluminum foil star for everyone to see. When the play was over, the child proudly announced that she had had the main part.

"You did?" her mother questioned.

"Yes," the daughter answered, "because I showed everybody how to find Jesus."

Show everybody how to find Jesus.... Isn't that what Jesus Himself was saying when He commanded, "Go ye therefore, and teach all nations..." (Matthew 28:19)? Isn't that what each one of us can do in our lives?

During the coming month, I'm going to ask God to guide me to the one special person He wants me to talk to each day. Well, not every single day, perhaps, but almost every day. I'll ask Him to let me be receptive to this person's need. I realize it might be a family member in trouble. Or an unhappy coworker. Or a friend who just needs someone to talk to.

I'm going to go to the stationery store and buy one of those little boxes of gold stars. After I've talked to—or tried to help—that special person, I'll stick a star on the page for the day in my pocket diary, where no one else will see it. The purpose isn't to congratulate myself; it's just a reminder that God answered my prayer, and He let me try to show someone how to find Jesus.

Dear Lord, now and in the coming year, use me to bring others just a little closer to You. —Eleanor Sass

Tuesday

4

And yet show I unto you a more excellent way.
—I Corinthians 12:31

At eleven years old, I loved to take scraps of wood and build rafts, ladders or houses for our dogs and cats. One morning a couple of friends and I collected enough lumber to build a clubhouse. In a few hours we had built the frame and nailed on shingles for siding. We used cardboard to cover the inside and we threw an old bedspread over the top for our roof. Since we had built the clubhouse on our patio, we also had a concrete floor.

After we finished, I called my mother and older brother to see our handiwork. My mother offered enough praise to satisfy me, but my brother was more analytical. He examined the clubhouse like a building inspector and finally said, "It's good, but we can make it better. Why don't we take this apart and I'll help you build your clubhouse back the right way. We can use the table saw and cut all the corners to fit. We can even build a gable roof."

I was hurt. I wasn't about to tear apart my clubhouse no matter how bad my brother thought it was. For the rest of the day, my pals and I held club meetings. But the next afternoon, my mother informed me that we were going to have to move our clubhouse to the back of the yard. "The neighbors are complaining that it's an eyesore," she said.

Reluctantly, we began the task of moving, but the clubhouse had been so poorly built that by the time we had it off the patio, it was falling apart. I felt so bad that we tore the clubhouse down and never rebuilt it.

If I had listened to my brother, I could well have had a clubhouse that lasted for several years. But because I was so proud of my own efforts, I couldn't bring myself to admit there was a better way. I've always remembered that old clubhouse and the lesson it taught me. Since then I have been listening to my "older Brother"—the One Who is "the Way, the Truth and the Life."

Lord, help me to put aside my pride and learn Your most excellent way.

—Brian Miller

Wednesday

5

For God alone my soul waits in silence....

—Psalm 62:1 (RSV)

"The polite part of speaking with God is to be still long enough to listen," wrote Ruth Graham in her perceptive book *Legacy of a Pack Rat.* And sometimes when she listens: "God says, as it were, 'Why are you praying? Do something!'" She went on to quote C. S. Lewis who in the same vein wrote, "It is so much easier to pray for a boor than go and see him."

The Bible tells us to pray without ceasing (I Thessalonians 5:17), but it also informs us that faith without works is dead (James 2:17). I suspect James uttered the latter to keep the super pious from using prayer and meditation as a dodge from involvement—visiting the sick, lifting the fallen, clothing the poor, sheltering the homeless, feeding the hungry, nurturing the young, listening to the lonely, assisting the old....

How do we keep those two things—faith and works—in balance? One way is to set aside a regular period during the day for both. Not that they are mutually exclusive. Brother Lawrence (who wrote *Practicing the Presence of God*) encouraged engaging in prayer and work *simultaneously.* While the saintly monk was washing pots and pans, standing at a monastery sink, he prayed, which may be the ideal solution for people who are always on the run.

To my knowledge there is no correlation between our posture and the potency of our prayers. Otherwise, Christ would have insisted that His disciples get on their knees and close their eyes when praying. If I read my Bible correctly, God's focus is on our heart condition, not our body position.

Remind us, Lord, that prayer is listening, too,
Receiving Your guidance, then following through.

—Fred Bauer

Thursday

6

And there we saw the giants.... —Numbers 13:33

Grandma and I had just settled down to visit when a piercing scream sent me running outside. Three-year-old Rebecca hurled herself into my arms. "A dragon!" she shrieked. "A dragon chased me!"

"Dragons are make-believe," I scolded.

"But I saw one!" Rebecca insisted. "He stuck out his tongue at me! He's hiding over there!" She pointed to a massive honeysuckle.

I looked. A four-inch green and gold gecko flicked its tongue, and I grabbed it. "Honey, it's only a lizard," I explained.

After much persuasion, she gingerly touched its back. "It looks like the dragons in my fairy tale book," she said.

So it did. The lizard was the exact size as the *picture* of a fire-breathing monster that held the princess captive in its lair.

Right now, like Rebecca's "dragon," my own problems seem larger than life: a child who can't find the right niche in life, financial troubles that threaten our farm existence, relatives with serious health problems. When the dragons seem insurmountable, I turn to God, Who frees me from disabling fear and helps me reduce problems to a realistic, manageable size. Then I can take action: I put my child in touch with a vocational counselor, take an additional part-time job to help with expenses and talk with my physician for wisdom in helping my mother manage emphysema.

Having done as much as I can do, I continue to seek counsel from the One Who can lead me through any eventuality, One Who can help me turn my dragons into lizards.

Lord of all things, I entrust You with this "dragon" that looms so large in my life: ______________________________________.

—Penney Schwab

Friday

7

Never criticize or condemn—or it will all come back on you. Go easy on others; then they will do the same for you. —Luke 6:37 (TLB)

My eight-year-old son Andrew and I went shopping for bright blue high-top canvas sneakers. There was only one other person in the shoe store with the sales clerk—a teenaged boy wearing loafers and no socks. He was paying for a pair of athletic shoes when we walked in. After he received his change, he walked over to the sport socks rack in the corner of the store.

The clerk went to the back room for a minute to find Andrew's size. I glanced up from my chair to see the boy shove a pair of fluffy white socks into his bag as he walked toward the front door. When the clerk returned, I whispered, "Did he buy a pair of socks?"

"No, why?"

"Well, I just saw him stuff a pair of socks into his bag." The clerk ran after the young shoplifter. As a firm believer in "tough" love, I felt that if the boy got caught now, perhaps he would end his life of crime at an early age.

The clerk returned, smiling. "Those were Jason's own socks that he brought in to try on with his sneakers."

I had misjudged and wrongly accused the boy. It was then that I decided to concentrate on gathering all the facts before opening my mouth... especially when dealing with fragile teenaged egos. Maybe if I make a list of my own faults and look at it periodically, I won't be so quick to criticize others.

Lord, help me to work on my own faults and go easy on everyone else.

—Patricia Lorenz

Saturday

8

As he thinketh in his heart, so is he.... —Proverbs 23:7

John Burroughs was one of America's best loved naturalists. In simple style, his books convey his avid enthusiasm and vast knowledge of nature. One day Burroughs was visiting a neighbor. She was familiar with his writings and particularly impressed with his knowledge of birds. As they sat on her front porch, she asked him, "Why is it there are so many birds at your place, but I have no birds at all in my yard?"

Burroughs smiled. For the last quarter hour he had been watching all sorts of birds flitter in her bushes, light in her shrubs, flutter in her trees. He replied, "You will not see birds in your yard until you have birds in your heart."

Sometimes all I see around me is sadness. The hopelessness of the homeless. The injustice of evil men prospering. The bitterness of unachieved goals. Slowly these begin crowding out the wonder, the optimism, the hope I once saw. Then I remember Burroughs' birds. And I know I must cultivate *inner* joy before I can find it in the world around me.

So today I'm going to look for love. I'm going to listen for the songs of birds and the laughter of children. I'm going to expect good things to happen. What good things can you find to cultivate today?

Oh, God, open my eyes and ears—and heart—to the wonders of life.

—Mary Lou Carney

Sunday

9

JOURNEY TO INNER BETHLEHEM
The Candle of Compassion

Suppose there are brothers or sisters who need clothes and don't have enough to eat. What good is there in your saying to them, "God bless you! Keep warm and eat well!"—if you don't give them the necessities of life?

—James 2:15–16 (GNB)

It is dark and snowing outside. As I light the second candle on my

Advent wreath, I snuggle into the comfort of my overstuffed chair. I remember another night some years ago. It was snowing then, too. But my mood was not nearly so peaceful.

The strap of a carry-on bag dug deep into my shoulders and my back ached. I carried fourteen-month-old Mandy onto the shuttle bus while my husband Jim maneuvered two denim bags filled with presents, formula and traveling gear. The Denver airport, jammed with holiday travelers like ourselves, had just closed for the night. Eighteen inches of snow was more than they could deal with. Tears of frustration burned my cheeks: Twelve hours of waiting, no place to spend the night, and only one remaining disposable diaper was more than I could deal with.

The bus driver let us off in front of the hotel and warned, "I think it's a lost cause. There isn't a vacant room around." He was right. There were no rooms available. The sympathetic man at the registration desk motioned to an available sofa in the corner of the lobby where we could wait for a cancellation. We accepted his offer. And, as I watched Jim trudge off to look for food and diapers, I thought of Mary and Joseph, seeking lodging in a crowded inn. How alone they must have felt, to be so far away from home, looking for a place to deliver God's Son into the world.

Tonight, remembering and journeying inward, I discover the sleeping candle of compassion. The kind of compassion offered by an innkeeper in Bethlehem and one in Denver.

This snowy night of Advent, as I light the second candle, I think of the many homeless Marys and Josephs in the world. And as I offer up a prayer on their behalf, it occurs to me there may be yet another kind of homelessness. Is it possible that there may be people in my own circle of acquaintances, even my own family, seeking another kind of shelter? I think of my sensitive six-year-old daughter Mandy confiding that a classmate at school doesn't like her. Isn't Mandy knocking at my door, seeking the comfort of my love and the shelter of my arms? Then I think of Jean. She left a secure job in Texas to attend seminary here in Louisville. Being uprooted is a kind of homelessness. I've been meaning to call. Perhaps I could offer Jean the warmth of our kitchen table by setting an extra plate for dinner.

True compassion is more than a fleeting thought for another, more than pity. It is opening the door, staring into the eyes of need and then doing something to meet that need... whether it be offering a young couple the use of a stable, inviting a lonely woman for dinner or holding a sad little girl until she drifts off to sleep.

Heavenly Father, this Advent help me to understand that compassion is best thought of as a verb instead of a noun. —Terry Helwig

Monday

10

Thou shalt love thy neighbour as thyself.

—Leviticus 19:18

I got off my subway in a glum mood, attacked by worries—term papers, office deadlines and missing my best friend who was traveling. *Everyone rushes around in New York,* I thought. *Including me. What's the point?* Heading home, I wasn't in the mood to wave to Ira, the dry cleaner, or to stop and watch Giuseppi, Luigi and Tomas toss dough high into the air of their pizza shop. I just wanted to pick up my evening paper and be alone. But when I stepped into the news shop, Raj, the shopkeeper, and a customer were debating a tabloid headline: "Drink 25 Quarts of Fruit Juice and Lose 10 Pounds Overnight." The customer shook his head, saying, "I don't believe it." Raj agreed it was deceptive.

Their solemn faces made me smile, and so I turned to the customer and jokingly said, "Now, be sure you drink those 25 quarts before going to bed tonight!" The men looked at each other, then burst out laughing. After a moment, I laughed, too. Not just at them, but at myself. After all, I had been feeling pretty solemn myself, about worries that in the long run, like a silly headline, wouldn't matter.

Surely, God wants me to get my work done. But He doesn't want me to get so wrapped up in doing that I forget to take time to *be*! That must be why He sprinkles my day with small encounters with Raj, Ira, Giuseppi, Luigi and Tomas. Just because I live in a big city doesn't mean I have to let small-town pleasures like friendly chats with good neighbors slip through my fingers.

Feeling trapped by your worries? Watch for those small, neighborly encounters that can remind you not just to *do*, but to *be*.

Lord, remind me: Live today—today! —Terri Castillo

Tuesday

11

For thou dost requite a man according to his work.
—Psalm 62:12 (RSV)

As I was growing up, I gave my little brother a lot of advice. He needed to learn good work habits, I rationalized, for he was too carefree, too full of high spirits. Imagine my surprise when his first-grade report card came back full of A's. What did my rambunctious brother know that I didn't? Whenever I came home late with armloads of books for the report I had left to do till the last minute, he was always in the street playing ball with his pals.

I chalked up his good grades to good luck, until the day school let out for Christmas vacation. I had dumped my books on the floor and was heading for my best friend's house, when I looked into his room. He was sitting at his desk busily scratching on his tablets with a thick pencil. "What are you doing homework for?" I scolded in typical big-sister fashion. "It's Friday afternoon. Go out and play! You don't have to go to school for two weeks."

"I always do homework as soon as school's over," he replied. His small face turned serious. "If I do the hard stuff first, then I can play all vacation and not have to worry."

Okay, I admit my brother was better than me at facing up to difficult responsibilities. Since then, I've been trying to adopt his "hard-stuff-first habit" for the last thirty years. But don't tell him I said so.

Father, when I want to avoid the tough or demanding job before me, give me discipline to tackle the "hard stuff" first, and then enjoy the fun of play that awaits me. —Linda Ching Sledge

Wednesday

12

This is how God showed his love among us: He sent his one and only Son into the world....
—I John 4:9 (NIV)

When it looked as though a business venture would keep an old friend of mine in England over the Christmas holidays, he saw to it that his wife and young daughter joined him there. Christmas Eve found them together in a London hotel, but just before bedtime, Robin, who was ten, came out of her bedroom in great distress. She had left the present she'd bought for her parents at home. Nothing my friends could say to her seemed to ease the youngster's disappointment.

On Christmas morning, however, Robin was as cheerful as ever. In the midst of opening her presents she stopped and with a touch of ceremony asked her mother and father to sit down because she had something to give them after all.

"I stayed up last night getting it ready," she said. Then, moving to the center of the room she turned, stood up straight, and began to speak these words:

"And Joseph went up from Galilee, out of the city of Nazareth, into Judea, unto the city of David, which is called Bethlehem...."

And on and on she went through the Christmas story according to Luke, never missing a word that she had stayed up late to memorize.

"And suddenly there was with the angel a multitude of the heavenly host praising God, and saying, glory to God in the highest, and on earth peace, goodwill toward men."

When Robin finished, she was surprised to find that her mother and father were silent. But after a moment they reached out and drew her to them and held her close.

My old friend says that it's still the best Christmas gift he and his wife have ever received, and the most unusual—something meant for them alone, and for everybody in the world.

Thank You, Father, for the wisdom of the young...and for the glorious Hope You bring each and every one of us this Holy Season.

—Van Varner

Thursday

13

Such as I have give I thee.... —Acts 3:6

"The presents you make are always the best!" I've repeatedly told our three children since their preschool days. Our home is filled with a priceless collection of papier-mâché objects, lumpy clay ashtrays, collages of family pictures and framed Scripture verses with illustrations.

A few years ago, we came up with a "present-you-can-make" idea for grandparents, which my husband Lynn's parents now claim is their favorite Christmas present. It's our own personalized, wall-hanging calendar, which is as much fun to make as it is to receive. Gather together lots of heavy, colored construction paper, a hole-puncher, scissors, glue, some yarn, a picture-calendar that comes in the mail this time of year, and a pile of family photos you're willing to give away.

We copy the format of any wall-hanging calendar. First, we cut the pages of the month off the new picture calendar, paste them on separate sheets of construction paper and make a collage of pictures and artwork to go with that month. We add a few captions, Scripture verses or monthly reminders, and tie the whole thing together with colorful yarn. Each child does his or her birthday month, and we divide up the rest of the pages. The result is a photo-summary of a year in the life of our family, which, according to our Mamma and Pappa, blesses them from their kitchen wall every single day of the year.

Why don't you create your own family-photo calendar for some far-away relative or friend this Christmas?

Lord, as the Christmas season approaches, let us find new ways to give ourselves to one another. —Carol Kuykendall

Friday

14

Break forth into joy, sing together.... —Isaiah 52:9

I'm listening to one of my favorite albums. The music always lifts me into the joy of Christmas. The goose bumps I get are like old friends.

The record is thirty-two years old. It was a present to my wife Sally while we were dating. I can still remember the anguish I felt when I heard the first scratch on it. Then another, and another. Each year I planned to buy a new copy, but somehow never found the time.

Then slowly these scratchy noises began to make the record even more special. Like a favorite old sweater, they warmed me with memories of Christmases we shared: our first one together in a drafty third-floor apartment and all the ones that followed.

The events of the past three decades have left their marks on me as well: when I've missed opportunities, or said the wrong thing to loved ones, or been hurt by a colleague. But I try to make friends with these scars and bruises the same way I've made friends with the scratches on my Christmas record. Because just as I listen for the skips that make my copy of the record unique, I know my aches are my own, unique to me, caused by my own experience, and complete with lessons that guide me to live better.

Are you smarting from the scratches that life inflicts? Let time help you heal them. You can help the process along, too, by making friends with your hurts. They're part of living and they have lessons for you. Remember: Like few other things in the world, those raspy imperfections are part of the record of your life.

And Lord, even with all our flaws and roughness, may the melody of Your Son's love resound through us. —Scott Harrison

Saturday

15

WINDOWS INTO WONDER
A Place of Safety

Arise, and take the young child and his mother, and flee into Egypt.... —Matthew 2:13

Imagine how Mary must have felt when she heard that King Herod was out to destroy her Baby, this precious new Child Who was a gift of the Spirit. How relieved she must have been when the angel appeared to Joseph in a dream, telling him that his little family could find safety in Egypt.

At Christmastime, I like to think of Jesus being born anew in my heart. The time I sense it best is after all the rush of card-writing, shopping, wrapping, decorating and baking is done, and I'm sitting in the darkened church with my spiritual family, holding my little lighted candle, and the first soft strains of "Silent Night" begin. My faith is freshened and renewed and, yes, reborn. But I know that, like Mary's Baby, this new little Child of the Spirit needs a safe place in which to grow. My renewed faith must be protected from Herod (all those things that try to distract me from God). This means finding my own quiet refuge, a place where I can go to pray, away from all the commotion and clamor of daily living. Usually, my sanctuary is the spare bedroom, but if it's occupied, I can always find another Egypt, whether it's in the storage room, laundry room or even the bathroom. If none of those places is available, there's always my car! The important thing is that I find a private place apart, where the fragile new rebirth of faith can be nurtured every day and from which it can emerge to do its work in the world.

Perhaps during this holy season, as Christ is reborn in your heart, you'll want to prepare a safe place for the Baby to grow, even after the crèche has been put away—a quiet place where you can be alone to pray. If you go there every day, you may soon find that the *real* sanctuary you have built is an inner one, a window into wonder that can never be taken away.

Together, we've looked through many windows into some of the most astounding dreams and visions in the Bible, but the real wonder of it is that, underneath all the ordinariness of our daily lives, there shines a quiet radiance that rivals any holy vision; that within our own contemporary lives, there is a chosenness as real as that of any biblical ancestor; that beyond our moments of spiritual dryness, a growing intimacy with God awaits, asking only for our acceptance.

Come, Lord Jesus. Be born in us anew. —Marilyn Morgan Helleberg

December Prayer List Reminder

Return to your Monthly Prayer List on the calendar opening page and review your requests. Give thanks for prayers answered, renew old prayers and add new concerns today. Then pray once again our *Family Prayer for December*.

Sunday 16

JOURNEY TO INNER BETHLEHEM
The Candle of Vision

"Martha, Martha! You are worried and troubled over so many things...." —Luke 10:41 (GNB)

Today, as I light the third candle of my Advent wreath, I find myself in the trap that befalls me every holiday season—*no time*. I still have a full box of cards to address, Christmas cookies to bake, and presents to buy, wrap and send.

As I stare into the flames, traveling inward, the story of Mary and Martha comes to mind. I picture Martha trying to brush away a damp curl on her forehead with the back of her floured hand. She has been working since daybreak in the warm kitchen. Her sister Mary was helping earlier, but now she sits at the Master's feet in the other room. Martha goes out to her. "Mary," she says, "I need your help." Martha looks to Jesus, expecting His support. But to her surprise, Jesus remarks, "Martha, Martha! You are worried and troubled over so many things, but just one is needed. Mary has chosen the right thing, and it will not be taken away from her" (Luke 10:41-42, GNB).

How like Martha I am, especially during the holidays. I hang a wreath, trim a tree, wind garland up the bannister, put out a crèche. Then I rush past the crèche to buy more flour for baking, presents for giving and paper for wrapping. At night I trudge sleepily past the crèche and fall into bed exhausted.

On this third Sunday of Advent, I wonder if Jesus isn't close by whispering, "Terry, Terry! You are worried and troubled over so many things, but just one is needed...." Traveling on those words, toward my inner Bethlehem, I discover the sleeping candle of vision—Mary's vision.

Too often, I look at the world through Martha's busy eyes. The Martha in me is my perfectionist side. When I invite twelve neighbors to lunch, the Martha in me insists on doing *all* the cooking herself. No shared potluck. While the others chat in enjoyment, I'm sprinkling just the right amount of dill onto the curry dressing, checking the place settings and turning the chicken.

What would Mary do differently? I have a feeling she might invite the neighbors over individually to share a cup of tea. Then she might set out a plate of cookies, look into their faces and use those moments to build a friendship.

With that thought, I walk past the box of unaddressed Christmas cards and pick up the telephone to call my blind friend Park. I've been promising to take him to lunch. And even though I'm still a little anxious about my Christmas preparations, I know they can wait. At this moment, reaching out feels very right.

Dear Lord, when I am pressured on all sides by life's demanding obligations, help me to see with Mary's vision. —Terry Helwig

Monday

17

Every good thing bestowed...is from above, coming down from the Father of lights, with whom there is no variation, or shifting shadow. —James 1:17 (NAS)

Last December, when I opened the boxes of Christmas decorations, I suggested that we throw our old ornaments away and buy everything new. "But we gave this one to Daddy," eight-year-old Geoffrey wailed as he dug through the boxes. It was a Styrofoam ball with plastic eyes and glasses and a mop of brown hair. The ornament looked exactly like my husband, and I remembered the hilarious time Geoff and I had making it.

"And what about this?" asked sixteen-year-old Tim, holding up a wooden triangle with clothespin figures of Joseph, Mary and Jesus. His Sunday school teacher had given it to him in third grade.

My husband, too, had found a treasure. He pulled out a paper plate trimmed with colorful string out of which stared a photo of Geoff's four-year-old face. "Geoffrey made this for me in nursery school!"

I had to admit that some ornaments were too precious to discard. I set aside the tiny baby tucked into a walnut I had given Tim when he was two. And how could we part with the Christmas mouse that fit on the top of the tree? We had inherited it from my brother when he and his wife moved away, and it always reminded me of him.

The tree was decorated before we knew it. As usual, it was lopsided and bottom heavy, for Geoffrey had piled on the ornaments as high as his arms could reach, and the clothespin Joseph kept falling off his wooden perch. But it was the best tree in the world. It was at once humble and grand, lowly and proud, intensely human and entirely sublime.

Like Jesus.

Christ Jesus, in every small gift bestowed, we see glimmers of Your greatness this Christmas season. —Linda Ching Sledge

Tuesday

18

You have sorrow now, but I will see you again and then you will rejoice; and no one can rob you of that joy. —John 16:22 (TLB)

That year Christmas looked bleak. I had just become a newly single parent and was facing life alone. For the first time ever, one of my children wouldn't be with me on Christmas: Jeanne, my oldest, was a foreign-exchange student in Yugoslavia. Then the annual New Year's Eve get-together in Illinois with my relatives, to which I had been looking forward, had been canceled. And it was my turn to host the huge neighborhood Christmas party.

But here's what happened that week: On Christmas Eve, my other three children all wanted to attend the traditional family service at our church. Later, they insisted upon another family tradition: reading the Christmas story from the Bible before we opened presents. At midnight, my friends Bob and Betsy whisked me off to the candlelight service at their church. Two days later, they offered to co-host the neighborhood party, and all the neighbors pitched in to help with the refreshments. Then on New Year's weekend, my out-of-town family came to my home, ending the holiday week with loads of laughter and love.

Because I gave in to the gentle nudgings and invitations of friends and family, that Christmas week became a memory I treasure. Sometimes it's hard to get through the Christmas season when you're alone. But if you stay open to letting others reach out to you, you may be surprised what happens during Christmas week.

God bless you... and know that someone in Oak Creek, Wisconsin, wishes you a very Merry Christmas.

Thank You, Lord, for family, friends, neighbors... and for Christmas. Happy birthday, Jesus! —Patricia Lorenz

Wednesday

19

For all things come of thee, and of thine own have we given thee. —I Chronicles 29:14

When we first moved to Washington, D.C., we bought a huge, run-down Victorian house. After months of hard labor we had restored it to such grace and charm, people called from blocks around to thank us.

That first Christmas we decided to decorate outside in celebration. "Wow, outdoor lights!" the children cried. "Let's put reindeers on the roof! And Santa climbing down the chimney."

"Wait," we told them. "If we put anything on the roof, it should feature the true reason of Christmas—the birth of Jesus." The tiny balcony in front was perfect for the stable. On one roof leading to it, we had the wise men riding camels; on the other, shepherds with their sheep. We made the figures ourselves—with everybody helping—cutting them out of some old linoleum rugs in the attic. Their dad mounted them to appear in silhouette. With amber lights behind them, these lifesize figures were so dramatic the newspaper took pictures. We even won a prize. People came from all over to see them.

But down the street was an elderly couple whose Christmas display had always been the neighborhood's major attraction, a dazzling display of elves and reindeers and Mr. and Mrs. Santa Claus. When we saw it, I felt almost guilty. "Oh, dear, I hope they don't think we were competing!"

Then, to our happy surprise, that dear couple invited us inside, where prominently displayed was a beautiful candle-lit crèche. "Your decorations are wonderful," they exclaimed, and told the story of their own: Both had been raised in strict homes that didn't allow even a Christmas tree, let alone Santa Claus. "We resolved if we had children, Santa would be welcome, too. Not as important as the Christ Child, goodness no! But as another symbol of what Jesus taught us—the joy of giving. To our sorrow, we were never blessed as you are. But we decided to have our Santa anyway and put him outside where everybody could enjoy him."

We smiled. "We're sure Jesus would approve," we said. "After all, this is to celebrate His birthday. He wants everybody to be happy, to become like little children."

Lord, thanks for the symbols of Christmas: holly and bells and a jolly saint who never asks to be rewarded. But most of all, Your most precious gift, a Baby in a manger. —Marjorie Holmes

Thursday

20

Give, and it shall be given unto you; good measure, pressed down, and shaken together, and running over.... —Luke 6:38

My mother recently shared a story with me about my grandmother. One day when my mother was a little girl in Elberton, Georgia, she walked down the dusty road that led to her home. A horse and buggy rumbled by and stopped. A lady asked, "Little girl, we've come for a picnic but forgot to bring something to spread our lunch on. Would you ask your mother if she has any newspaper we can borrow?"

My mother ran to the house while the lady waited. "Mama," she called, "there's a lady down the road. They're having a picnic and she forgot to bring something to spread their lunch on. She wants to know if you have any newspaper she can borrow."

My grandmother nodded, wiping her hands on a worn apron and going to a drawer. Carefully she pulled out her freshly starched and ironed linen tablecloth—her only tablecloth. "We don't have any newspaper, dear, but this will do nicely," my grandmother said, smiling.

When I think of that story now, I smile at my grandmother's grand gesture. How extravagant it was, lending her treasured tablecloth to a stranger—and for a picnic! But, of course, Jesus talked about grand gestures of giving: going the extra mile, giving up your cloak, turning the other cheek. It reminds me that when I give, I shouldn't just give the sweater I'm tired of, the money that's left over at month's end, the time that would be free anyway. Those things are worthy, but sometimes I should do what Grandma did: Give from the heart—freely and extravagantly!

Father, teach me not to count the cost but, like Grandma, to become a joyful giver. —Marion Bond West

Friday

21

He will leave the other ninety-nine... and go and look for the lost sheep. —Matthew 18:12 (GNB)

Prickly leaf-points stung my wrist. I was helping my husband Jim thread the last strand of miniature Christmas lights through the holly branches. The results were well worth a few scratches. Our two twenty-foot hollies towered above us like giant, twinkling cones. Momentarily anyway.

A gust of wind rustled the trees. Lights flickered and the middle of one tree went black. Jim and I eyed each other, trying to remember whose turn it was *this year* to find the bad connection. Evidently, it was mine!

I patiently pushed a new bulb into socket after socket. Not until I neared the end of the fifty-light strand did the whole string of lights come alive again. "I found it!" I exclaimed to Jim as I raised the strand above my head.

My satisfaction might mirror, to a small degree, the feeling of the shepherd seeking his lost sheep. Jesus says that the shepherd feels far happier over finding that one sheep than over the ninety-nine that did not get lost. My Christmas lights help me better to understand that parable. No wonder there is such joy when a lost one is found! For finding the lost may be the difference between darkness and heavenly light.

Lord, thank You for leaving the ninety-nine and seeking out the one. Without that kind of love, I might never have been found.

—Terry Helwig

Saturday

22

Blessed is he that considereth the poor.... —Psalm 41:1

The clothing rooms operated by our ministry are stocked through donations from generous Christians. Wonderful, love-filled gifts are shared! We just received fifty handmade baby quilts to supply warmth and beauty for infants whose cribs may be cardboard boxes. We have bright knitted caps and mittens for schoolchildren, "in" shirts and slacks for teenagers and sturdy work clothes for job seekers.

But we get other "gifts," too. Yesterday a woman brought a bag of ripped, threadbare jeans covered with oily stains. Noticing my nose wrinkle (they smelled terrible!) she snapped, "Poor people shouldn't be picky! If they are really in need they'll wear these and be grateful."

Her comment reminded me of a story I once heard. A little girl came home from Sunday school and asked her mother for some food to fill a Thanksgiving basket for a poor family. The mother rummaged through the pantry and fished out a couple of cans of anchovies. "Take these," she said. "They've been on the shelf for years, and none of us likes them anyway."

The child's face fell in disappointment. "But, Mother," she said quietly, "if we only share what we don't want, we're not helping the poor. They are helping us."

Holidays are a traditional time for giving to those who lack the luxuries—and necessities—of life. As you plan your gifts this year, take time to ask, "Will my gift glorify Christ? Will it help the receiver? Or does it only help me?"

Lord Jesus, Giver of all good things, help us to give wisely, compassionately and with love.
—Penney Schwab

JOURNEY TO INNER BETHLEHEM
The Candle of Sacrifice

For God so loved the world, that he gave his only begotten Son....
—John 3:16

Today, I strike a match and light the fourth candle. As I stare into the flames and journey inward, toward the Bethlehem of my soul, I remember the story of another woman's journey.

She was on her way to visit a missionary church in Ghana. She traveled many hours over potholed roads, and the jeep that carried her broke down thirty-seven times. In a village several miles from the church, she saw a line of people nearly three blocks long. "What are they waiting for?" she asked the driver. "Kerosene," he replied. "It's very, very scarce."

Later, after a strenuous mountain climb, the woman arrived at the place where she would be staying. She was given a warm welcome, then led up a narrow, winding stairway to her room. The glow of a kerosene lamp hanging on the wall kept her from stumbling in the dark passageway. She remembered the strenuous climb and the long line back in the village, and suddenly knew that the lamp, hung there for her comfort and safety, had been placed there by one of the tired, needy villagers at great cost and sacrifice.

Today, as I journey inward, I am reminded of another lamp—a star, hung centuries ago above a stable in a little town called Bethlehem. This bright star in a darkened sky pointed to the place where God made His greatest sacrifice, the place where His only Son was to be laid in a manger so that the world might be given a new Light by which to see.

Perhaps in my small way I, too, can sacrifice in order to bring light into my world. My time, for instance. Most of my prayers are said on the run or just before dropping off to sleep. Perhaps I can give up an hour of sleep, a TV program or even a weekend for more prayer, reflection and meditation. When I'm spiritually renewed, I have more to give to others.

During this next week, I think I'll pause each day, turn on the telephone answering machine, relax in the recliner and listen to the cardinals chirping outside the window. Twenty minutes of quiet and reflection can fill me with peace. So much so, that I just might have the extra patience and understanding needed for my family and friends.

Amid those thoughts, on this fourth Sunday of Advent, I discover the sleeping candle of sacrifice. I light it, promising to give up more time for deeper prayer. It won't be easy, but I think my sacrifice of a little time each day can sustain the blessings of Christmas and illumine in me a more loving attitude, patient spirit and thankful heart.

Dear Lord, help me give up time so that I may find the time to be with You. —Terry Helwig

Monday 24

JOURNEY TO INNER BETHLEHEM
The Christ Candle of Love

I am the light of the world. —John 9:5

Today is Christmas Eve. The grandfather clock in the hall dongs six times. And in the still shadows of early morning, I light the fifth candle on my Advent wreath.

The fifth candle, the Christ candle, plays an important role in our church's Christmas Eve service. Late in the service, our minister takes a small, unlit candle and approaches the altar where the Christ candle burns. Lighting his candle in its flame, he begins the passing of that flame.

I remember last year how candlelight reflected off his glasses as he carried his flame toward the two ushers waiting to pass the flame to the congregation. Rustling noises filled the pews as everyone readied their candles. My husband Jim lifted his candle toward the usher, then turned and passed his flame to our daughter Mandy, sitting beside him. Mandy tilted her candle toward me. A drop of warm wax fell on my hand as my candle burst into flame. Then I turned and edged toward the man sitting beside me. In every pew, neighbor turned to neighbor. And gradually, one by one, the entire sanctuary filled with the flickering light of two hundred tiny flames. Looking again at the Christ candle, burning serenely at the front of the church, I realized that each of us had symbolically received and passed on the love of Christ.

The powerful symbolism of that moment remains with me, even now, as I journey toward my inner Bethlehem. Staring into the flames of my Advent wreath, this Christmas Eve, I discover the sleeping candle of Christ deep within me. And as I light the Christ candle within, I know a thousand other flames can spring from it, if only I am willing to share that light.

And perhaps sharing that light is easier than I think. I remember caroling last week at the convalescent home where a frail gentleman was seated in a wheelchair in front of me. He wore a bulky gray sweater that made him look like a giraffe in elephant's clothing. His mouth gaped in a smile until a nurse unknowingly knocked off one of his navy blue slippers. She was gone before he could protest. As we sang, his black-stocking foot fished unsuccessfully on the floor for his slipper. Minutes passed. His foot kept moving. Then blushing, I stepped forward, knelt beside him and pulled the slipper onto his foot. I thought of Jesus washing the disciples' feet saying, "[I have] come not to be served but to serve" (Matthew 20:28, RSV). When I looked up, the man's grateful eyes met mine and something passed between us. I think it was the flame of the Christ candle.

It seems that the flame can be passed quite simply... by washing a foot or slipping on a shoe. Perhaps, as Mother Teresa says, "It is not how much we do, but how much love we put into the doing."

Lord, help me to keep the Christ candle burning within, by turning in love toward my brother and sharing its light. —Terry Helwig

Tuesday
25

JOURNEY TO INNER BETHLEHEM
The Candle of Surrender

They saw the young child with Mary his mother, and fell down, and worshiped him: and when they had opened their treasures, they presented unto him gifts; gold, and frankincense, and myrrh. —Matthew 2:11

It's Christmas Day. A day of gift-giving. As I light the candles on my wreath, a melody plays in my head. It's a song my daughter has sung over and over this past month as part of the church Christmas play. It's the song of a young camel boy who joined a caravan accompanying the wise men as they journeyed toward Bethlehem. Upon arriving at the stable, the wise men offered their gifts of gold, frankincense and myrrh. Even the churlish attitude of the caravan cook changed as she offered the Christ Child her freshly baked bread. But the camel boy had nothing. Whispers went through the caravan as he came forward empty-handed. *What could he possibly have to give?* Then the camel boy gazed into the manger and sang to the Christ Child, "Me. My gift is me."

The words of the song became even more poignant when the lights above the stage dimmed and pictures of children flashed on a large screen. Many of the toothless smiles belonged to the children of the parents sitting in the audience. A picture of my own Mandy flashed across the screen. Through blurry, proud eyes I looked out on the stage of children, whose little voices still echo in my memory.

As I stare into the flame of my candles and journey inward, I discover another sleeping candle—the candle of surrender. Today, I light it and surrender all.

I surrender all my hopes and dreams. I surrender the fantasy I have of an *ideal* me, who lives in a big-windowed dream house overlooking the ocean. She wakes at sunrise every morning and sits on a deck listening to waves crashing against the shore. The *ideal* me understands the meaning of life and death, doesn't get angry, loves everyone and knows what God wants her to do with her life.

But I also give God the *real* me. The one who wakes up fifteen minutes too late, gobbles a piece of toast on the run, drives Mandy to school and can't begin to comprehend the meaning of life and death. The *real* me gets angry, finds it hard to love some people and keeps asking, "Is this what I'm supposed to be doing, God?" And even though I may never be *ideal* and live in a many-windowed house overlooking the ocean, I give God thanks for the *real* me that lives in a cozy house in the suburbs overlooking a child's swing.

On this day of giving gifts, I surrender myself and all that I am—all the burning and sleeping candles that lie within. Kneeling before the manger, in my inner Bethlehem, I give to God—not only for today, but the whole year through—"All that I am. All that I ever hope to be. . . ."

Heavenly Father, as I blow out the candles on my Advent wreath, please accept my gift of me. And may my inner candles continue to burn with the eternal flame of Your Love. Amen. —Terry Helwig

Wednesday

26

There is a time for everything. . . .

—Ecclesiastes 3:1 (NIV)

It's the day after Christmas. And all that beautiful foil wrapping paper I impulsively bought just before the holidays still sits in its packaging, intact and untouched. As soon as I laid eyes on the gold wrap with iridescent snowflakes, I knew I had to have it. But I kept saving it—afraid to open it, lest I use it all up. I waited for just the right gifts to wrap with it, but I waited too long. Christmas has come and gone.

Regretfully, I put the foil away in the attic with the other Christmas leftovers. Then I wonder... *Are there other things in my life that have spoiled because I'm cautiously "saving" them? Or special moments that have passed because I'm wistfully "waiting" for the right time?* Like Grandma's cameo. It sits in a dusty box while I wait for just the right occasion to wear it. And that new Madeline L'Engle book has been on my bedside table for months, because soon I'm sure I'll find those uninterrupted hours to read it. I've been meaning to have that new couple at church over for dinner, but I'm waiting to get the house in tip-top shape. And as soon as I can clear up my schedule, I'm going to begin that correspondence Bible study course.

I come down from the attic to see fresh snow falling. I look around at the post-Christmas clutter and at my two children, dutifully taking down ornaments. Remembering the unused foil, I decide to make the most of this moment. "Come on, kids!" I yell, racing for my parka. "Let's go out and build a snow fort!" Laughing, we run out into the iridescent beauty. And with the cold wetness of fluffy flakes caressing my face, I make myself—and God—a promise. No more foolish waiting; no more imprudent hoarding. With His help, I'll grasp *all* the special moments God has in store for me—and use *everything* I have for His glory.

I long to seize the wonders and opportunities You've given me, Father. And I won't wait for someday—I'll do it today!

—Mary Lou Carney

Thursday

27

And though I bestow all my goods to feed the poor, and though I give my body to be burned, and have not charity, it profiteth me nothing. —I Corinthians 13:3

One year my husband and I spent a weekend as volunteers in a shelter for the homeless in Atlanta. I'd read an article that said the homeless were America's invisible people. *Well, that certainly isn't true here,* I thought, as we arrived at the shelter door. I could see plenty of them.

While men wandered in from the streets, I busied myself in the kitchen. I inspected the pantry, stirred and re-stirred the stew, cleaned the sink. The men seemed to keep their distance. I didn't talk to one all evening.

But the next night after dinner, an old man came and stood at the kitchen door. His gray hair was blown in wild tangles around his ears. I seemed to recognize his face vaguely from when I'd handed out plates of food. "My name is Al," he said. "I sure wish you would give me a hug."

I stared at him, wishing I had a pot to stir, a plate to fill. Anything but this. Some of the men had mental problems and strange requests were not so unusual. Still I hoped I hadn't heard right. "Did you say hug?" I asked weakly.

He nodded, a look of pleading in his watery old eyes. "My daughter used to hug me a long time ago," he said.

Suddenly I saw beyond the wild hair and dirty coat right into his heart. I knew it was not the men who'd kept their distance, but *I*. Even in the middle of a shelter, the homeless had been invisible to me. And I understood, perhaps better than ever before, that love was not only doing something *for* somebody, it was touching their lives with my own. It was crying with them, laughing with them, accepting them as individuals and sharing my own heart.

I looked at Al. Then I wrapped my arms around him and hugged him tight.

Lord, teach me not to hide behind my good works, but to open my eyes and heart to the people around me. —Sue Monk Kidd

For the Lord your God is bringing you into a good land, a land of brooks of water, of fountains and springs, flowing forth in valleys and hills.

—Deuteronomy 8:7 (RSV)

I had always been a sedentary person, but a few years ago, after putting on some unwanted pounds, I decided to change my ways. My husband Vincent and I buckled down to a long, hard winter where we learned to eat right and exercise. When summer finally arrived, I felt elated with my trimmer figure.

Then some friends invited us on a hiking trip in upstate New York. Not being naturally athletic, we were reluctant to accept at first. But in our new and improved health-conscious state, we decided to give it a try.

I started hiking gingerly, but soon realized that with my newly conditioned body, I was perfectly capable of keeping up with everyone else. I was stretching, bending, reaching...and loving it. "Let's go four miles tomorrow," I said.

On the next hike, we walked rough paths that led to breathtaking views of the scenery around us. We tramped through green clover and admired the young tiger birch standing delicately among tall maples and evergreens. We learned to identify mountain laurel, boxwood and beautiful wildflowers. We spent hours watching tiny green frogs hopping and sunning in a water lily-strewn pond. Once, we even hiked five miles just to visit with a family of beavers that had recently set up home in the overflow from a nearby duck pond. The new experience held so many wonderful surprises!

Since then, we've been hiking many times. But if we had not made the long, painful effort of getting ourselves in shape, we never would have found this magical world of water lilies and frogs, beavers and birches.

How's your "fitness" quotient today? Caring for our bodily needs—in both eating right and exercising—is part of our spiritual calling, for our "body is the temple of the Holy Spirit" (I Corinthians 6:19, RSV). Our temples, well cared for, hold spiritual treasures, unimaginable, both within and without us.

Keep me at it, Lord. Help me stay fit to discover all the wonderful surprises You've put in Your world. —Mary Tomaselli

Saturday

29

"Therefore do not be anxious about tomorrow, for tomorrow will be anxious for itself."

—Matthew 6:34 (RSV)

You know how some children drive their parents crazy by asking, "Why?" My precocious eight-year-old son Geoffrey is a worrier who asks a more potent question: "What if?" Here's how a typical conversation with him goes:

"It's snowing outside," I observe.

"What happens if the road freezes up?" he asks.

"The snowplow will dig us out."

"What if it breaks down?"

"Then the city will use the sand trucks."

"What if they run out of sand?"

"Then they'll use salt."

"What if the salt doesn't melt the ice."

"Salt *always* melts ice," I say triumphantly.

"What if this salt doesn't?" he asks.

Geoffrey isn't being rude. He's a careful, thoughtful child who perceives the perilous nature of the world. Ultimately, I am able to satisfy Geoffrey's questioning because I know that what he wants is not information but solace. I tell him not to worry, and he believes me—not so much because of what I say but because of the authority I have and the love I show.

I understand Geoffrey because he's a lot like me. When the question "What if?" races pell-mell through my mind today, I'll turn to the best Authority of all—Christ's wise words in the Gospels—to dispel my doubt and fear about tomorrow.

Lord, what if *I truly believe what You say about the lilies of the field and the birds of the air....* —Linda Ching Sledge

Sunday

30

Delight thyself also in the Lord; and he shall give thee the desires of thine heart. —Psalm 37:4

Just before the New Year, a Sunday school teacher once asked her senior-high class this question: "What would you like to accomplish next year that you didn't this year?" The answers she received, a laundry list of wishes, were not surprising—lose weight, learn to ski, make more friends, save more money (for a car), study harder, be more helpful, read more (and watch less TV), be more regular with prayer and Bible study....

"With God's help," she told the class, "you can achieve any worthwhile goal. But you must do more than wish something, you must work at it." Then, she shared a little story about a boy who had the reputation of being the village smart aleck. "'Why, you think you're even smarter than Mr. Evans, a playmate ridiculed. (Mr. Evans was known in those parts as the wisest man around.) 'I probably am wiser,' the boy answered impudently, and furthermore he said he could prove it with a riddle that even Mr. Evans could not solve. When they located the town sage, the boy raised cupped hands to the man's wrinkled face and said, 'I am holding a sparrow—is it dead or alive?' Mr. Evans looked puzzled for a minute, then smiled when he realized the ruse. If he answered alive, the boy would crush the bird; if he answered dead, the bird would be presented intact. Mr. Evans decreed neither. 'It is,' the wise man responded, 'as you wish it.'"

And the same can be said for you and me in the New Year. Like a coin, the year can be spent foolishly or wisely. If you choose wisely, make God your vision and His will your goal, you can turn 1991 into the most fulfilling, productive, exciting, glorious year of your life. It is as you wish it.

In the New Year...

Lord, show me Thy will,
then help me to dare,
Put hands on my wishes,
and feet on my prayers.

—Fred Bauer

Monday

31

Renew a right spirit within me. —Psalm 51:10

Once every year, Mother had us children sort our toys into three piles: *Keepers*, *Throwaways,* and *Worth Passing On*. The keepers were put back neatly, the throwaways carried out to the trash and the others were taken to the fire department, where they were repaired and given to needy children for Christmas.

As this year ends, I plan to sort through the events of 1990, to see what I really want to keep (such as my new prayer time, an old friendship renewed, greater honesty in little things); what needs to be thrown away (that old grudge, jealousy, the mistake I couldn't change); and what is worth passing on to others (words of praise about a friend's talent, a book that helped me so much, inspiring thoughts from a workshop). Maybe you'd like to join me in this, by sorting through your own year, listing and offering all to Jesus for safekeeping, disposal or passing on.

Keepers:	*Throwaways:*	*Worth Passing On:*
________________	________________	________________
________________	________________	________________
________________	________________	________________

Loving Lord, I lay all of these 1990 things at Your feet. Safekeep my treasures, repair my brokenness, take away what I no longer need, and help me to pass on what I've gained.

—Marilyn Morgan Helleberg

Day Brightener

BENEDICTION

Go on your way in peace.
Be of good courage.
Hold fast that which is good.
Render to no man evil for evil.
Strengthen the fainthearted.
Support the weak.
Help and cheer the sick.
Honor all men.
Love and serve the Lord.
May the blessing of God be upon you
and remain with you forever.

—Gloucester Cathedral

Thank-You Notes to God

1

2

3

4

5

6

7

8

9

10

11

12

13

14

15

16 __________

17 __________

18 __________

19 __________

20 __________

21 __________

22 __________

23 __________

24 __________

25 __________

26 __________

27 __________

28 __________

29 __________

30 __________

31 __________

A FAMILY AFFAIR

What makes *Daily Guideposts* special is you, your family and friends joining with other readers all across the country and spending time getting to know your family of *Daily Guideposts* writers. The happy surprise this year is that the writers have brought along *their* families to meet you as well. So, gather around and get acquainted.

FRED BAUER and his wife Shirley who live in Princeton, New Jersey, marked their 35th anniversary in a very special way last year. They took a trip to South America, including Peru, Ecuador and the Galapagos Islands. "Visiting the Inca ruins of Machu Picchu, swimming with sea lions in Galapagos and fishing for piranhas are memories that won't soon fade," says Fred. He is pictured here with his granddaughters Jessica, 5, and Ashley, 3.

GINA BRIDGEMAN is a 1988 winner of the Guideposts Writers Workshop contest, and writes for a living as a publicist for Musical Theater of Arizona. But her most enjoyable writing experience was collaborating with her father, broadcaster Joe Garagiola, on his book *It's Anybody's Ballgame*. Gina, her husband Paul, and their new first-born son Ross live in Scottsdale, Arizona. For fun, Gina and Paul sing with the Masterworks Chorale, a 100-member chorus that performs with the Phoenix Symphony Orchestra.

Last year MARY LOU CARNEY decided to make more time for family activities with her husband Gary and their two teenagers, Amy Jo, 17, and Brett, 14. "I knew the kids were growing up when I poured a bowl of cereal and found the prize still inside!" laughs Mary Lou. While Mary Lou is busy writing children's books, Gary keeps his active excavation business going. Trips from their Chesterton, Indiana, home to a nearby Lake Michigan beach and racquetball games helped keep the Carney family close last year.

JOHN COEN's life is bustling with the activities of parent, community-minded citizen and farmer. He and his wife Cherry, who live in Wellsville, Kansas, keep busy parenting three young daughters: Whitney, 5, Jessica, 3, and Chelsy, 21 months. They also are involved in numerous community and church activities. But those aren't the only things that keep the Coens occupied. They have 80 cows to milk and a 300-acre farm to tend. "It's very demanding, but we are happy to be able to work close to the land and be involved with nature in a working relationship."

B.J. (Betty Jo) CONNOR and family (husband Michael, daughter Nichole, 11, and son Sean, 7) spent three glorious, whirlwind days touring Washington, D.C., last spring. They visited monuments, memorials and museums, pedaled paddle boats in the Tidal Basin, and ate dinner in Chinatown. Highlights of 1988 for the Connors, who live in Chattanooga, Tennessee, included caring for their third foster baby Whitney, and returning to their home state of Pennsylvania for a wedding and for Christmas.

ERIC FELLMAN and his wife got to play proud parents while their three sons played ball last year. Oldest son Jason, 12, was voted "Most Improved" player on his Little League team. Middle son Nathan, 10, helped his brother's team to a championship season. Youngest son Jon, 8, started soccer and found a niche as a "pretty good" goalie. The Fellmans live in Pawling, New York, where Eric is editor-in-chief at the Foundation for Christian Living.

ARTHUR GORDON and his wife Pam, who live in Savannah, Georgia, made a trip to China last year. Their most memorable sight? The 6,000 life-size terra-cotta warriors buried near Xian more than 2,000 years ago, guarding the tomb of an ancient emperor. In addition to traveling, family life and all his various projects, Arthur is the general editor of *Daily Guideposts*. He is pictured here with Pam and son Mac, 32.

When OSCAR GREENE was a young teacher in East St. Louis, he would often eat at a local café. A friendly waitress decided to introduce him to a young woman he'd confessed he'd admired. Now he and that "very proper and nice young lady," Ruby, have been married for 47 years. This past year, Ruby completed her 35th year in the choir at their church Grace Episcopal of West Medford, Massachusetts, while Oscar served on the committee to help choose a new pastor. Oscar is pictured here with grandsons Shaun, 17, and Jeremy, 11.

"Is it possible that after six years of marriage and two years of parenting, our lives have settled into a comfortable routine?" asks RICK HAMLIN. In the morning, Rick travels through Manhattan to his job as *Guideposts* magazine's features editor. Meanwhile, on days the baby-sitter comes to watch son Willy, 2, wife Carol pursues her writing career (she writes an advice column in *Child* magazine). When evening comes it's Rick and Willy's play-time.

Last year SCOTT HARRISON and wife Sally went on a very special trip to Greece and Turkey. The high point for the Harrisons was St. Paul's adopted city of Ephesus. "To stand in the amphitheater where Paul spoke gave me a new sense of closeness to that great apostle," says Scott, who's pictured here with then 3-months-old grandson CJ, now 2. Back at home in Mechanicsburg, Pennsylvania, Scott keeps busy with his medical career and his family.

MARILYN MORGAN HELLEBERG reflected on her life a lot last year: "I'm learning to live more congruently, aiming to make my actions more closely match who I really am." For Marilyn, that includes being more assertive and being more direct about her feelings, including expressing the negative ones when appropriate. Marilyn lives in Kearney, Nebraska, and is pictured here with her family dog Oscar. She spent last year cultivating close ties with grown children John, Karen and Paul.

Feeling very much like a new bride and wearing a fragrant magnolia corsage on her dress, TERRY HELWIG renewed her wedding vows to husband Jim this past year after 20 years of marriage. Her favorite guest was daughter Mandy, 7, who smiled and watched from the first pew. The Helwigs, who live in Louisville, Kentucky, vacationed in the Great Smoky Mountains last summer.

MARJORIE HOLMES and her husband Dr. George Schmieler, who live in McMurray, Pennsylvania, are both "as happy as ever!" Last year Marjorie's favorite trip took her and George back to her hometown Storm Lake, Iowa, where Buena Vista College dramatized her early best-selling book of nostalgia *You and I and Yesterday.* The next day, George and Marjorie led the homecoming parade in a bright red Model T and were presented with the game ball from the football match, autographed by the whole team.

After ten years of writing in a corner of the family den in her Anderson, South Carolina, home, SUE MONK KIDD finally got a beautiful, book-lined study all her own. She spent Friday nights last fall in the bleachers, cheering on her son Bob, 16, who plays defensive lineman on the Hanna High School football team. Daughter Ann, 13, is a budding writer herself, creating short stories and poems. The entire Kidd family went off to Mexico last year where Sue and her husband Sandy celebrated their 20th wedding anniversary.

CAROL KNAPP says last year was "one big surprise package for our family." They outgrew their mobile home and found a two-story house tucked away in the woods of Big Lake, Alaska. "We didn't meet a single requirement for buying, but that didn't stop us. I just kept repeating Jesus' promise, 'Knock and it will be opened to you.'" Five months later the Knapps moved in, and Carol "learned faith really does open doors." Carol and her husband Terry, have four children—Tamara, 15, Phil, 13, Kelly, 12, and Brenda, 11.

As CAROL KUYKENDALL and lawyer-husband Lynn's homemade Christmas cards told friends last year, "The branches on our family tree are growing stronger... with more spaces in between." Son Derek, 18, and daughters Lindsay, 16, and Kendall, 13, are growing up, and with everybody going in different directions, sometimes moments like "the five of us sitting side by side on the same church pew" seem extraordinary. Yet the Kuykendalls, who live in Boulder, Colorado, have had some special times together, including a weeklong trip to the California coast last spring.

ALETHA JANE LINDSTROM has had a year "filled with simple pleasures," such as long walks around the Lake Michigan summer home she shares with her husband Carl (Andy). "I return from the beach with pockets sagging with beautiful glass and fascinating stones." For the first time since their son Tim was born, Carl and Aletha spent Christmas alone at home in Battle Creek, Michigan, while Tim and his wife Jessica flew to Germany to see her parents.

"A new phase of life has begun at the Lorenz household—college!" says PATRICIA LORENZ, of Oak Creek, Wisconsin. Daughter Jeanne, 20, is a freshman in college in California, after taking two years off after high school. Julie, 18, is a freshman at the University of Wisconsin, Stevens Point. Michael, 17, a high-school senior, will be in college next year studying music. Andrew, 10, in 4th grade, keeps the kitchen cabinets covered with his artwork and stories.

Back when BRIAN MILLER of Mounds, Oklahoma, was a crew chief on a helicopter gunship in Vietnam, he made a "foxhole commitment" to the Lord, and carried it out when he returned to his home state. He and his wife Sandy have spent the past 22 years working at the Bethesda Boys' Ranch for delinquent boys. Together they raise their six children: Ben, 20, Jeff, 19, Phil, 18, Matt, 16, Beth, 15, and Becca, 14.

Dr. NORMAN VINCENT PEALE has written 36 books, and now, in his 9th decade, he has no intention of slowing down—he's currently at work on books number 37 and 38! Dr. Peale received several awards last year. The New York Academy of Dentistry gave him their Merit Award. He received the Orator's Hall of Fame Bowl Award. But the award that was, perhaps, dearest to his heart was the Outstanding Alumnus Award for Ohio's Foundation of Independent Colleges. Dr. Peale is a loyal alumnus of Ohio Wesleyan University in Delaware, Ohio.

RUTH STAFFORD PEALE needs all of her executive skills for her life with Dr. Peale. She serves as president, co-editor and publisher of *Guideposts,* and chief executive officer of the Foundation for Christian Living. Mrs. Peale is proud of her granddaughter Lacy Peale, daughter of son John and his wife Lydia, who graduated from Dickinson College in Carlisle, Pennsylvania, last year, as well as her 7 other grandchildren. She is also more than proud that this June she and Dr. Peale will be celebrating a happy and remarkable 60 years of marriage.

In 1990, ELEANOR SASS will celebrate her 27th year at Guideposts. "I'm astounded when I realize how much time has passed!" Ellie says. "That must be a sign that I enjoy my work." Her skiing vacation in Colorado last year was Ellie's fifth trip to that state. "Next to New York," says Manhattan-dweller Ellie, "it is the state I love best." She is pictured here with her dog Heidi at her apartment window, which she writes about this year at the beginning of each month.

DANIEL SCHANTZ's daughters Teresa and Natalie have left home, and their dad still misses them. "When you've been a father for eighteen years, though your kids have left home, you still aren't finished with those fatherly emotions." Dan and wife Sharon, both teachers at Central Christian College in their hometown of Moberly, Missouri, have taken the time to become closer to each other. Last year, for instance, they went on a 25th anniversary trip to New England, visiting homes of authors such as Nathaniel Hawthorne on the way.

PENNEY SCHWAB and her husband Don are still, "by the grace of God," living on their farm near Copeland, Kansas. She is executive director of United Methodist Western Kansas Mexican-American Ministries. She and Don have especially enjoyed visiting their children: Patrick and wife Patricia, Michael, and Rebecca. An addition to the family is Nysse, a cinnamon-colored Chow, who now joins Penney and her other dog Dobie on walks.

ELIZABETH (Tib) SHERRILL and her writer-husband John are proud of their three grown-up children and their families. Oldest son John Scott, a country and western musician, his wife Meg and their daughter Kerlin, 11, live in Nashville. Tib's middle son Donn, a sales rep, his wife Lorraine and their 3 children Lindsay, 7, Andrew, 5, and Daniel, 3, live in Miami. Tib's daughter Liz, a psychiatric social worker, lives in the Boston area with her geneticist husband Alan and son Jeffrey, 3. The Sherrill's live in Chappaqua, New York.

LINDA CHING SLEDGE, a teacher at Westchester Community College, and her husband Gary, an editor at Reader's Digest, make their home in Pleasantville, New York. Linda was a Cub Scout den mother for 8-year-old Geoffrey and 6 of his pals, and the Sledges continue to team-teach a teenage Sunday school class. And Tim, 16 years old, went traveling as a youth ambassador to the Soviet Union last year!

For TONI SORTOR and her family of Harrington Park, New Jersey, the big news is that her daughter Laura, 25, is getting married this March. Laura's husband-to-be Ed Mazzella has been with Laura for eight years and Toni says, "Ed's been part of the family forever, it seems." Meanwhile, son Jim, 21, is studying industrial design at the University of Bridgeport; youngest son Steve, 18, graduates from high school this year; and husband Bill works as a financial consultant.

For *Guideposts* magazine's editor VAN VARNER, one of the subjects that has interested him especially is "Who are the inspiring people?" and what are the qualities that the people who inspire us all possess? When he asked Dr. Norman Vincent Peale what he thought, Van reports, "Dr. Peale told me that the inspiring people he knew all had the ability to make him feel good about himself. Often too they have the talent to make you accomplish something you didn't think you could do." This past year Manhattanite Van made an eight-day voyage from Hawaii to California.

LEE WEBBER and his wife Peg are as different as night and day. Peg is five foot six; Lee's six foot six. She's not interested in cars; he's fixed up 9 vintage Volkswagens just for fun (in fact, he drives one now!). She's conservative; he loves taking a chance on anything. She grows flowers; he grows vegetables. But the Santa Rosa, California, couple love sharing a marriage that's lasted 45 years. Lee says, "Maybe because we're so different we don't make demands on each other. We can each do our own thing and meet again, refreshed, at dinner."

MARION BOND WEST and her husband Dr. Gene Acuff moved toward their second year of marriage continuing to commute from Stillwater, Oklahoma (his home), to Lilburn, Georgia (her home). They continue to believe they can sell both their houses and one day have "our house." Marion is a proud grandmother of three—to daughters Julie's, Jamie and Kate, and Jennifer's, Alex. Sons Jeremy and John now work and still live in Georgia.

BEHIND THE SCENES...

A special, first-time introduction to the names and faces of a few behind-the-scenes family members who help produce this year's *Daily Guideposts*.

TERRI CASTILLO has been senior editor of *Daily Guideposts* for the past 7 years. She makes sure that the book is filled with a variety of writers and spiritual lessons year after year. Originally from Hawaii, she loves bustling New York City where she attends night school.

BETTY GOLD is managing editor at Guideposts Books, making sure that all the material gets typeset and to the printer on time. She lives in Queens, New York, with her husband Alan, sons Adem and Karl, and their dog Julia. What she likes most about Guideposts is working with people from all across the country, and learning that their problems and joys are the same as the ones in New York.

HOLLY JOHNSON is a free-lance graphic designer specializing in book design. Originally from Louisiana, she now divides her time between New York City and Pennsylvania. Her husband Don Davis is an artist, and together with their cat Joey they enjoy both city life and the countryside.

ANNE MOISEEV grew up in Michigan, but now makes her home in Springfield, New Jersey, with husband Neil, daughter Laura, 7, and son Robbie, 4. When she's not copyediting *Daily Guideposts*, driving two carpools and serving as president of her congregation's Women's League, she is a lap for her cat Golda.

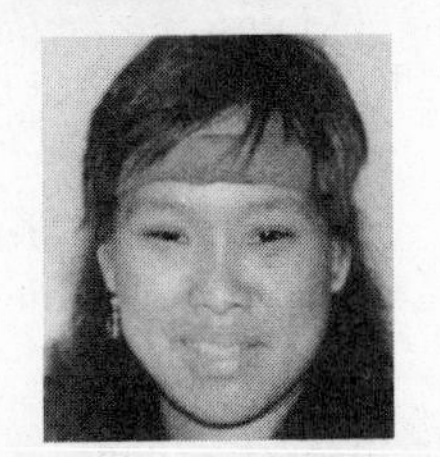

STEPHANIE SAMOY is an editorial assistant who helps with *Daily Guideposts*—from recordkeeping to editing. She moved to New York City 2½ years ago from Tucson, Arizona. On her off-hours, Stephanie is a volunteer at the National AIDS Crisisline, enjoys dancing and riding her bike.

Full-time free-lance indexer MARY TOMASELLI says that indexing *Daily Guideposts,* which she's done since 1986, is one of her more delightful assignments. Last year Mary and her husband Vincent won a week's cruise down the Pacific Coast of Mexico.

FIRESIDE FRIENDS

Our family affair wouldn't be complete without our *Fireside Friends*. Their occasional visits throughout our year bring added warmth, sunshine and family closeness.

ROBIN WHITE GOODE is associate editor on the Guideposts Bible Study Program. Besides starting a graduate program in English last year, she and her art director-husband Harley who live in Monsey, New York, are proud of their newly started daily calisthenic exercise program.

For MARY JANE MEYER last year was the beginning of her 25th year of marriage to husband Smokey. She's a volunteer for the literacy council of her hometown Enid, Oklahoma, and she's active in her church's prayer circle.

LINDA NEUKRUG and her husband Paul live in Walnut Creek, California. A temporary office worker, Linda enjoys studying sign language.

STEPHANIE ODA, originally from Ireland, makes her home with husband Kaz and son Jason, 10, in Darien, Connecticut. She's also an editor at Morehouse-Barlow, an Episcopal publishing house.

TAMMY RIDER left her native Minneapolis in the fall to start attending McCormick Seminary in Chicago. She hopes eventually to work in an inner-city ministry.

GEORGIANA SANCHEZ is a Native American who teaches at California State University at Long Beach, where she lives. She and her husband Fred have five children.

Last year, VICKI SCHAD spent nearly 2 weeks with her parents in Lubec, the coastal Maine village where she grew up. She lives with husband Jim and their two sons in Vassalboro, Maine.

TERESA SCHANTZ is a Guideposts Youth Writing Contest winner and lives in Lake Ozark, Missouri. Her dad Daniel Schantz also writes for *Daily Guideposts*.

DEBBI SMOOT, her doctor-husband David and their three children added a new family member—a "Heinz 57 variety" dog named Maddie—to their family home in Salt Lake City, Utah.

SHIRLEY POPE WAITE and her husband Kyle make their home in Walla Walla, Washington. In addition to teaching continuing education classes, Shirley is an active church worker.

After a "lifetime" of parenting (homemade, adopted and foster children with disabilities), BONNIE WHEELER is working full-time as an accounting clerk. She and her husband Dennis live in Hayward, California.

THE READER'S GUIDE

A handy, three-part index to all the selections in DAILY GUIDEPOSTS, 1990.

SCRIPTURE REFERENCE INDEX

An alphabetical index of Scripture references to verses appearing either at the tops of devotionals or, on occasion, within the text. Chapter and verse numbers are in bold type on the left. Numbers in regular type, on the right, refer to the Daily Guideposts page(s) on which the complete verse can be located.

FIRST FEW WORDS INDEX

An alphabetical index to the first few words of Scripture verses appearing either at the top of the devotionals or within the text, as well as the first few words of poetry, prose quotations, and songs appearing in the book. Numbers given refer to the Daily Guideposts *pages on which these can be located.*

AUTHORS, TITLES AND SUBJECTS INDEX

An alphabetical index to devotional authors; titles of special series, poems and songs; proper names of people, places and things; holidays and holy days; Biblical persons and events appearing in the text; and subjects with sub-heading breakdowns that will help you find a devotional to meet that special need. Numbers refer to the Daily Guideposts *page(s) on which these can be located.*

A Note from the Editors